New Rules for Global Markets

New Rules for Global Markets

Public and Private Governance in the World Economy

Edited by

Stefan A. Schirm
University of Bochum
Germany

First published 2004 by
PALGRAVE MACMILLAN
Houndmills, Basingstoke, Hampshire RG21 6XS and
175 Fifth Avenue, New York, N.Y. 10010
Companies and representatives throughout the world

PALGRAVE MACMILLAN is the global academic imprint of the Palgrave
Macmillan division of St. Martin's Press, LLC and of Palgrave Macmillan Ltd.
Macmillan® is a registered trademark in the United States, United Kingdom
and other countries. Palgrave is a registered trademark in the European
Union and other countries.

ISBN 1–4039–3264–6

This book is printed on paper suitable for recycling and made from fully
managed and sustained forest sources.

A catalogue record for this book is available from the British Library.

Library of Congress Cataloging-in-Publication Data
    New rules for global markets : public and private governance in the world
economy / edited by Stefan A. Schirm.
        p. cm.
    Includes bibliographical references and index.
    ISBN 1–4039–3264–6 (cloth)
    1. International economic relations. 2. Commercial policy. 3. Foreign trade
regulation. 4. State, The. 5. Regionalism. 6. International business enterprises.
7. International trade agencies. 8. International organization. 9. Corporate
governance. I. Schirm, Stefan A., 1963–
HF1359.N483 2004
337—dc22   2003065250

10 9 8 7 6 5 4 3 2 1
13 12 11 10 09 08 07 06 05 04

Printed and bound in Great Britain by
Antony Rowe Ltd, Chippenham and Eastbourne

Contents

Part II States as Actors in Global Economic Governance

4 Governance by Negotiation: The EU, the United States and China's Integration into the World Trade System 67
Hubert Zimmermann

5 The Resilience of National Institutions: The Case of Banking Regulation 87
Andreas Busch

6 Global Governance: From Fordist Trilateralism to Neoliberal Constitutionalism **109**
Christoph Scherrer

List of Tables and Figures

Tables

Figures

Notes on the Contributors

Andreas Busch is University Lecturer in Comparative European Politics at the University of Oxford and a Fellow of Hertford College.

Heribert Dieter is Senior Research Associate at the German Institute for International and Security Affairs, Berlin.

Jörg Faust is Senior Research Associate at the German Development Institute, Bonn.

Doris A. Fuchs is Assistant Professor of Political Science at the University of Munich.

Sieglinde Gstöhl is Assistant Professor of Political Science at the Humboldt University, Berlin.

Robert Kaiser is Assistant Professor of Political Science at the Technical University of Munich.

Dirk Nabers is Research Fellow at the Institute of Asian Affairs, Hamburg.

Andreas Nölke is Lecturer in Political Science at the Free University of Amsterdam.

Lothar Rieth is Doctoral Student of Political Science at the University of Tübingen.

Christoph Scherrer is Professor of Political Science at the University of Kassel.

Stefan A. Schirm is Professor of Political Science at the University of Bochum.

Manuela Spindler is Lecturer in Political Science at the University of Mannheim.

Hubert Zimmermann is DAAD Visiting Professor of Political Science at Cornell University, Ithaca, NY.

Preface

Which rules will govern the world economy in the twenty-first century? As cross-border economic flows and private actors' mobility grow, national economic policy and international organizations do not seem to live up to expectations. The spread of financial crises, conflictual international trade negotiations and the increasing power of private actors suggest the necessity of a new political architecture for the world economy. Does economic globalization require new strategies for global governance? Can new rules for global markets promote trade as well as development and stabilize financial markets? Why do national strategies for global governance diverge considerably? How do states govern transnational economic flows individually and multilaterally? Which role does private business play for the setting of the rules of the game? Are regional institutions and international organizations suitable for the construction of cross-border public goods and for the management of the world economy?

In addressing these questions, this volume follows distinctive parameters. It focuses strictly on the governance of economic flows, whereas other publications frequently include security, culture or environmental issues, thus mixing up different political logics. While sticking systematically to 'governing the economy' as the central issue area, the analysis is carried out on all levels of existing and possible governance – the national, the regional, the multilateral and the private transnational. With this approach, the book looks at a unique range of policy making levels encompassing public as well as private governance. All chapters analyse global economic governance following theoretical claims and providing empirical evidence. One of the distinct features of this book is that it allows for theoretical variation. While some chapters explicitly follow a rationalist approach, others use constructivist theory; some follow a liberal approach to economics, others employ 'critical' theories; some use quantitative methods while others use qualitative ones.

All chapters follow an actor-centred analysis of public and private authority in global governance. The authors identify those actors, which promote change, are affected by change, and shape the rules for a globalized world economy. Thus, 'globalization' and 'governance' are not taken as unspecific and vague forces, but analyzed, following an actor-centred approach. In addition, this volume represents the first contribution to the debate on global governance from a distinctively European point of departure. While American colleagues might be better located to understand the governance of the world economy through the market, Europeans might be better situated to realize the governance of markets through rule-setting. Living in the great European complexity, the German scholars united in this volume offer an analysis of the rules for an ever more complex world economy, without proposing the regulatory institutions former generations of scholars would have preferred.

This volume is the result of a book-making workshop on 'Global Economic Governance' which I organized as one of the chairs of the Section for International Relations of the German Political Science Association (DVPW). The workshop followed a call for papers and brought together 25 expert colleagues in lively and inspiring debates in Arnoldshain near Frankfurt (Main) on 10–12 April, 2003. The papers were distributed in advance and were commented on by designated discussants and other participating scholars. I am indebted to the authors, discussants and participants for their thoughtful contributions to our workshop. The authors deserve special thanks for the thorough and rapid revision of their papers in light of my comments.

Special thanks go to the Volkswagen Foundation for generous financial support of the workshop in Arnoldshain. I am grateful to Louis Pauly for crossing the Atlantic and stimulating our debates in Arnoldshain. Also, I would like to thank the Fritz Thyssen Foundation for funding productive months at the Munk Centre for International Studies, University of Toronto, where I did most of the editing work. Many thanks go to Sandra Wassermann for organizational support and research, to Keith Povey for scrutiny with the copy-editing and especially to Amanda Watkins of Palgrave Macmillan for competently steering the publication of this project.

STEFAN A. SCHIRM

Abstracts of Chapters

The Divergence of Global Economic Governance Strategies
Stefan A. Schirm

The chapter fulfils first chapter duties in introducing the subject. In addition, it explains the divergence of national attitudes to global economic governance (GEG). First, a short account is given of globalization, its impact on politics, the reasons for financial crises, and the need for new governance. Second, the debate on the necessity for GEG and the main proposals for a new GEG are examined. Because these proposals diverge considerably, the third section is dedicated to an analysis of divergence in a case study comparing the attitudes of the German and the US government towards a reform of the International Monetary Fund. As power-based explanations do not convince, I argue that the variation in the positions of governments on GEG can best be explained by the influence of domestic institutions and norms on national strategies for global economic management. In the fourth part of the chapter I then evaluate the debate on GEG strategies according to the criteria of adequacy, viability, and legitimacy in trying to qualify what can be a 'better' GEG.

The Stability of International Financial Markets: A Global Public Good?
Heribert Dieter

Throughout the 1990s, instability and crises have been a feature of international financial markets. Both currency and credit crises have been a burden for borrowers, and, in some cases, for lenders. Consequently we have to ask whether increased financial stability is desirable. In the chapter, I argue that improved financial stability is a global public good: many would benefit, no player could be excluded, and the use of the public good would not reduce its availability. However, achieving financial stability is not a simple task. Some frequently discussed measures, for instance the Tobin Tax, will not provide sufficient financial stability. More useful would be the creation of a global lender of last resort.

Democratization, Financial Crises and Global Governance
Jörg Faust

This chapter provides insights about the domestic sources of financial crises in young democracies and subsequent implications for global economic governance. Nested within the convergence/divergence debate of economic globalisation, the theoretical argument and the empirical findings suggest that young democracies are especially vulnerable to financial turmoil. Confronted with strong economic distribution conflicts endemic to the process of democratization, governments in young democracies often tend to strongly orient their policies toward short-term legitimacy gains. Political uncertainty and institutional fluidity thus tend to provoke problems of time-inconsistent policies during the period of capital account opening. Furthermore, the empirical findings suggest that within a sample of 32 unconsolidated democracies, the vulnerability to financial crises increases with the degree of political fragmentation. Finally, the analysis focuses on the implications for the debate on global governance, as the findings indicate a tension between two central goals of global governance with respect to developing countries, the support of democratization and the promotion of market-led development.

Governance by Negotiation: The EU, the United States and China's Integration into the World Trade System
Hubert Zimmermann

This chapter analyses, in a comparative perspective, American and European policies toward China's integration into the world trade system, in particular the negotiations on its accession to the WTO (1986–2001). It is argued that the shape of an actors' institutional constellation in different phases of the negotiation (agenda-setting, negotiation and ratification) influences its preferences and negotiating efficiency in a systematic and characteristic way. Whether geopolitical, societal interests or international institutions have an influence on the negotiating behaviour of the US or the EU is therefore determined to an important degree by their respective institutional set-up. Thus, for example, the EU acts much more on geopolitical preferences than the USA, and it is more consistent and efficient in international negotiations. However, the EU is faced with a lingering legitimacy problem, which might endanger the ratification and/or implementation of its international agreements in the future.

The Resilience of National Institutions: The Case of Banking Regulation
Andreas Busch

The debate about globalization has so far not been able to resolve the dispute between those who predict the 'erosion' and 'decline' of the nation state, and those who predict its 'revival' because of the 'new tasks' it faces. This chapter argues that the root cause for this disagreement lies in different theoretical models that underlie the debate on both sides of the issue, and that both are well-founded. Only empirical research can therefore advance the debate. The chapter goes on to present evidence from four countries (USA, UK, Germany and Switzerland) in the area of state regulation of the banking sector since 1974. It argues that domestic institutions function as strong filters for globalization, and that they produce quite different policy dynamics and outcomes in the four countries, thus supporting fully neither of the two initial theoretical positions.

Global Governance: From Fordist Trilateralism to Neoliberal Constitutionalism
Christoph Scherrer

The chapter introduces research on global economic governance done by neo-Gramscian authors. This research is distinctive by focusing on class in international relations and by a relational understanding of hegemony. A central question of this neo-Gramscian research is whether an international class of capitalists has emerged. Some authors have answered in the positive. This chapter, however, maintains that hegemony in the international realm is still exercised by the American state, though its foreign economic policies have been greatly influenced by internationally-oriented corporations and that these actors have increasingly found allies among economic elites in other countries. The chapter explores the move from a Fordist (Christian-Social Democratic) project, which included workers and their representatives, to a neoliberal constitutionalist project, which protects private assets from state interference.

The Role of Business in Global Governance
Doris A. Fuchs

In the view of many observers, business is one of the primary beneficiaries if not causes of the 'decline of the state' in a globalizing world. However, a sound analysis of the role of business in global governance is still lacking. In order to overcome this deficiency, this chapter provides a systematic integration of two disparate debates, one on 'new' forms of political activity by business and one on the power of business and its implications, and an embedding of the respective arguments and evidence in a sound theoretical framework. On the basis of this exercise, the chapter demonstrates that in our fascination with the newness of global governance, we should not ignore 'old' forms of political activity by business. These play a crucial complementary role in the current political game. In addition, the chapter draws our attention to a particularly noteworthy expansion in higher dimensions of business power.

Transnational Private Authority and Corporate Governance
Andreas Nölke

Compared to the various forms of intergovernmental or public–private cooperation, transnational private self-regulation is a rarely studied case of global economic governance. Furthermore, existing research on transnational self-regulation has neglected the issue of corporate governance. Transnational private self-regulation appears to be at the core of current pressures for convergence of national models of capitalism. Three features of private self-regulation are singled out for a more detailed study, namely the work of rating agencies, private codes of 'good corporate governance' and the transnational harmonization of accounting standards. The chapter concludes that the increasing role of transnational private self-regulation raises important normative concerns and, more particularly, asks for the identification of alternative agency.

Corporate Social Responsibility in Global Economic Governance: A Comparison of the OECD Guidelines and the UN Global Compact
Lothar Rieth

This chapter focuses on private business as one of the central actors in global economic governance. It explains the rise of business ethics and corporate social responsibility (CSR) and in particular why transnational corporations (TNCs) only act in response to particular, predominantly voluntary, governance mechanisms and not to others. Governance mechanisms are defined as instruments that ask TNCs to comply with provisions concerning human rights, labour and environment, such as the OECD guidelines for multinational enterprises, the UN Global Compact or standards such as the Social Accountability 8000. Based on the assumption that TNCs have to take moral and ethical aspects into consideration, the concept of authority is crucial to TNC behaviour. The concept is based on three elements: power, interest and legitimacy. I argue that only if governance mechanisms meet these three elements are TNCs willing to change their behaviour in accordance with provisions laid out in these governance mechanisms. In a case study I show that the Global Compact has a comparative advantage to other governance mechanisms by fulfilling this condition.

Mechanisms of Global Trade Governance: The 'Double Standard' on Standards in the WTO
Sieglinde Gstöhl and Robert Kaiser

The setting, implementation and enforcement of international standards is a case in point of global governance as it involves networks of public and private actors across different levels. This article examines how the World Trade Organization (WTO), instead of setting its own standards, 'imports' them from other international bodies by making such references either in its agreements or dispute settlement rulings. Under WTO law, national regulation of imports is basically restricted to product standards, whereas standards of process and production methods (PPM) may not be applied to foreign goods and services. We argue that this 'double standard' is due to the member states' fear of interference, their conflicting interests and the WTO's institutional context. The dichotomy seems durable and the future incorporation of environmental and social PPM standards into WTO treaties thus unlikely.

ASEAN +3: The Failure of Global Governance and the Construction of Regional Institutions
Dirk Nabers

The chapter falls within the framework of the debate between rationalists and constructivists in the international relations community. I argue that the IR community should not overstress the variation in metatheoretical orientations, such as rational choice capturing the logic of consequentialism and social constructivism covering either the logic of appropriateness or the logic of arguing. Since both modes of action are ideal types that hardly ever happen in real life, one should rather stick to a combination of the two. I illustrate my arguments through the analysis of the ASEAN plus three process. The development of this new institution in East Asia, comprising the ten members of ASEAN plus China, Japan and South Korea is an obvious test case for the problems connected with global governance, since it originates in the Asian Crisis of 1997/1998, which is seen as an example of the failure of global financial institutions – most notably the IMF and the World Bank.

New Regionalism and Global Economic Governance
Manuela Spindler

The chapter picks up the discussion of one strand of global governance theory that relates patterns of global change to a shift of political authority from states to transnational market actors. It investigates into the consequences of an overall changing balance between those forces at the regional level by raising the question of transformation and change from old to new regionalism. Drawing on case studies on the APEC Forum and the European internal market done in a wider research project, it will be shown how groups comprising strong globally oriented businesses such as the Pacific Economic Cooperation Council, the APEC Business Advisory Council and the European Round Table of Industrialists contribute to the adoption of a 'marketized' and thus 'open' politics of regionalism. The strength and influence of those actors has to be taken into account when theorizing regionalism in the global political economy. The chapter thus concludes by pointing to the shortcomings in the literature on regionalism, and suggests a framework of understanding that does not leave out the new role of transnational market actors.

Part I

Causes and Strategies of Global Economic Governance

1

The Divergence of Global Economic Governance Strategies

Stefan A. Schirm

Introduction

The globalization of the world economy since the 1970s is increasingly integrating national economies and blurring the distinction between internal and external economic developments. This process has promoted growth and competition, but was overshadowed by severe financial crises such as in Asia and Mexico, which led to recessions in the directly affected countries and were contagious to the respective regions, to world trade and stock markets. These crises suggest the need for an improved political management of the world economy as existing mechanisms seem not to perform adequately. Thus, global economic governance (GEG), defined as the multilateral, rule-based management of the world economy by public and private actors, is both a subject for empirical analysis and a normative, prescriptive debate on the future of the political management of globalization.

On the one hand, structures and actors that constitute and perform governance can be analysed empirically. This 'real world' of GEG stretches from the performance of international organizations such as the International Monetary Fund (IMF) and the World Trade Organization (WTO), which superseded the General Agreement on Tariffs and Trade (GATT) over regional cooperation such as the European Union as a possible 'role model' for governance up to more informal mechanisms such as the Financial Stability Forum and the Global Compact. The latter includes transnational corporations (TNCs) and non-governmental organizations (NGOs) such as environmental groups and trade unions as well as the United Nations.

On the other hand, the second dimension of global economic governance, the 'proposed world' of GEG, can be found in lively debate in the media, academia and among political practitioners from governments as well as from private economic actors and NGOs. Here, a wide spectrum of proposals is discussed which ranges from an improved surveillance of economic flows and a reform of international organizations, over the strengthening of developing countries' participation up to the strict regulation of the global economy.

The background for increased analysis and debate on global economic governance in the last decade lies essentially in the perceived need for better regulation or management of the world economy due to the financial crises in the 1990s. The Peso Crisis in Mexico 1994, the Asian Crisis in 1997/98 as well as financial crises in Russia, Argentina, Brazil and Turkey show similar patterns: all of them were not restricted to the affected countries but had global repercussions and involved globally mobile capital and can thus be attributed to the globalization of the world economy. As the intensity as well as the frequency of these crises are perceived to be stronger than before the 1990s, politicians and analysts embarked in a debate on the present state and the possible future of the multilateral management of the world economy. Besides the financial markets, world trade is a second focus of the debate because liberalization through the WTO apparently became more controversial and complex on issues such as agriculture as well as labour and environmental standards. This chapter is dedicated to the basic questions on the need for global governance, the cause for diverging national positions on global governance and to the evaluation of the proposed strategies for GEG: does the global economy need better governance, and if so, which one?

The chapter will deal with these questions in four steps. First, a short account is given on the empirical background for GEG; this relates to globalization, its impact on politics and the need for GEG. Second, I debate on the necessity for GEG and present the main proposals for a new GEG. Because these proposals diverge considerably, the chapter thirdly analyses the reasons for divergence in a case study comparing the attitudes of the German and the US government. As power-based explanations of governmental attitudes to GEG do not convince, I argue that the variation in the positions of governments on GEG can best be explained by the influence of domestic institutions and norms on national strategies for global economic management. Fourth, the chapter concludes by suggesting criteria for the evaluation of the proposed strategies in trying to qualify what can be a 'better' GEG.

The global economy and its crises

Globalization, defined as the increased share of cross-border economic activities in total gross domestic product, has risen sharply since the 1970s. Therefore, we can observe an expansion of cross-border movements of goods and services as well as of investment and of speculative capital. The latter constitutes the most advanced global market: financial markets are more 'global' than trade and division of labour (investment). In this chapter, the term 'globalization' is used as synonym for 'global markets', which seems more precise, because in this way the term is restricted to the economic dimension and provides the definitional distinction between 'the market' and 'the state' necessary for any analysis of the interaction between the two.[1] Global markets function in accordance with the logic of profit maximization of private, transnational, and potentially globally-operating actors. Therefore, global markets are clearly distinguishable from the allocation of public goods as undertaken by governments, which are restricted by the confines of the nation-state and aim in principle at the common weal. To avoid the impression of simplification and reductionism, four caveats on the relationship between the state and global markets must be made:

(1) The development of global markets is not a process occurring independently from the policies of national governments. States and global markets mutually influence each other. Without the liberalizing policies of nation-states and multilateral organizations (IMF, GATT/WTO), global markets would not have emerged in the present form. I do not argue here that states are powerless against global markets, or that regionalism will inevitably occur, as Ohmae (1995) suggests. On the contrary, states continue to shape economic developments and seem to maintain autonomy for diverging national institutional settings and policies (Hall and Soskice 2001; Mosley 2000; Schirm 2002b; Weiss 1998).

(2) Global markets are, historically speaking, not a new phenomenon. The cross-border integration of production and capital flows was very strong at the end of the nineteenth century (Hirst and Thompson 1996: 2). This era of openness ended with the two world wars and the world economic crisis after 1929. In the 1950s and until the 1970s, 'embedded liberalism' (Ruggie 1982) shaped the economic policy of the industrialized world; that is, a mix of restrictions of capital movement, fixed exchange rates, relatively open trade in goods and inward-oriented neo-Keynesianism. Assessing the impact of globalization today means looking at its rise since the 1970s.

(3) The term 'global' does not imply that economic transactions are predominantly global. It only indicates that the share of cross-border activities is increasing in proportion to global output. Global actors do not necessarily operate in every country or worldwide. Rather, their activities are in the process of global expansion and extension to a growing number of countries. Transnational activities in finance, trade and production focus to 60–80 per cent on the OECD countries of Europe, North America and East Asia.

(4) Only a small portion of the GNP also of the OECD countries is created by transnational activities. Investment, production and consumption are still predominantly 'domestic'. TNCs continue to be primarily shaped by their 'underlying nationality' (Pauly and Reich 1997: 4).

Decisive for the relevancy of global markets today is the growing share of transnational trade, investment and finance in total GNP since the 1970s.

The core characteristics of the development of global markets are the transnational integration of national economies and the easing of cross-border transfers of resources for private actors. As a consequence, economic policies that meet the expectations of global markets can be 'rewarded' more strongly than before, while policies that do not follow the requirements of world market competition can be 'punished' more strongly by a withdrawal or a withholding of mobile resources. Global markets, especially foreign direct investment (FDI), can be attracted, for example, by liberal policies, low costs for labour, high skill levels, good infrastructure, social stability and large markets. If governments ignore the expectations of global markets, it can be assumed that the respective country will suffer effects such as a weakening of its currency (inflationary pressures) and a withholding or a withdrawal of investment (less production and jobs) to a greater extent than in the 1960s. In addition, transnational activities make the financing of the government's budget difficult, as mobile actors can escape taxation more easily than immobile actors (*The Economist* 31 May, 1997: 17–19).

As a consequence, the costs of redistributive, inward-oriented interventionist policies such as neo-Keynesianism and import substitution industrialization rise as deficit spending becomes more expensive and tight regulations hinder competitive production (Garrett 2000). At the same time, incentives for world market-oriented reforms rise as they can stimulate the inflow of investment as well as production and trade (Frankel 2000: 59f.). This pressure is accentuated by the potentially global allocation possibilities for transnational actors, which make states compete as locations for mobile resources. Transnational actors also attain greater political 'voice' *vis à vis* governments as they can threaten – with more credibility than inward-oriented actors – to relocate their activities abroad ('exit'), if the government does not provide more profitable conditions.

The financial crises of the 1990s and their predecessor, the Latin American debt crisis of the 1980s, can be considered 'globalization crises' with respect to their causes and consequences (Schirm 2000: 377f.). They became possible only due to the rapid expansion of global financial markets since the 1970s. This financial globalization enabled the governments of developing countries to complement internal savings with external resources in order to promote development, often industrialization. The expanded volume, geographical reach and mobility of private capital flows – as well as the respective governments' decision to take out loans – were the precondition for the integration of newly industrializing and developing countries into financial markets. This integration in turn triggered the crises when financial markets became disenchanted with the economic policy of these countries: the crises of the 1990s can be interpreted as a result of the rapid and partly speculative withdrawal of capital due to economic policies perceived as detrimental to the profit expectations of private actors.

The policy 'grievances' in newly industrializing and developing countries from the point of view of private transnational actors were alternatively or cumulatively:

- insufficient capacity to earn hard currency (suggesting external payment problems)
- overvalued exchange rates (suggesting devaluation and stock value losses)
- nepotism and bad management in the banking and real estate sectors (suggesting instability and defaults)
- governmental interventionism (suggesting market distortions) and
- heavy indebtedness of public entities (suggesting inflationary tendencies).

In addition to these internal reasons for the crises of the 1990s, 'herd behaviour' and high-risk speculation by private actors decisively contributed to the instant magnitude of the crises. The partly incorrect judgement of the economic situation and inadequate conditions for support (intensifying recession rather than alleviating it) by the IMF made the prevention of the crises and moderate behaviour of private actors difficult (see Blustein 2003).

Besides the transnational causes of the crises – more capital going more rapidly to more countries – their consequences reached a global dimension. In the countries directly affected, the crises often led to severe economic recession, impoverishment of broad segments of the population, to the halt of investment activities and sometimes to political instability. Thus, Latin America experienced a developmentally 'lost decade' due to the debt crisis in the 1980s, Mexico almost had to relinquish its market driven economic model in 1995 and the Asian crisis in 1997/98 ended the myth of the unstoppable success of the 'Tiger' countries. The consequences of these crises were not restricted to the directly affected countries but were contagious also for neighbours, such as Argentina during the Mexican Peso Crisis ('Tequila Effect') and South Korea during the Asian Crisis. In addition to a frequent regionalization of crisis symptoms, geographically distant markets were also severely affected through a breakdown of trade and investment. Therefore, jobs and profits in industrialized countries also suffered from crises in Asia and Latin America due to the reduction of exports and to worldwide stock market losses as a consequence of the crises. The increasing integration of national economies thus not only eased access to capital but also allowed the impact of financial crises to spread geographically as well as to trade and production.

Proposals for global economic governance

In the light of these crises, various proposals were made by governments, private business, international organizations, NGOs and academics for better management of the world economy, especially of financial markets.[2] These proposals usually rest on an analysis of the present state of global governance through international organizations – from the IMF to G7 – and suggest reforms of the status quo. Simplifying, we can distinguish four different approaches to GEG put forward in recent years: (1) approaches advocating free markets and self-discipline of countries and economic actors, (2) a focus on better global supervision and management of markets, (3) propositions for a stricter regulation of markets, and (4) a democratization of governance by empowering NGOs and developing countries. These approaches sometimes overlap and can be seen as different points on a continuum of attitudes towards the role of markets and towards economic policy in general.

Free markets and self-discipline

This group of proposals basically argues that governance distorts market processes and competition, and thus leads to an inefficient allocation of resources. International rescue and management activities in financial crises, through the safety-net of IMF loans, would provoke 'moral hazard' in giving private investors as well as governments of developing countries a stimulus for risky and crisis enhancing behaviour. Bail-out guaranties generate moral hazard problems and lead to a misallocation of resources. Therefore, the activities of the IMF should be restricted to short-term emergency aid to countries that perform well, and its financial resources should come increasingly from capital markets and not only from member countries. Such a privatization of IMF functions is partly advocated by US authorities and was a recommendation of the Meltzer Commission (2000) which evaluated international financial institutions on behalf of the US Congress. An elimination of the IMF is proposed only by the very conservative corner in the US political spectrum, which sees the IMF as a counterproductive waste of US taxpayer's money. In sum, the free market position on GEG advocates stronger self-discipline by private transnational actors as well as by national governments, and sees multilateral management and financial help as a distortion of market efficiency only viable in case of systemic crises or short-term emergency aid (Frenkel and Menkhoff 2002: 242; Haggard 1998: 6).

Better global supervision and management

An enhanced supervision of economic flows and rules, and a better management of perceived market failure is advocated by this approach. This 'improving the status quo' group also includes international organizations currently in charge of GEG, such as the IMF and the World Bank. According to this line of thought, international organizations should be reformed or newly created in order to provide codes of conduct, more transparency and a coordination of economic policy and private activities. Along these lines, the Financial Stability Forum (FSF) was established. This includes the G7 governments, the IMF, the World Bank, the Bank for International Settlements (BIS), the OECD and national authorities for the supervision of the banking and insurance sector (Griffith-Jones 2000: 119). Other new initiatives are G20, including G7 as well as newly industrializing countries (NICs) (such as India, Brazil and China), and the creation of the Global Compact including transnational corporations (TNCs) and the United Nations. These new international governance bodies remain in the realm of non-binding consultations. A binding character was attained with the Basle Accord of the BIS on banking standards. Also proposed are measures to enhance transparency, such as a weekly publication of risk analyses, currency reserves and the balance of payments situation of developing countries and NICs by the IMF. Another open question is the bailing in of private actors into the costs of rescuing crisis-ridden countries. Transnational banks, investors and speculators should not only benefit from publicly financed rescue packages by the IMF, but should also contribute to the costs. This argument is shared by the free market group.

The supervision and management approach also includes proposals for 'good governance' criteria for the recipient countries of international help. In a milder form than that suggested by the free market group, this second line advocates self-discipline through demanding a sound economic policy from developing countries in order to qualify for governance support. In an imagined continuum from total free markets to a planned economy, most good governance criteria can be located on the economic policy spectrum practised in the OECD-world of North America and Western Europe. Developing countries' economic policy should not only be stable and, in principle, market driven, but also allow for correction of market failures, managed sustainable development, poverty alleviation, social security nets, environmental protection and so on. Governance innovations such as the bailing in of private actors, enhanced surveillance and good governance conditions are to be achieved in a 'public–private-partnership' (Reinicke 1997: 133).

Stricter regulation of markets

The traditional left in industrialized countries is among the strongest supporters of the interventionist approach to GEG: globalization is to be contained and rolled back by control and taxation of capital movements, national industrial policy (subsidies), protection of uncompetitive sectors and so on. This group proposes governance by governmental intervention and often sees a 'race to the bottom' of labour and environmental standards caused by globalization as well as a fundamental destabilization of the world economy by liberalized financial markets. Therefore, governments should multilaterally engage in setting global standards as a precondition for trade, restricting the free movement of transnational flows, and augmenting the power of developing countries in GEG (Helleiner 2001; Naiman 2000) and in civilizing 'Casino Capitalism' and 'Mad Money' (Strange 1986, 1998). Trade unions who see jobs and labour standards in industrialized countries threatened by trade with developing countries advocate a regulation of globalization in order to prevent 'social dumping'. They are often joined by employers who see their profits threatened by competition from abroad often labelled as 'unfair'. The demands for multilaterally agreed and binding labour and environmental standards are rejected by most NIC governments, fearing for their competitiveness and criticizing these demands as hidden protectionism. The conflict between the demand for labour and environmental standards by the Clinton administration on the one hand, and India's and Brazil's demands for trade liberalization in agriculture on the other hand were a central reason for the failure of WTO's 'Millennium Round' in Seattle in 1999.

A much debated proposal is the taxation of capital movements ('Tobin Tax'), which can be considered part of the 'interventionist approach' if it proves to be prohibitive, thus substantially reducing transnational flows. But it can also be an element of the global management and supervision approach, if merely stabilizing flows by making quick withdrawals costly. The variations of the Tobin Tax idea correspond to these positions. France, Germany and Canada are among the proponents of a moderate approach aiming at crisis prevention, the USA rejects all versions of a Tobin Tax as detrimental to growth and efficiency, and radical NGOs such as ATTAC favour the prohibitive version. Proposals on currency regimes – from fixed exchange rates and target zones to floating – mirror the continuum from strict regulation to free movement.

Democratization of governance

Proposals for a democratization of global governance follow two lines of thought. First, it is argued that those countries affected by the crises and NGOs representing the 'civil society' should have a greater say because they are directly involved whereas the industrialized countries are not. Second, GEG should be approximated to the 'one country – one vote' principle of the General Assembly of the United Nations in order to fulfil the equal rights philosophy of the UN (Commission on Global Governance 1995: 187f.). As a consequence of this reasoning, developing countries should dominate international organizations such as the IMF and the World Bank. Until now, the IMF and the World Bank follow the idea that voting power corresponds to financial engagement in the respective institution. Therefore, the G7 countries control them. Developing countries and some academics advocate the principle 'no harmonization without representation' (Helleiner 2001: 250), which implies that those who bear the cost of economic adjustment to global financial markets should also have the dominant say. In addition, it is argued that NGOs such as groups on environmental protection, women's rights, farm worker interests, rights of indigenous people should also have a greater participation in GEG as they are more directly affected than governmental officials and offer specific knowledge on relevant questions (Scholte 2002).

Why do governmental attitudes to global economic governance diverge?

Considering the global dimensions and repercussions of the financial crises of the 1990s, one would expect all countries to share a similar willingness to improve the management of the world economy. This is not the case. Even comparing the positions of industrialized countries that are similarly integrated into the global economy shows considerable differences in their various approaches to GEG. In the following case study, I analyze governmental attitudes in Germany and the USA. Both countries were negatively affected by the financial crises of the 1990s; firstly, through losses in exports to the crisis-ridden regions and secondly through downturns on the capital markets and stock exchanges.[3] Therefore, both countries share an interest in the stabilization of global financial markets and in the prevention and the better management of crises. This similar interest does not translate into similar positions on GEG, exemplified in the following with respect to the core element of global financial governance, the IMF.

Basically, the Bush administration favours a downsizing of the IMF's influence by restricting its funding and its functions. The IMF should focus its programmes to short-term emergency aid and should finance its activities increasingly through the capital market. The existing practice of publicly financed or guaranteed lending is seen in a critical light. As outlined above, US policy makers emphasize the need for the self-discipline of economic actors and the danger of moral hazard when publicly financed international organizations such as the IMF offer a safety net for 'wrong' behaviour too (Birdsall 2000; Frenkel and Menkhoff 2002). On the other hand, the German government wants the IMF to expand its publicly financed resources as well as to enlarge its programmes and policy conditions beyond short-term financial stabilization towards poverty alleviation. In addition, the developing countries and the 'civil society' in form of trade unions, farmers associations and NGOs are to participate more strongly in the IMF's decision-making process (Hofmann 2002: 15).

Why do these national attitudes towards global economic governance diverge? The differences between US and German approaches can hardly be explained by conventional theories of international relations. Following power based approaches, the USA should have a high interest in strengthening the IMF's influence on recipient countries and the world economy because the USA dominates the Fund's policy more than any other country. The USA has the largest number of votes and is the only member country with a veto power share of 17 per cent of voting rights (fundamental decisions requiring 85 per cent). Some see the IMF as an instrument of the USA to promote American economic and strategic interests through 'soft' (Joseph S. Nye 1990) and 'structural' (Susan Strange 1988) power. However, the USA proposes restricting the IMF's funding and functions while medium-sized powers such as Germany favour its strengthening. One might argue that the US position is driven by the feeling that negotiating solutions for financial crises bilaterally with affected countries would give the USA even more power. However, this argument does not seem convincing as the USA explicitly wants to share the financial burden with other donors and does not show attempts at pursuing bilateral financial rescue.

One could also argue that the USA opposes a strengthening of the IMF because any upgrading of the Fund's functions would require a democratization of the Fund, which in turn would weaken US dominance. Looking at the richest body of evidence on 'international institutions and democracy' actually allows us to dismiss this argument. Strengthening the EU was not accompanied by substantial democratization and weakening of the influence of the large member states. Another power-based approach, party politics as an independent variable, also seems to be only partially able to explain the divergence at stake here. Even though the democratic Clinton administration is supposed to have been more multilateral than its republican successor's policy, it also did not favour an upgrading of the IMF's functions and funding. Similarly, the social–democratic Schröder government's position on the IMF resembles the attitude of his Christian–democratic predecessor Kohl to a large extent.

I argue that the influence of domestic norms and institutions on foreign economic policy making is better suited to explain the differences in attitudes towards GEG than approaches based on national power or party politics. An 'institutional constructivist' approach following domestic norms and institutional settings is plausible, because the field of international political economy (IPE) at stake here matters more to the domestic level *and vice versa* than, say, international security, as it is more about those socio-economic issues relevant in the national policy-making process. In addition, an 'institutional constructivist' approach seems better suited, because domestic institutions and dominant norms mutually constituting each other offer an explanatory model more adequate for the analysis of path dependent behaviour by governments and of the contents of attitudes than those of power-based approaches.

Dominant norms are those basic values of a given society which reach sufficient commonality (are they shared by a majority of citizens?) as well as specificity (are their meanings clear for all?) to influence the political decision-making process (Boekle, Rittberger and Wagner 2001: 109f.). Looking for norms which might contribute to explaining national attitudes towards global economic governance, it seems plausible (1) to focus on the socio-economic field at stake in global economic governance, (2) to search for process norms guiding policy decision making, and (3) to identify what society considers to be the primary task of the state in this field. I propose 'consensual decision making' as the core policy process norm and 'public solidarity' as the central policy contents norm for countries such as Germany and France. For the USA and, to a certain extent, also the United Kingdom, dominant norms seem to point more at 'competitive decision making' ('the winner takes all') and 'individual freedom/self-responsibility' (solidarity conceived as private charity and not as a governmental stronghold).

A socio-economic institution with possible relevancy here is the organizational pattern through which societal interests are channelled and mediated into the governmental decision-making process. This refers to the institutionalization of the political role of intermediate organizations (situated between population and government in the political process) in the socio-economic field, such as trade unions and employer associations. Germany can be classified in this regard as a corporatist country, where trade unions and employer associations have a powerful and autonomous participation in guiding the economic development. Corporatist groups can be distinguished from other interest groups by their institutionalized influence on economic regulations and their institutionalized inclusion into the governmental decision-making process. On the other hand, competition and market oriented countries such as the USA see their economic policy decided by the government and only marginally submitted to the institutionalized influence of organized interests. The norm of consensual decision making figures here as the cultural side of corporatism.

Looking at the attitudes of Germany and the USA towards GEG through the prism of the respective societal norms and institutions leads to a better understanding of the differences. The attitudes correspond to norms and institutions dominant internally in the two societies.[4] Of course, there is variation of attitudes inside both administrations and, of course, the daily business of the two nations' bureaucracies is shaped more by pragmatic and technical considerations than the official positions of their political leaders. In order to grasp the official positions, I have looked at speeches by the heads of government (Bush and Schröder) as well as those of top level politicians from the responsible departments or ministries in the USA (Treasury) and Germany (Finance, Foreign Affairs). I have searched these speeches: (1) for instances for the norms 'self-responsibility/competition' (USA) and 'solidarity/consensus' (Germany), and (2) for a replication of domestic institutions following the lines of 'corporatism/coordinated market' (Germany) and 'governmental autonomy/free market' (USA). These are, of course, simplifications of the more complex social realities in the two countries, but seem plausible as tendencies of the diverging underlying orientations.

In his recent keynote speech on the global financial architecture, the 'Millennium Challenge Account' address at the Inter-American Development Bank on 14 March, 2002, President Bush stated as the lead motive: 'Greater contributions from developed nations must be linked to greater responsibility from developing nations' (Bush 2002: 1). This clearly reflects a liberal economic philosophy with individual responsibility ranking first and financial aid being linked not primarily to 'solidarity' but to greater commitment to self-responsibility by the recipients. On the German side, Chancellor Schröder writes in a recent article on globalization, that 'the world needs a truly democratic trade and financial regime' (Schröder 2002: 4). By ignoring economic asymmetries and advocating equal rights and or influence for all countries, this position obviously follows the domestic pattern of consensual and corporative decision making. At the same time, it suggests equality between the donors and the recipients of financial aid flows. This position is clearly in contradiction to that of President Bush by stressing solidarity and not self-responsibility.

When it comes to the reach and character of the IMF's programmes, both governments again diverge along the lines of those socioeconomic norms and institutions relevant domestically. Treasury Secretary Paul O'Neill declares that in order to prevent financial crises and better resolve them, the IMF should follow 'a market-oriented approach to the sovereign debt restructuring process' (O'Neill 2002: 2). The Under Secretary in the US Treasury Department, John Taylor, states: 'The policy challenge is to move gradually in the direction of less reliance on large official packages ... The United States has indicated that it does not support an IMF quota increase.' As Secretary O'Neill has said, 'Limiting official resources is a key tool for increasing discipline over lending decisions' (Taylor 2002: 3). The latter clearly aims at avoiding the moral hazard of a publicly guaranteed safety net.

The US Treasury stresses the US trust in the self-regulation of market mechanisms when stating: 'Investors have become much more skilled at differentiating between countries and markets based on fundamental economic assessments, with the result that contagion has fallen dramatically' (Taylor 2002: 3). In addition, the Deputy Treasury Secretary, Kenneth W. Dam, proposes that the IMF should reduce the reach of its programmes and focus on his core duties such as 'helping to strengthen monetary, fiscal, exchange rate, financial sector, and debt management policies. In the last decade, the IMF became too involved in matters outside of these core areas' (Dam 2002: 3). In sum, the US position stresses different roles for donors and recipients of aid, the self-responsibility of all actors, trust in free market mechanisms, the wish to avoid moral hazard as well as the goal of limiting IMF programmes to emergency aid in situations of financial turmoil.

On the other hand, the Deputy Minister in the Germany Foreign Ministry, Kerstin Müller, wants the IMF (as the World Bank) to be involved in programmes to fight poverty and to include the civil society in its decision-making process (Müller 2003: 2). This position follows the norm of solidarity and expands the IMF tasks way beyond its responsibility for financial market stability. The German Finance Ministry (Bundesministerium der Finanzen, BMF) supports and developed this position further in an official statement on the IMF meeting in April 2003 when it stated that sovereign debt should not to be left to market mechanisms, but should be dealt with multilaterally in the IMF, which is supposed to expand its programmes to poverty reduction and should include the 'civil society' in its policy-making process (BMF 2003: 5). In the same paper, the BMF stresses the 'partnership among equals between industrialized and developing countries' and the need to 'strengthen the voice of developing countries in international institutions' hereby explicitly including the IMF (BMF 2003: 6). Taken together, the German position shows less trust in markets than the US attitude, clearly promotes international 'solidarity' by asking the IMF to expand its programmes beyond financial stability to poverty alleviation, and advocates corporatist and inclusive decision-making by asking for an empowering of developing countries and civil society actors.

In sum, looking at institutions and norms as independent variables offers a more plausible explanation of the diverging attitudes of countries similarly affected by global financial crises than power based approaches to international relations and foreign policy. The manifest interest in GEG is shared by both countries examined here as it follows from the increasing integration of national economies into the world market. The desired form of GEG and the need for governance are not shared as they reflect national patterns which apparently remain largely unchanged by globalization.

How can we evaluate global economic governance proposals?

The need for global economic governance and its form are contested between developing and industrialized countries, between NGOs, TNCs and governments and even among members of the G7 and the OECD, such as Germany and the USA. These political actors follow societal norms and institutions as shown in the previous section and might also be motivated by special interests, power and ideological goals. This is perfectly legitimate for political actors. As academic observers, we must deal with an additional question: How can we evaluate the proposals beyond the analysis of governmental and group specific behaviour? How can we analyze the proposals following an issue specific, problem bound logic? For this purpose, I will propose three criteria for the evaluation of the different proposals: (1) adequacy: capacity to solve the problem, (2) viability: probability of implementation, (3) legitimacy: democratic accountability of governance. The criteria overlap and might enforce each other. Of course, these criteria are only a selection from the list of all imaginable criteria. The first two were chosen following their plausible relevance in meeting the empirical puzzle of this chapter: How can global governance better manage economic crises? The third criterion seems a necessary component of any policy and is therefore indispensable to global governance.

Adequacy

In order to solve the problem 'global financial crises', any governance strategy has to face three challenges, as the reasons for the crises seem to have been domestic in the respective developing country, transnational with the financial markets, and international considering erroneous forecasts and management by the IMF. A tighter supervision of speculative movements through multilateral banking, stock exchange and investment standards along the national rules given in industrialized countries can be an adequate contribution to the stabilization of capital flows. If complemented by a reform of the IMF and 'good governance' conditionality for a transparent, stable and in principle market-driven policy of sustained development in developing countries, the supervision strategy offers the best prospects for managing the problem at stake. The interventionist approach to GEG might indeed also minimize the problem by strongly reducing transnational economic flows through prohibitive controls and taxation but would, at the same time (depending on its prohibitive level) reduce the growth and wealth potential of the international division of labour. In addition, the interventionist approach faces the problem that global markets can only be cut back if all countries participate. If individual countries or small groups would introduce controls and taxes, global markets would in principle avoid these locations and operate in different countries.

The free market approach actually does not fit to the criteria of 'adequacy' as it does not see any problem which would require global governance. Instead, the crises are seen as a natural reaction of the markets to 'wrong' economic policies. This self regulation should not be distorted by governmental management, which only enhances inefficient behaviour through the moral hazard of a safety net. The democratization approach seems to be of ambivalent relevance, as an increased power of developing countries in international organizations might make, say, the IMF programmes more relevant to the specificities of the country at stake, but might also transfer the often paternalistic and inefficient policy making in the developing world to the IMF. In addition, a democratization of the IMF would lead to a withdrawal of resources by some industrialized countries and would therefore weaken the IMF's ability to help.

Viability

The probability of an implementation of any approach has to be judged with considerable scepticism. The USA is split between those who do not see a necessity for further governance instruments or structures with regard to financial governance, and those who advocate strong labour and environmental standards as a precondition for further trade liberalization. These standards are strongly opposed by leading developing countries such as Brazil and India. Within the G7 and the OECD, we find clear differences along the lines between Germany and the USA shown in the previous section. Again, the approach best suited seems to be the supervision approach as it rests on a moderate market philosophy which is, with all differences in detail, shared in principle by most industrialized countries and by many developing countries that have liberalized their economies in the 1990s. In addition, this approach builds upon the existing institutions and structures of GEG, such as the IMF, the WTO and the World Bank whose very existence is not seriously put into question – only by some radical free marketers in the USA.

The free market approach does not seem viable as it is only advocated by important actors in the USA. The interventionist approach is supported in more countries but does not reach acceptance in the OECD and among NICs. Even the reformed social democratic parties in Western Europe by and large favour the supervision approach on the domestic level over interventionist regulation. Only some NGOs and the traditional left seem to support a roll back of globalization. The democratization approach, on the other hand, is not only shared by NGOs and leftist parties in the industrialized countries, but also by most developing countries. It aims at changing the control of resourceful international organizations such as the IMF and the World Bank, which are currently dominated by those countries which finance them. Therefore, this proposal does not seem viable, as the majority of the industrialized countries is not willing to let other countries that are considered economically less competent (to put it politely) decide on the way their taxpayers' money is spent.

Legitimacy

The free market approach is problematic in so far as it suggests a shift in power from politics to markets which are per se not politically accountable. The supervision and the interventionist approaches both propose new political regimes, institutions and rules and thus have to deal with the question of how to make new global governance 'architecture' democratically accountable in a manner comparable to, say, national governance in the OECD world. The democratization approach, which tries to solve the accountability problem of the other three approaches, also encounters difficulties when analyzed closely. Democratization through the empowering of developing countries in international organizations might reduce the accountability of international decision making as these countries, on average, do not meet the same standards of democratic legitimacy internally that are met by the industrialized countries dominating international organizations at the moment. The often authoritarian and oligarchic political structures of developing countries, including most NICs, do not have the same standard of accountability met by OECD governments efficiently controlled by independent parliaments and courts, educated voters and a critical press. This applies to many but not all NICs and developing countries. Rewarding democratic and stable countries such as Chile and Taiwan through stronger influence in global governance could be a means to broaden GEG legitimacy and stimulate good governance.

Also, the legitimacy and adequacy of 'democratizing' international resources must be questioned. A large part of the flows of resources to developing countries expected by proponents of a reform of the distribution of power in international organizations would probably bypass the majority of the population due to a very asymmetrical distribution of wealth common in many developing countries. A stronger participation of NGOs raises similar legitimacy problems because NGOs are usually not structured democratically internally and often represent special interests. In the end, democratically accountable governments seem to be the only actors who possess legitimacy and the ability to balance special interests in the process of global governance. NGOs might contribute as advisors with special qualifications, say, on environmental, gender or labour issues, but not as decision makers.

Conclusion

Does the global economy need better governance, and if so, in which form? The analysis of the state of global economic governance and of the proposals for its reform showed that the diverging national answers to this question are strongly influenced by domestic institutions and norms: what constitutes 'better' governance depends largely on the socioeconomic patterns dominant in the respective governments' society. Thus, national attitudes and behaviour towards GEG are forcefully explained by an 'institutional constructivist' approach to IPE focusing on domestic institutions and norms mutually constituting each other. The evaluation of the proposals according to the criteria of adequacy, viability and legitimacy led to the result that governance as supervision and management of markets, socially balanced and sustained by democratically accountable governments, best meets the criteria. As most governmental actors share the impression that some kind of GEG is needed, and most of them converge on the smallest possible denominator around the approach just mentioned, 'better' governance is to be expected.

The future form of GEG will probably be influenced by the experiences with the management of transnational political, economic and social issues many countries have had with the regional governance. Regional cooperation shapes politics and economics increasingly in ever more regions, and in ever more issue areas. In the last decade, the European Union implemented its single market as well as the monetary union, while new institutions came into existence, such as the Common Market of the South in South America (Mercosur), the North American Free Trade Agreement (NAFTA) and the Free Trade Agreement of ASEAN in South-East Asia. Thus, globalization and financial crises were accompanied by regionalization processes which partly aim at the same goals as GEG. Bringing economic liberalization into line with stability and sustained development, enhancing growth and preventing or managing crises are at the core of regional cooperation. Therefore, the patterns of behaviour, as well as the institutions and rules for public and private authority developed at the regional level, can deliver a blueprint for global economic governance.

Notes

1 For a theoretical conceptualization of the impact of globalization on domestic politics and for empirical evidence, see Frankel 2000; Garrett 2000; Schirm 2002a.
2 For an overview on the proposals for GEG, see Brett 2000; Frenkel and Menkhoff 2002; Griffith-Jones 2000; Hopkinson 2000; Kreile 2000; Nunnenkamp 2001, 2002; Rodrik 2000; Sandholtz 1999; Schirm 2000; Time for a Redesign? A Survey on Global Finance, in *The Economist*, 30 January, 1999.
3 Of course, one can argue that the USA actually benefited from the Asian crisis by attracting the subsequently footloose capital. But this is only true for some groups and in the short term. I believe that global financial stability is of national interest to the USA in the medium–long term and for the economy as a whole.
4 On the power of institutions and norms in shaping domestic economic policy answers to globalization, see Schirm 2002b.

References

Birdsall, N. (2000) 'The World Bank of the future: Victim, villain, global credit union?', in *The Brown Journal of World Affairs*, 7(2), 119–27.

Blustein, P. (2003) *The Chastening. Inside the Crisis That Rocked the Global Financial System and Humbled the IMF*, 2nd edn, New York: PublicAffairs.

BMF (Bundesministerium der Finanzen) (2003) 'Zu den Themen der IWF-Frühjahrestagung', 12/13, April 2003 in Washington, DC, Berlin 9 April, 2003, taken on 3 May, 2003 from *http://www.bundesfinanzministerium.de/Anlage18089/ Themen-der-IWF-Fruehjahrstagung-am-12./13.-April-2003-in-Washington-D.C.pdf*

Boekle, H., Rittberger, V. and Wagner, W. (2001) 'Constructivist foreign policy theory', in Rittberger, V. (ed.), *German Foreign Policy Since Unification. Theories and Case Studies*, Manchester: Manchester University Press, 105–37.

Brett, E.A. (2000) 'Global governance in an unstable world', in *The Brown Journal of World Affairs*, 7(2), 95–105.

Bush, George W., The White House (2002) 'The Millennium Challenge Account', speech of the US President at the Inter-American Development Bank, Washington, DC, 14 March, 2002, taken on 3 May, 2003 from *http://www.whitehouse.gov/infocus/ developingnations/print/millennium.html*

Commission on Global Governance (1995) *Our Global Neighbourhood*, Oxford: Oxford University Press.

Dam, Kenneth W., Department of the Treasury (2002) Remarks of the Deputy Secretary on 'The Role of the United States in the Global Economy' delivered to the Center for Strategic and International Studies, Washington, DC, 11 September, 2002, taken on 3 May, 2003 from *http://www.ustreas.gov/press/releases/po3411.htm*

Frankel, J. (2000) 'Globalization of the economy', in Nye, J.S. and Donahue, J.D. (eds), *Governance in a Globalizing World*, Washington, DC: Brookings Institution Press, 72–85.

Frenkel, M. and Menkhoff, L. (2002) 'Reform proposals for a new international financial system', in Fendt, R. and Lins, M.A. Del Tedesco (eds), *Uneven Architecture. The Space of Emerging Countries in the International Financial System*, Sao Paulo and Rio de Janeiro, Fundação Konrad Adenauer, 227–50.

Garrett, G. (2000) 'The causes of globalization', in *Comparative Political Studies*, 33(6/7), 941–91.

Griffith-Jones, S. (2000) 'Proposals for a better international financial system', in *World Economics*, 1/2, 111–33.

Haggard, S. (1998) 'Why we need the IMF', in *IGCC Newsletter* (Institute for Global Conflict and Cooperation), San Diego, CA, 14(1), 6–7.

Hall, P.A. and Soskice, D. (2001) 'An introduction to varieties of capitalism', in Hall, P.A. and Soskice, D. (eds), *Varieties of Capitalism. The Institutional Foundations of Comparative Advantage*, Oxford: Oxford University Press, 1–68.

Helleiner, G.K. (2001) 'Markets, politics and globalization: Can the global economy be civilized?', in *Global Governance*, 7(3), 243–63.

Hirst, P. and Thompson, G. (1996) *Globalization in Question. The International Economy and the Possibilities of Governance*, Cambridge: Polity Press.

Hofmann, M. (2002) 'Good global governance: ja. Aber "Wie"?', in *Kommunikation Global* (IPS-CIC), 3(36), 14–17 (Article of a high ranking official (Ministerialdirektor) of the German Ministry for Economic Development an Cooperation).

Hopkinson, N. (2000) 'Managing the global economy: Prospects for a new financial architecture and economic recovery', in *The Brown Journal of World Affairs*, 7(2), 129–40.

Kreile, M. (2000) 'Deutschland und die Reform der internationalen Finanzarchitektur', in *Aus Politik und Zeitgeschichte*, B 37/38, 12–20.

Meltzer Commission, US Congress (2000) Report of the International Financial Institution Advisory Commission, Washington, DC, in *http://www.house.gov/jec/imf/meltzer.htm*

Mosley, L. (2000) 'Room to move: International financial markets and national welfare states', in *International Organization*, 54(4), 737–73.

Müller, K., Auswärtiges Amt (2003) Rede von Staatsminisiterin Kerstin Müller beim OECD-Forum, Paris, 29 April, 2003 (Speech of the German Deputy Foreign Minister at the OECD-Forum), taken on 3 May, 2003 from: *http://www.auswaertiges-amt.de/www/de/aussenpolitik/aussenwirtschaft/foerderung/ausgabe_archiv?archiv_id=4380&typ e_id=3&bereich_id=8*

Naiman, R. (2000) 'From protests to policy: Reducing the destructive power of the international financial institutions', in *The Brown Journal of World Affairs*, 7(2), 107–17.

Nunnenkamp, P. (2002) 'IWF und Weltbank: Trotz aller Mängel weiterhin gebraucht?', Kiel Discussion Papers No. 388, Institut für Weltwirtschaft, Kiel.

Nunnenkamp, P. (2001) 'Umbaupläne und Reparaturarbeiten an der internationalen Finanzarchitektur: Eine Zwischenbilanz aus deutscher Perspektive', Kiel Working Papers No. 1078, Institut für Weltwirtschaft, Kiel.

Nye, J. (1990) *Bound to Lead*, New York: Basic Books, 32.

Ohmae, K. (1995) *The End of the Nation State: The Rise of Regional Economies*, New York: Free Press.

O'Neill, P., Department of the Treasury (2002) Testimony of Treasury Secretary Paul H. O'Neill before the Senate Committee on Banking, Housing and Urban Affairs, Washington, DC, 1 May, 2002, taken on 3 May, 2003 from http://www.ustreas.gov/press/releases/po3062.htm

Pauly, L.W. and Reich, S. (1997) 'National structures and multinational corporate behavior. Enduring differences in the age of globalization', in *International Organization*, 51(1), 1–30.

Reinicke, W.H. (1997) 'Global public policy', in *Foreign Affairs*, 76(6), 127–38.

Rodrik, D. (2000) 'Governance of economic globalization', in Nye, J.S. and Donahue, J.D. (eds), *Governance in a Globalizing World*, Washington, DC: Brookings Institution Press, 347–65.

Ruggie, J.G. (1982) 'International regimes, transactions, and change: Embedded liberalism in the postwar economic order', in *International Organization*, 36(2), 379–415.

Sandholtz, W. (1999) 'Globalization and the evolution of rules', in Prakash, A. and Hart, J.A. (eds), *Globalization and Governance*, London: Routledge: 77–102.

Schirm, S.A. (2002a) *Globalization and the New Regionalism. Global Markets, Domestic Politics and Regional Cooperation*, Cambridge: Polity Press.

Schirm, S.A. (2002b) 'The power of institutions and norms in shaping national answers to globalization: German economic policy after unification', in *German Politics*, 11(3), 217–36.

Schirm, S.A. (2000) 'Global economic governance? Globalisierung, Staat und die Prävention weltwirtschaftlicher Krisen', in Scherpenberg, J. van and Schmidt, P. (eds), *Stabilität und Kooperation: Aufgaben internationaler Ordnungspolitik*, Baden-Baden: Nomos, 377–92.

Scholte, J.A. (2002) 'Civil society and democracy in global governance', in *Global Governance*, 8(3), 281–304.

Schröder, G. (2002) 'Das Zeitalter der Chancen. Sicherheit, Modernisierung und Gerechtigkeit in der Globalisierung', in *Die Neue Gesellschaft – Frankfurter Hefte*, 49(5), 271–76.

Strange, S. (1998) *Mad Money*, Manchester University Press.

Strange, S. (1988) *States and Markets*, London, New York: Pinter Publishers (2nd edn).

Strange, S. (1986) *Casino Capitalism*, Oxford: Blackwell.

Taylor, J.B., Department of the Treasury (2002) Speech of the Under Secretary of Treasury for International Affairs on 'Strengthening the Global Economy: A Report on the Bush Administration Agenda', delivered at the Annual Meeting of the National Association for Business Economics, Washington, DC, 30 September, 2002, taken on 3 May, 2003 from *http://www.ustreas.gov/press/releases/2002930214479428.htm*

Weiss, L. (1998) *The Myth of the Powerless State*, Ithaca, NY: Cornell University Press.

2
The Stability of International Financial Markets: A Global Public Good?

Heribert Dieter

Introduction

The financial crises of the past ten years have intensified the debate on a new international financial architecture. Since the Mexican crisis in 1994 and 1995, financial markets have frequently been hit by severe crises: since 1945, there has been no decade with as many financial crises as the 1990s. The turmoil also affected countries which were, prior to the crisis, considered to be model pupils.

The Asian crisis was particularly striking. That crisis was not limited to one economy, but affected an entire region. Furthermore, there were virtually no warnings in advance. Both this inability to forecast and the dimension of the biggest economic crisis since World War II have caused concern. But, since 1998, several other financial crises hit developing and transforming countries. The crisis in Russia in 1998, the Brazilian crisis in 1999, the Turkish crisis in 2001, the default of Argentina and the turmoil in Brazil in late 2002 show that financial markets in recent years have been characterized by frequent instability.

For developing countries the volatility of capital flows is a particularly worrying aspect. While in 1996 about $230 billion of private capital (net) was flowing to developing countries and emerging markets, in 2000 these flows were reduced to a mere $30 billion. Even more problematic is the development of bank credit. In 1996, the net flow of private bank credit to all developing countries was $24 billion (net), in 2000 there was a net *outflow* of $124 billion (see Table 2.1). In 1997 and 1998, public inflows partly filled the gap.

For developing countries and emerging markets, these trends are very problematic. These difficulties are not only caused by outflows of capital. In the event of substantial capital inflows, these often contribute to an unwanted overheating of the economy. After the dismantling of capital controls in many developing countries and emerging markets, the central banks of these countries are confronted with a dilemma. To reduce the trend

Table 2.1 Capital flows to developing countries and emerging markets,[a] 1993–2003 (billions of $US)

	1993	1994	1995	1996	1997	1998	1999	2000	2001	2002	2003
Private capital, net	139.1	147.5	211.5	228.8	102.2	62.1	84.8	29.4	24.9	62.4	64.9
Direct investment, net	57.6	81.4	98.2	114.4	141.7	153.6	164.0	158.0	172.1	151.3	160.9
Portfolio investment, net	87.6	112.8	42.7	90.2	46.7	−0.1	34.3	−4.3	−42.6	−3.0	−4.0
Other private borrowing, including bank credit, net	−6.1	−46.8	70.5	24.1	−86.2	−91.5	−113.4	−124.3	−104.6	−85.9	−91.9
Public capital flows, net	50.3	5.5	26.5	−2.3	68.3	69.9	12.2	0.2	15.4	20.6	18.2

[a] Developing countries, countries in transition, Israel, Singapore, South Korea, Taiwan. A minus indicates an outflow of capital.

Source for 1993 and 1994: IMF World Economic Outlook, October 2001, p. 9. All other years: IMF World Economic Outlook, October 2002, p. 12.

towards overheating, the central bank ought to raise interest rates. In the absence of capital controls, the rise of interest rates in an emerging market frequently encourages banks and companies to increase their borrowing abroad. This in turn increases the vulnerability of the entire economy in the event of a change in sentiment; that is, when lenders abruptly stop rolling over existing debt.

Nevertheless, the reversal of capital flows to an emerging market is the more dramatic event. For banks, companies and the government, a massive reversal of capital flows represents a task that is hard to shoulder. In such a situation, the short maturities of loans, chosen because of lower interest rates on short-term credit, backfire. Entire economies can be forced to repay a substantial part of their foreign debt within weeks. In the event of instability, private lenders tend to panic and thereby they put fuel into the fire. Once the fire is lit, both lenders and portfolio investors tend to rush to the exit at the same time. It should be noted that such a panic also puts enormous pressure on the exchange rate. If domestic borrowers are forced to repay their loans, most of the time denominated in foreign currency, the dramatically rising demand for foreign exchange forces the central bank, in the case of fixed rates, to use its foreign reserves. In the case of flexible rates, it directly weakens the exchange rate.

These developments are somewhat surprising. The supporters of a comprehensive liberalization of financial markets had promised a very different outcome. The liberalization of capital markets should have led to substantial advantages for developing countries. The cost of financing an investment in a developing country should have been lower due to the use of cheap foreign savings. The competitiveness of companies should have risen. Instead, what we witness is at best a mixed blessing. Phases of higher efficiency are followed by periods of financial crises. On balance, the cost of this liberalized system to developing countries appears to be higher than the benefit. This assessment is underlined when the reversal of capital flows to all developing countries and emerging markets is considered: these economies do not obtain the capital they need, yet they suffer from the disadvantages of liberalized financial markets. It is necessary to make a differentiation. There are different types of capital flows with differing levels of risk and differing effects on financial stability. The most problematic capital flows are foreign credits with a short maturity. Significantly less risky are foreign credits with a maturity of several years as well as foreign direct investment. The latter category in particular has shown very little volatility over recent years. From 1993 to 2003, foreign direct investment to all developing countries rose steadily and was affected by a moderate decline (see Table 2.1).

In this chapter, I do not intend to suggest a grand strategy for the re-regulation of international financial markets. Instead, I am looking at a number of specific proposals that can make a contribution towards more stable financial markets. First, I look at some definitions: What constitutes a global public good, and how could financial stability be defined? Second, I discuss a proposal for a tax on currency transactions, the so-called Tobin tax. Thirdly, I look at the institution that is of utmost importance for the international financial markets, the International Monetary Fund (IMF). The IMF continues to be the single most important institution that governs financial market regulation. Particularly important is the future role of the IMF and its lending policies. I will argue that the IMF should be transformed into a global lender-of-last-resort; that is, that the IMF should in the future lend more freely than in the past. The downside of such an approach, however, will be that borrowing countries will have to accept a reduction of their sovereignty in exchange for easier access to emergency funding. Finally, the issue of exchange rate regimes will be discussed briefly.

Are stable financial markets a global public good?

The currently discussed proposals for a re-regulation of international financial markets focus on the creation of a new global regime for these markets. A solid framework for these markets is the aim. In national financial markets, we have had these conditions for many years. All national financial markets of OECD countries are highly regulated. For instance, there are detailed procedures in the event of the bankruptcy of a borrower. But there are responsibilities for lenders as well. In national markets, no lender can escape his obligations. All lenders have to contribute to the orderly solution of a bankruptcy; that is, they have to accept a partial reduction of their claims. Furthermore, national financial systems do have a powerful lender-of-last resort, the central bank. In the event of a crisis, these lenders of last resort provide the financial sector with its essential fuel, liquidity.

Developing countries and emerging markets do not have access to those instruments. They do not have developed, deep financial markets. Therefore, companies have to borrow abroad to finance investment. But the current system does not provide these countries with sufficient support in the event of a crisis; rather the contrary. In the past, financial crises were often abused. Countries had to implement measures that were in the interest of the financial industry of OECD countries, but against the interest of the affected developing country.

The provision of a stability-enhancing framework for international financial markets can also be described as a global public good. A stable international financial system would be characterized by both non-rivalry and non-excludability. Consumption of this good would not reduce its availability for other countries, and no country could be excluded from using that public good. It can only be provided by the collective effort of national governments, yet the non-provision causes costs for all players, both private and public, in all countries. The classic example of a public good is clean air. Once produced, it is impossible to limit the enjoyment of clean air, because everyone can breathe it. Furthermore, the marginal cost of allowing another person to breathe the clean air is zero. If one can limit the use of the public good geographically, it is a national public good. If the benefits can be used by all countries, it is a global public good (see Development Committee 2000: 1f.). So, in reality, there are a lot of potential global public goods, in particular with regard to the environment, but also with regard to health. If research would provide a vaccine for a prevalent deadly disease *and* the knowledge would be made available to all countries concerned, this would constitute a global public good. The vaccine itself, however, would be a private good, since it would be characterized by both rivalry and excludability.

However, it has to be asked how universal a public good has to be in order to qualify a public good as global. Inge Kaul, Isabell Grunberg and Marc Stern have suggested three criteria:

(1) Firstly, a global public good has to cover more than one group of countries. A public good that can only be enjoyed by one geographically defined group of countries would consequently have to be characterized as a regional public good (see Kaul *et al*. 1999: 10). At the same time, a public good that could only be enjoyed by a group of countries characterized by a specific level of economic development would also disqualify as a global public good.[1]
(2) A second criterion concerns the socio-economic reach of a public good. The benefits must not only reach more than one group of countries, but also a broad spectrum of the global population (see Kaul *et al*. 1999: 11).
(3) Finally, the generational aspect has to be considered. A global public good has to benefit neither just the old, nor just the young. It has to provide intergenerational equity (see Kaul *et al*. 1999: 11).

Thus, the definition of a true global public good is marked by universality. It has to benefit all countries, all socio-economic groups, and all generations. But such a pure global public good is rare. A useful and pragmatic qualification is: 'An impure global public good would tend towards universality in that it would benefit more than one group of countries, and would not discriminate against any population segment or set of generations' (Kaul *et al*. 1999: 11).

The World Bank has further clarified the definition of global public goods and has given reference to development issues: 'global public goods are commodities, resources, services – and also systems of rules or policy regimes with substantial cross-border externalities that are important for development and poverty-reduction, and that can be produced in sufficient supply only through cooperation and collective action by developed and developing countries' (Development Committee 2000: 2).

Considering that definition, a stable financial system would be a policy regime that could only be provided by collective action of developed and developing countries. The World Bank definition helps to understand the political dimension of a stable international financial system. It cannot be produced by single countries nor by groups of countries. Consider exchange rates. Developing countries that trade both with the dollar-zone and the euro-zone cannot have a stable real exchange rate unless there is stability in the exchange rate between dollar and euro. Not even the OECD countries on their own could produce financial stability. For instance, financial stability would have to curb the playing field for speculators, in particular for certain types of hedge funds. These, however, are primarily registered in offshore financial centres; that is, in small developing countries. If the OECD countries wished to limit speculation against their own currencies, they would need the support of those offshore financial centres.[2]

A stable international financial system would be a benefit to all economies. However, although virtually all countries would benefit, the stabilization of the international financial system would also create losers. Those that are currently making a profit, either from speculation or from providing insurance against speculation, would suffer, and these players are resisting change in the system. Although this applies primarily to the foreign exchange markets, similar points can be made with regard to the credit markets.

After having discussed whether financial stability is a global public good, another definition is required. What is financial stability?

There are different ways of approaching this issue. First, financial stability, like beauty, always lies in the eyes of the beholder. Therefore, financial stability is a global public good, but its presence or absence is defined from the perspective of national economies. Second, one could simply assume that financial stability is characterized by the absence of credit and currency crises. This definition, however, is both vague and unrealistic. First, not all turbulence in financial markets necessarily is a financial crisis. Second, capitalist development without crises appears to be impossible: crises are a necessary element of the development of an economy. So it is *severe* crises that have to be addressed. Financial crises that unsettle entire societies and have negative consequences for an economy beyond the short term are the expression of financial instability. Consequently, their absence would constitute financial stability.

However, that definition needs further clarification. In principle, there is need for stability at two levels: both exchange rates and financial flows should be stable. A real exchange rate that does not fluctuate is neither achievable nor necessary. Any definition of stable exchange rates will contain an element of arbitrariness. The main question here is: Which fluctuations require insurance? – that is, hedging. It appears to be realistic to assume that a variation of the real exchange rate of, say, less than ±5 per cent in one year would be sufficiently stable to enable those affected by exchange rate fluctuations (that is, those trading goods and services as well as those borrowing and lending abroad) to accommodate those fluctuations quite easily. Needless to say, there is no exact justification for this assumption. But greater fluctuations than ±5 per cent are not easily accommodated and cause difficulties for traders. Considering this, an exchange rate that fluctuates to a greater degree should not be considered stable. But what about financial flows?

The easiest yet coarse way of making financial flows stable is to prohibit them. Although this appears to be a dramatic proposal at first, this approach has been quite common in the past. In the Bretton Woods system, capital flows were highly regulated; that is, many transactions needed government or central bank approval. Current account transactions were not subject to restrictions, capital account transactions were. A definition of stable capital flows would have to consider the size of capital flows relative to GDP. A change of capital flows of more than 2 per cent of GDP from one year to another would be considered an unstable situation, whilst a lower figure would be considered a stable situation. This is, again, an arbitrarily set level that is inviting criticism. Nevertheless, a change of capital flows of more than 2 per cent of GDP per year can cause difficulties both in the event of inflows and in the case of outflows.

Stability of international financial markets would then be defined by three elements: the absence of severe financial crises, exchange rate fluctuations of less than ±5 per cent and variations in the capital account of less than 2 per cent per year.

One might think that national monetary stability is also an element of financial stability. However, I do not think that this is a necessary condition. Internal stability, first of all expressed in the stable value of the national currency, does not in principle require the cooperation of other countries and multilateral institutions. It is therefore not of prime importance for the discussion of stability in international financial markets.

When discussing the need for change in the regulation of international financial markets, we have to take into consideration that change is nothing new in that field. In the twentieth century, the regulation both of exchange rate regimes and international capital flows has been changing frequently. There has been a tendency for the repetition of past mistakes: phases of deregulation in the 1920s, tended to be followed by financial crashs, which in turn created calls for more regulation. The highly regulated 1930s were then followed by a system that was much more intensively regulated than the 1920s, but less so than the 1930s. As the memory of the consequences of deregulation faded, the Bretton Woods system lost political support and disappeared. It was gradually replaced by today's liberal system, which provides neither stable capital flows nor exchange rate stability. As in the 1920s, deregulation and liberalization has produced dramatic excesses in financial markets, namely in the USA. Speculation and greed have produced the biggest bubble the world economy has ever seen, and it is to be expected that overcoming the bubble of the 1990s will depress the world economy for much of the first decade of the twenty-first century.

Just consider one indicator: the price/earnings ratio for shares in the S&P 500 index, the most accurate American share market index, skyrocketed in 2001 when *historic* profits were taken into account. Until 2001, expected profits and historic profits were developing in a parallel. In 1999, price/earnings ratios on historic profits briefly were above 30, but in 2001 they reached an average of above 60 (see Bank für Internationalen Zahlungsausgleich 2002: 120). That means that the average share in the S&P 500 was traded at a price which represented 60 years' profits. Needless to say, this means there is only one direction of American share prices, and that is down. The consequences for the American economy and the world economy are severe: America will probably need a decade to get rid of the party's hangover, and the rest of the world will have to live with depressed demand from the USA for the medium term. Considering these trends, in a few years we might witness a greater willingness in America to support multilateral regimes that stabilize the international financial markets, but for the time being this continues to be wishful thinking.

As already mentioned, today's system reflects a change of political priorities, in particular in comparison with the system of Bretton Woods, operational from 1945 to 1971. In the Bretton Woods system, the interests of the financial sector were subordinated under the wider interest of societies for a stable development of the economy. Also, the experiences with unregulated markets in the 1920s were still sufficiently well-remembered to encourage policy makers to limit the power of financial markets. In other words, the liberalization of financial markets from the beginning of the 1970s was not only a push for more efficiency of the financial sector, but also reflected the increased political influence of the financial sector and a declining interest in a steady development of the entire economy (see Underhill 2001).

Could a Tobin tax provide financial stability?

After financial stability has been defined, the next step is to explore some potential measures for achieving that goal. In 2001 and 2002, an old proposal by James Tobin made the headlines again. Many critics of globalization hope that the introduction of a Tobin tax would solve two problems at the same time. The tax would stabilize exchange rates and simultaneously provide a source for financing development in the developing countries.

After the collapse of the Bretton Woods system, Tobin had suggested a small tax of 0.1 to 0.25 per cent on cross-border currency transactions. The idea was to make speculation against currencies less attractive by increasing transaction costs. Tobin's proposal is based on earlier suggestions by John

Maynard Keynes, who had advocated the use of taxes for the stabilization of financial markets. In 2001, both the French and the German heads of government supported the careful evaluation of the instrument. Numerous non-governmental organizations, amongst them WEED in Germany and ATTAC, have made the introduction of the Tobin tax a central element of their reform proposals. Despite the widespread support that the Tobin tax enjoys, it does not appear to be an instrument that can provide the expected results.

The central weakness of the Tobin tax is that all international movements of capital are implicitly considered harmful. Thousands of useful and entirely harmless transactions are put into the same category with destructive speculative movements of capital (see Flassbeck and Noé 2001: 1367). This is unnecessary and leads to additional cost that negatively affects international trade. The argument that such a small tax will not harm trade is not convincing when taking today's mode of transnational production into consideration. A product and the associated payments will cross the borders of national economies a few times before the end product reaches the customer. Therefore, a Tobin tax would have a cumulative effect. Furthermore, doubts remain whether the Tobin tax can reach its primary goal; that is, the avoidance of severe currency crises. Speculators who wish to attack an exchange rate will not be discouraged by a tax of 0.1 to 0.25 per cent. When profits of 30 per cent and more are expected, such a small tax does not have any effect (see Nunnenkamp 2001: 16; Frenkel and Menkhoff 2000: 66). Two studies by the European Commission and the German Ministry of Economic Co-operation and Development come to the same conclusion. The main goal, the stabilization of exchange rates, will not be achievable with the Tobin tax (see Commission of the European Communities 2002: 44; Spahn 2002: 4).

On a more general level, it is not clear whether raising transactions costs is always a powerful instrument against speculation. Consider, for example, real estate markets. Transaction costs vary from country to country, but they are quite high everywhere. According to the logic of the Tobin tax, real estate markets should be characterized by very few speculative excesses. There is no empirical evidence that supports such a judgement (see Shiller 2000: 227).

Also, stock exchanges with higher transaction costs do not show any signs of greater stability compared with exchanges with lower transaction costs (see Shiller 2000: 227). An example for a stock exchange with relatively high transaction costs is, surprisingly, the London Stock Exchange. Since 1694, the government has collected a so-called stamp duty at a rate of 0.5 per cent, to be paid by the buyer of a share. This transaction tax today is the oldest tax collected in the United Kingdom. The revenue from this form of taxation is considerable. In the fiscal year 1999–2000, the British Treasury collected more than €5 billion from this stamp duty. This is a fourfold increase from 1994–95. Despite the relatively high level of taxation, the London Stock Exchange has been as volatile as any other exchange in Europe. The reduction of speculation cannot be demonstrated with this example.[3]

A Tobin tax could eventually even have destabilizing effects for exchange markets. A reduction of the level of liquidity by reducing turnover can raise the volatility of exchange markets (see Paqué 2001). This is particularly so in the case of developing countries, where turnover is quite low already (see Commission of the European Communities 2002: 44). An example for the negative consequences of the reduction of liquidity in exchange markets is the South African case. In October 2001, the South African government wanted to curb speculation against the rand and introduced measures to limit the trade in foreign exchange. These measures contributed to the collapse of the exchange rate towards the end of 2001. Finally, it cannot be ignored that the successful implementation of a Tobin tax most probably requires its worldwide introduction. Even if just one financial centre in every time zone would not participate, this could result in a cost disadvantage for the other financial centres bearing the Tobin tax. In the medium and long term, this could lead to a relocation of currency trade to those financial centres that would not participate in the collection of the Tobin tax.

Although there are both conceptual and political reasons for questioning the usefulness of a Tobin tax, the debate about it is nevertheless beneficial. Governments do have a responsibility for shaping globalization and for the stability of financial markets in particular. Globalization has not led to powerless governments. Rather, policy makers have for a long time ignored their responsibility for the regulation of markets and have hoped for their self-regulation. The frequency of severe financial crises and the growing resistance against unregulated financial markets, as well as the debate on the Tobin tax, may encourage the governments in OECD countries to evaluate carefully the economic and political advantages of improved regulation.

On the other hand, the debate on the Tobin tax may also have exactly the opposite effect. The debate distracts attention from the real problems of international financial markets and the willingness to consider complex economic problems might be reduced (see Flassbeck and Noé 2001: 1368). This danger is evident both in policy making circles and in the anti-globalization movement. The temptation appears to be high. By imposing a Tobin tax, its supporters hope to achieve both the stabilization of financial markets and to gain a solid source for the financing of development. Miraculously, two of the most pressing problems of the global economy will be solved at the same time. Unfortunately, neither will be achieved with a Tobin tax. Without going into a detailed discussion, I would like to point out that other instruments (for example, on aviation fuel) appear to be far more realistic; they promise to provide a stable flow of money and can be implemented much more easily (see Commission of the European Communities 2002: 91).[4]

In view of the substantial weaknesses the Tobin tax shows in its original form, modified variations have been proposed. Paul Bernd Spahn has suggested a two-tiered tax. The first level would cover all currency transactions and would be exactly like the original Tobin tax with one difference – the tax rate should be extremely low; that is, between 0.005 and 0.02 per cent. This part of the tax would provide some revenue, although the amount collected would be very small. The stabilization of exchange rates would be achieved with the second tier. Spahn's idea is that a country's exchange rate should float within a pre-defined exchange rate band. Around the central exchange rate, administratively set, the exchange could fluctuate freely within a band of, say, ±3 per cent. Outside this exchange rate corridor, a high tax of between 50 and 100 per cent would be applied (see Spahn 2002: 21ff.). This tax should be implemented unilaterally by all those transformation countries, developing countries and emerging markets that wish to stabilize their exchange rate (see Spahn 2002: 27).

Spahn appears to have made a very convincing proposal. Both aims of the Tobin tax, the stabilization of exchange rates and the generation of revenue, appear to be achievable. The ability to implement it unilaterally (that is, without consent of the USA or the IMF) would be another major advantage. However, as often happens, if something looks too good to be true it probably is. The Spahn tax requires preconditions which, if provided, would make the implementation of the Spahn tax unnecessary.

The critical point is the spatial reach of the tax. The currency of any country is not only traded in its own financial markets, but also in other financial markets and, quite important, in offshore financial centres. To avoid currencies being affected by speculative attack, one would have to limit the trade of the currency to those financial markets that can be reached by a country's jurisdiction. These are only the country's own financial markets. Only there can the Spahn tax be levied. In other financial markets and, in particular, in offshore financial centres, the implementation of the tax requires the consent of the authorities in charge of those markets. It is hard to see why, say, the British authorities should implement a tax in London that is used for the stabilization of the Brazilian Real. And it is even more farfetched to expect that from an offshore financial centre. The consequence is that for the successful implementation of the Spahn tax, one would need capital controls. But if a country implements capital controls, it does not need a Spahn tax, because capital controls as such offer a sufficient protection against speculation. In other words, without capital controls, the Spahn tax would not work, and with capital controls it would not be required.

Considering these limitations, one could also imagine that a Spahn tax ought to be levied by companies operating as clearing houses for international currency trade. But the problem again is that this would be beyond

the jurisdiction of a given country. A private company registered in a third
country cannot be forced to levy the tax of the country that wants to stabilize its exchange rate. Even if the clearing house could be forced to do so,
this would only create an incentive to establish a competing company, with
a differing legal construction, to be set up in order to avoid the Spahn tax.

The bottom line is, neither the Tobin tax nor its modified version, the
Spahn tax, can make a decisive contribution to the stabilization of exchange
markets.

The role of the IMF: should it become a global lender of last resort?

Financial stability cannot be provided without a lender of last resort. In
financial markets, panic is a regular feature. Market participants can be
affected by collective fear. As soon as an isolated reversal of the assessment
of, say, an emerging market turns into mainstream thinking, the affected
country has an urgent need for liquidity. Take, for instance, South Korea in
late 1997. The country was rapidly facing illiquidity because no bank was
willing to roll-over existing short-term loans. But Korea was not insolvent.
It simply needed temporary liquidity; that is, it needed an international
lender-of-last-resort. The obvious candidate for such a task is the
International Monetary Fund. The question therefore is: In future crises,
should the Fund provide liquidity faster and more generously than in
the past?

Following the Asian crisis, the Fund created new instruments in particular for liquidity crises. The Supplemental Reserve Facility (SRF) was introduced in 1997, followed by the Contingent Credit Lines (CCL) in 1999. SRF
is a credit facility that can be used by countries that are confronted with an
unexpected disruption in the markets ('a sudden and disruptive loss of market confidence') that leads to a current account crisis. The SRF can only be
used by countries that implement measures which are considered by the IMF
as strengthening the confidence of markets.[5] The CCL are supposed to work
as a defence shield against so-called contagion effects from financial crises
in other countries. The provision of liquidity should help to reduce the
spreading of a crisis. Pre-qualification is compulsory.[6]

The importance of these aspects is underlined when the recent financial
crises are more carefully considered. At least some of these financial crises
were deepened, if not caused, by a sudden squeeze of liquidity. The affected
economies were temporary illiquid, but not insolvent. After the provision of
liquidity, the economy recovered rapidly, a so-called V-shaped development
of the crisis. In such cases, the delayed provision of liquidity leads to an
avoidable deterioration of the economic situation.

If one agrees that liquidity should be provided faster and more generously,
it has to be asked in what form this liquidity should be provided. Three

options are available:

(1) As in the past, the IMF could provide fresh liquidity only up to a certain, pre-set level and could ask for the implementation of conditions;
(2) Alternatively, the IMF could provide liquidity if countries have pre-qualified. This is the approach chosen for the CCL. The problem is that up to now, no country has applied for the CCL;[7]
(3) The third possible solution would be to expand the IMF and to turn it into a global lender of last resort. In this case, member countries could go to the IMF and could draw liquidity without limitations and conditions (see Fischer 2000).

The third option is both the most radical and the simplest option. It would create in the international field an institution that is considered indispensable in national financial markets: one function of central banks is to operate as national lenders of last resort.[8] In the nineteenth century, Walter Bagehot defined what a lender of last resort should do: it should lend freely, at penalty rates, against good collateral (see Fischer 2000: 9). In an international context, economies would gain access to liquidity if they would be willing to pay interest rates above pre-crisis market rates and if they would be able to provide collateral with a marketable value.

Stanley Fischer, First Deputy Managing Director of the IMF until summer 2001, has highlighted the need for liquidity in a financial crisis and has underlined the need to understand the dynamic of a financial crisis. In an economy with an open capital account, the national central bank cannot provide the foreign currency that is needed by both the public and the private sectors, because even a well equipped central bank only has limited foreign reserves. In such a situation, only an international lender of last resort can help.

Fischer explains his call for the creation of an international lender of last resort with the increasing volatility of international capital flows and with contagion effects that could be witnessed during the past crises. The instability of international financial markets caused by unfounded panic can, so Fischer argues, be eliminated by the existence of an international lender of last resort (see Fischer 2000: 16).

Fischer's remarks are interesting for a number of reasons. At the end of his work at the IMF, Fischer admitted that capital flows are volatile and that there are contagion effects. Financial crises do affect countries that coincidentally are located in a specific region struck by a crisis or, even less predictable, that are considered to lie in the same category; for example, are an emerging market. While such an assessment is nothing new for many observers of recent financial crises, for Stanley Fischer it is. In particular regard to the Asian crisis, he continued to argue that the main reasons for the crisis are to be found in the countries themselves, not in the behaviour of players on financial markets.

The implementation of the proposal to create an international lender of last resort, however, is complicated for conceptual as well as for political reasons. The least complicated issue is the level of interest that has to be found: it has to be above the pre-crisis level, but below the level that commercial banks are charging in the height of the crisis.

Much more complicated is the provision of adequate collateral. For an international lender of last resort, the identification of collateral that has a marketable value is not easy. For instance, the level of future export earnings cannot be estimated easily. Exports of raw materials are the easiest option. There exists an example for such a procedure. In the Mexican bail out in 1995, the country had to provide its future earnings from the export of crude oil as collateral. Although the Mexican bail out was successful, Mexico had to pay a price and had to accept a temporary reduction of its sovereignty. However, such a reduction of sovereignty happens in any financial crisis that requires support from abroad. Therefore, one could argue that a restriction of sovereignty is the price for a financial crisis, whatever the chosen instruments.

Even if the identification of sufficient collateral were possible, another point requires clarification: What should be done if the temporary liquidity crisis turns into a permanent solvency crisis? The international lender of last resort would then have to have the right to draw on the collateral. For such a proceeding, the existence of an international bankruptcy court or some other institutionalized procedure would be useful.

Apart from these conceptual problems, enormous political obstacles would have to be overcome. If the IMF were transformed into an international lender of last resort, this would constitute a major change in the character of the institution. The Fund would be converted into a cooperative bank in which the smaller stakeholders would have far reaching rights for the use of liquidity. The political influence of the larger OECD countries, and the USA in particular, would be reduced, because IMF lending could no longer be used to gain political and economic concessions from the country in financial distress. The Fund would be an institution that its member countries could use in the event of a crisis without having to surrender their sovereignty.

Although there appears to be a greater willingness to shape international financial markets in a more impartial way than in the 1990s, the transformation of the IMF into a lender of last resort might be too much for most IMF countries. It would require that substantial amounts of money are transferred to the Fund, and subsequently to member countries in trouble, without conventional conditionality applying. For many governments this would be unacceptable simply because an abuse of these credit lines cannot, by definition, be ruled out.

Nevertheless, from a theoretical perspective, the call for an international lender of last resort is consistent. If capital controls are scrapped and cross-border movements of capital are liberalized, central banks lose important instruments that have to be provided at a global level. Consequently, one can argue that as long as there is no international lender of last resort, capital controls should constantly be used.[9] Developing countries and emerging markets in particular should not completely liberalize capital flows into and out of their economies.

At the same time, the problems that are associated with the transformation of the IMF into a lender of last resort force groups of countries to develop their own regional liquidity funds. In particular, East Asian countries have both increased their own reserves as well as started to develop a regional liquidity fund (see Dieter 2000; Dieter and Higgott 2002; Kim *et al.* 2000). Although the implementation of a regional liquidity fund is confronted with both economic and political problems in East Asia, the underlying idea remains valid. Every financial system needs a lender of last resort, whether regional or global.

Exchange rate regimes and the trilemma of international finance

Stability of exchange rates is a central element of financial stability. The debate on the appropriate exchange rate regime for developing countries and emerging markets has gained momentum following the collapse of the Argentinean currency board in 2002. It is important to take into consideration that stable exchange rates in the periphery of the world economy are hard to achieve as long as volatility continues to exist between the Dollar, the Euro and the Yen. In a number of recent financial crises, in particular the crises in Asia and in Argentina, fluctuations of exchange rates in the core of the world economy played an important role. In Asia, the countries that had tied their currencies to the Dollar suffered a severe blow to the competitiveness of their companies when the Dollar appreciated against the Yen and the European currencies. In Argentina, the continuing strength of the Dollar reduced the competitive position of exporters and import competing domestic producers.

Without a mechanism for the stabilization of exchange rates between Dollar, Euro and Yen, developing countries will not be able to provide stable exchange rates of their own currencies. However, currently, the call for at least an exchange rate band is not receiving a great deal of support on both sides of the Atlantic, let alone in Japan, which has more dramatic economic problems to solve.[10]

For a short while, the options available to developing countries and emerging markets with regard to their exchange rate regime appeared to be either a currency board or fully flexible rates. This was the so-called bipolar view. Without going into the details of the debate, it has become increasingly clear that neither option is convincing. Argentina has shown the downside of a currency board, and neighbouring Brazil has demonstrated the severe disadvantages of flexible rates. If both currency boards and fully flexible exchange rates are excluded, a number of intermediate regimes are still available. Both corner solutions, however, have one thing in common: central banks have to be rather passive in both systems. In all intermediate regimes, the central bank has a much more prominent role to play and is more or less actively trying to influence the exchange rate.

However, intermediate exchange rate regimes have a common disadvantage. They do not work very well if capital flows are fully liberalized. With high, volatile capital flows, central banks have problems stabilizing exchange rates. The underlying dilemma is described in the impossible trinity of international finance. Monetary policy tries to reach three goals at the same time: independence of monetary policy, unrestricted flows of capital and stable exchange rates. However, it is impossible to reach more than two goals at the same time. Monetary policy can only choose between the following three options:

(1) A stable exchange rate and an independent monetary policy – this option requires the use of capital controls; or
(2) Unrestricted capital flows and an independent monetary policy – in this case the exchange rate will have to be flexible; or
(3) Unrestricted capital flows and a stable exchange rate – the central bank gives up an independent monetary policy and concentrates its activities on the stabilization of exchange rates (see Frenkel and Menkhoff 2000: 11ff.; Fischer 2001: 8).

The first option describes the Bretton Woods system. Capital controls were a central element of that monetary regime. These controls are necessary to enable the implementation of an independent monetary policy. For instance, in the absence of capital controls, the lowering of domestic interest rates would lead to an outflow of capital with subsequent pressure on the exchange rate. Bretton Woods was a stable financial system for more than twenty years. Moreover, Bretton Woods was a period of rapid economic growth of the global economy. Another example is China, which also generated exceptional growth over a long period of time. During the Asian crisis, China could maintain its fixed exchange rate vis-à-vis the Dollar primarily because of the tight capital controls it implements.

The second option describes our current system in the OECD outside the Eurozone. Exchange rates fluctuate, capital flows are more or less unrestricted and national monetary policy enjoys a certain autonomy, at least in the larger OECD countries.

The third option is plausible from an economic point of view, but not politically. The reason is that in such a scenario, monetary policy has to give absolute priority to the stabilization of the exchange rate. The consequence is that the central bank may have to raise interest rates even if that is counterproductive for the domestic economy. In democratic societies, very few interest groups would support such a monetary policy. Neither trade unions nor employers' associations are willing to accept a stable exchange rate as the primary target of monetary policy. Also, many sectors of an economy are not affected by changes in the exchange rate and would therefore not support a policy that ignores the consequences for the domestic economy.

Before World War I, such policies were implemented under the gold standard. The participating countries made the stability of the exchange rate an absolute priority of their economic policy. In the three core countries of the gold standard – France, Germany and the United Kingdom – the gold reserves and the convertibility at a given exchange rate were defended regardless of the short-term cost for the domestic economy (see Eichengreen 2000: 51). The political opposition against these policies was limited, mainly because trade unions were too weak to argue their case: full employment was not yet on the political agenda.

The bottom line is, stable exchange rates and an independent monetary policy are only achievable with capital controls.[11] For developing countries and, to a degree, emerging markets, there are many reasons why they should not liberalize capital flows completely. Whereas the contribution of stable exchange rates to the economic growth of an economy is well documented, liberalized capital flows do not always have the same positive effects. Selective restrictions of capital flows should be the norm, not the exception, for developing countries.

Although restrictions on capital flows can be implemented unilaterally, it would be positive if the IMF would support their implementation. Without such support, many countries will be reluctant to return to capital controls, partly because their implementation will, at least in the medium to long term, require the support of the IMF and the major financial centres. National capital controls could be implemented more effectively if international cooperation on the control of capital movements were strengthened. As long as this does not exist, the illegal export of capital is no big risk. If the money is not detected at the border, there is no future risk for the exporter of capital. In the case that receiving countries would also have to report the import of capital, the sustainability of capital controls would greatly rise.

Conclusion

For too long, the call for a better regulation of international financial markets did not receive much attention. In virtually all OECD countries deregulation and liberalization enjoyed support. Financial markets in particular were left to themselves. This, however, was wrong: the internationalization of financial markets is calling for the implementation of regulations that exist in all national markets at the global level. One example is the creation of an international lender of last resort.

The provision of financial stability is a task for the political sphere. It is unrealistic to expect markets to do this job. The governments of European Union countries in particular should accept this responsibility and should push a new order for international financial markets. The EU could play an important role in this field. The absence of a common policy in international financial affairs is, following the successful introduction of the Euro, much more obvious than before. For many years, Europe has spoken with one voice concerning international trade. This common policy partly explains why the EU has such a strong position in shaping the agenda on international trade. What a contrast to finance: Europe is hardly heard, primarily because it speaks with many voices.

Reaching financial stability would make a contribution to the development of a more stable and more just world economy. If this stabilization is not achieved, the current liberal economic order might be at stake. Similar to the developments that followed the Great Depression, much more than financial markets could be at risk. Countries may decide to isolate their economies from the world market. The collapse of the multilateral trading order may be the consequence. If financial markets are not providing the benefits that the proponents have been promising, the partial retreat from the global economy appears to be both plausible and possible. The recent reactions that followed the collapse of the Argentinean economy give an indication: this discussion may have already begun in some developing countries. The recent wave of migration from Argentina to Italy and Spain demonstrates that unless financial stability can be achieved in the developing world, people may simply decide to migrate to countries that have greater financial stability.

Notes

1   In other words, there cannot be a global public good that brings benefits only to some developed countries. For instance, a regime for the protection of foreign direct investment would not qualify for a global public good. Kaul *et al.* describe this as a club good (Kaul *et al.* 1999: 10).

2   Needless to say, the toolbox of OECD countries is better equipped than those of developing countries. Bank supervisors could probably ban business with offshore centres, which would quickly dry up those loopholes.

3   Not surprisingly, there is a movement that calls for the abolition of the stamp duty. See their homepage at *www.StampOutStampDuty.co.uk*

4   However, even a fuel tax collected within the European Union would create certain problems; for example, the treatment of aircraft flying to intercontinental destinations. If the tax were too high, there would be an incentive to refuel the aircraft just outside the EU.

5   SRF credit has a maturity of 12 to 30 months. The interest rate is the basic rate of the IMF plus a spread of 3 to 5 per cent (see IMF Survey Supplement, vol. 30, September 2001: 12).

6 The interest rate charged on CCL credit is lower than on SRF (see IMF Survey Supplement, vol. 30, September 2001: 12).

7 One can only speculate why member countries have not yet applied. An important aspect most probably is that financial markets may already interpret the application of a country for CCL as a sign of a looming financial crisis. Instead of strengthening a country, CCL might lead an economy into turmoil in financial markets. Therefore, the British government has demanded an improvement of CCL conditions to make their use more attractive (*Financial Times*, 30 November, 2001: WE 2).

8 Of course, the IMF cannot, by definition, become a true lender of last resort. This would require the Fund to be able to create liquidity, which it cannot. However, a Fund that has substantial resources at its disposal can operate as a quasi lender of last resort. In practice, this differentiation might not be of great importance.

9 In the absence of a global lender of last resort, rollover options can provide a partial substitute.

10 Nevertheless, immediately after the Asian crisis, 11 out of 29 experts of a working group of the American Council on Foreign Relations supported the call for a target zone between the major currencies. Among those advocates of more stable exchange rates were the economist Fred C. Bergsten, the former chairman of the Federal Reserve Bank, Paul Volcker, and the hedge fund manager and successful speculator, George Soros (see Council on Foreign Relations 1999: 129).

11 Stanley Fischer, for many years the most important figure in the IMF, accepts this conclusion and asserts that the implementation of capital controls permits a stable exchange rate. In Fischer's opinion, the problem is the declining efficiency of capital controls. Over time, the evasion of capital controls rises (see Fischer 2001: 10).

References

Altvater, E. (2003) 'Eine neue Finanzarchitektur oder das öffentliche Gut der Finanzmarktstabilität', in Mahnkopf, B. (ed.) *Globale öffentliche Güter – für menschliche Sicherheit und Frieden*, Berlin: Berliner Wissenschaftsverlag, 163–83.

Bank für Internationalen Zahlungsausgleich (2002) 72, June, *Jahresbericht*, Basel: BIZ.

Bhagwati, J. (1998) 'The capital myth. The difference between trade in widgets and dollars', in *Foreign Affairs* 77(3), May–June 1998, 7–12.

Braga de Macedo, J., Cohen, D. and Reisen, H. (eds) (2001) *Don't Fix, Don't Float. The Exchange Rate in Emerging Markets, Transition Economies and Developing Countries*, Paris: OECD.

Buiter, W. and Sibert, A. (1999) 'UDROP – a small contribution to the new international financial architecture', Centre for Economic Performance, London: London School of Economics and Political Science, Working Paper, May.

Cohen, B.J. (1998) *The Geography of Money*, Ithaca and London: Cornell University Press.

Commission of the European Communities (2002) 'Responses to the challenges of globalisation: A study on the international monetary and financial system and on financing for development', Working document from the Commission Services, Brussels, DOC/02/04.

Council on Foreign Relations (1999) *Safeguarding Prosperity in a Global Financial System. The Future International Financial Architecture*, New York: Council on Foreign Relations.

Development Committee (2000) 'Poverty reduction and global public goods. Issues for the World Bank in supporting global collective action', Joint Ministerial Committee of the Boards of Governors of the Bank and the Fund, DC/2000-16, 6 September.

Dieter, H. (2000) 'Monetary regionalism: Regional integration without financial crises', Warwick: Centre for the Study of Globalisation and Regionalisation (CSGR) Working Paper 52/00.

Dieter, H. (1998) *Die Asienkrise: Ursachen, Konsequenzen und die Rolle des Internationalen Währungsfonds*, Marburg: Metropolis Verlag.

Dieter, H. and Higgott, R. (2002) 'Exploring alternative theories of economic regionalism: From trade to finance in Asian co-operation', Warwick: Centre for the Study of Globalisation and Regionalisation (CSGR), Working Paper 89/02, January 2002.

Eichengreen, B. (2000) *Vom Goldstandard zum Euro. Die Geschichte des internationalen Währungssystems*, Berlin: Wagenbach.

Eichengreen, B. (1998) 'Capital controls: Capital idea or capital folly?', Mimeo, November.

Feldstein, M. (1998) 'Refocusing the IMF', in *Foreign Affairs* 79(2), March–April 1998.

Fischer, S. (2001) 'Exchange rate regimes: Is the bipolar view correct?', taken on January, 2001 from *www.imf.org/external/np/speeches/2001/010601a.htm*

Fischer, S. (2000) 'On the need for an international lender of last resort', *Essays in International Finance*, no. 220, November, Department of Economics, Princeton University.

Flassbeck, H. and Noé, C. (2001) 'Abkehr vom Unilateralismus', *Blätter für deutsche und internationale Politik*, 11, 1359–69.

Frenkel, M. and Menkhoff, L. (2000) *Stabile Weltfinanzen? Die Debatte um eine neue internationale Finanzarchitektur*, Berlin, Heidelberg: Springer Verlag.

Garten, J.E. (1999) 'Lessons for the next financial crisis', in *Foreign Affairs* 78(2), March–April 1999, 76–92.

Griffith-Jones, S. (1998) *Global Capital Flows. Should they be Regulated?*, Basingstoke: Palgrave.

James, H. (2001) *The End of Globalization*, Cambridge, MA, Harvard: Harvard University Press.

Kaplan, E. and Rodrik, D. (2000) 'Did the Malaysian capital controls work?', Paper prepared from an NBER Conference on Currency Crises, Mimeo, December.

Kaul, I., Grunberg, I. and Stern, M.A. (1999) 'Defining global public goods', in Kaul, I., Grunberg, I. and Stern, M.A. (eds), *Global Public Goods. International Cooperation in the 21st Century*, New York and Oxford: Oxford University Press, 2–17.

Kenen, P. (2002) 'Old issues and new initiatives', *International Finance* 5(1), 23–45, Mimeo, March.

Kim, T.-J., Ryou, J.-W. and Wang, Y. (2000) *Regional Arrangements to Borrow Seoul*, Korea Institute for international Economic Policy.

Krueger, A. (2001) 'International financial architecture for 2002: A new approach to sovereign debt restructuring', Address given at the American Enterprise Institute, 26 November, 2001 *www.imf.org/external/np/speeches/2001/ 112601.htm*

Mahnkopf, B. (ed.) (2003) *Globale öffentliche Güter – für menschliche Sicherheit und Frieden*, Berlin: Berliner Wissenschaftsverlag.

Nunnenkamp, P. (2001) *Umbaupläne und Reparaturarbeiten an der internationalen Finanzarchitektur: Eine Zwischenbilanz aus deutscher Perspektive*, Kiel: Kieler Arbeitspapiere No. 1078, October.

Paqué, K.-H. (2001) 'Kein Bedarf an Sand im Getriebe', in *Frankfurter Allgemeine Zeitung*, 20 October, 2001: 15.

Pastor, M. and Wise, C. (2001) 'From poster child to basket case', in *Foreign Affairs*, 80(6), November–December, 60–72.

Shiller, R. (2000) *Irrational Exuberance*, Princeton: Princeton University Press.

Spahn, P.B. (2002) 'Zur Durchführbarkeit einer Devisentransaktionssteuer', Gutachten im Auftrag des BMZ, Frankfurt am Main, February.

Stiglitz, J. (2002) *Die Schatten der Globalisierung*, Berlin: Siedler Verlag.

Underhill, G. (2001) 'State, markets and governance: Private interests, the public good and the democratic process', Inaugural Lecture delivered on 21 September, 2001 at the Universiteit van Amsterdam, Amsterdam: Vossiuspers.

3
Democratization, Financial Crises and Global Governance

Jörg Faust

> The most common and durable source of factions has been the various and unequal distribution of property. Those who hold and those who are without property have ever formed distinct interests in society.
>
> James Madison

Introduction

In the last two decades, one of the most contested disputes in the fields of comparative politics and international relations has been about the impact of globalization on national policies. Within this debate, the most far-reaching arguments predict an increasing convergence of national economic policies as a result of the trend towards free trade and free finance. In a nutshell, these arguments are deduced from theories of international trade and interjurisdictional contestation, assuming that the increasing mobility of goods and capital leaves national policy makers with few choices but to accommodate their policies to the interests of those who own the most mobile production factors. While it may be too early to finally judge the empirical robustness of those explanations, since the empirical effects only show up more clearly in the long run, the underlying assumption is that policy makers already adopt similar strategies in the course of increasing economic globalization. However, there is increasing empirical evidence for 'open economy politics' (Bates 1997) in the sense that national policy responses to economic globalization diverge in important policy fields at least in the short and medium term.[1] More cautious variations of the convergence argument therefore tend to stress the point that even if the trend towards free trade and free finance poses similar challenges to national policy makers, concrete policy designs and their economic impact still strongly respond to specific configurations of domestic actors and institutions.[2] Thus, divergent policy responses and their subsequent implications for resource allocation should be considered in the process of international institution building to meet the normative expectations connected to the global governance discourse. From this background, the following analysis puts further emphasis on the divergence argument by focusing on the causes of financial crises in emerging democracies.

While, especially since the 1980s, dozens of developing countries had to face extreme financial embarrassment, the latest wave of twin crises – the combination of banking and currency crises – during the 1990s seemed to differ in one important aspect, as many of those countries had at least partially removed their capital controls (Haggard and Maxfield 1996).[3] The similarity to previous episodes of financial turmoil consisted in the fact that most of the affected countries again opted for pegging the local currency to a foreign currency. The overall aim of these macroeconomic exchange rate regimes was to create or sustain low inflation by 'importing' the stability of a foreign currency and, at the same time, financing growth through the inflow of external (portfolio) capital. However, such a policy made developing countries vulnerable to the withdrawal of volatile international capital. From a perspective of the convergence argument, it therefore seems no surprise that several scholars have made the changing international financial system and its OECD-based supporters responsible for recent crises.[4] From a divergence point of view however, such interpretations as the early structural dependency theories tend to ignore the filtering functions of domestic political institutions. While on the one hand, external shocks and contagion effects have played an important role as triggering factors of financial crisis, disregarding the influence of domestic aspects leads to inconsistent explanations, as not all developing countries have responded in the same way to the challenges of economic globalization. With regard to the origins of financial crisis in developing countries, this observation leads to the question of how to explain why policy makers in some developing countries were obviously doing better than others?

In line with the divergence argument, there is increasing empirical evidence that connects financial vulnerability to domestic issues, such as bad governance and imprudent regulation. Yet, it seems of some surprise that no systematic attention has been given to the fact that most of the countries affected by twin crises in the 1990s were in a process of democratization.[5] Therefore, I will try to combine the concept of time inconsistencies (Kydland and Prescott 1977) with respect to its implicit assumptions on distributional conflict (Scharpf 1997) with actor-centred research on democratization (Przeworski 1991; Weingast 1997). I will put forward that emerging and unconsolidated democracies are especially exposed to financial crisis, if they are confronted with political fragmentation as a consequence of the inherent distribution conflicts of democratization. Even if the transformation from illiberal order to liberal democracy promises welfare gains in the long run, the endogenous distribution conflicts of democratization increase the danger of political fragmentation often followed by time-inconsistent policies and macroeconomic vulnerability.[6] Thus, in a context of political fragmentation, the combination of capital account liberalization, respectively increasing state debt and pegged exchange rates, is a dangerous attraction because it is often oriented rather towards short-term legitimacy gains than towards long-term oriented development. Just as the combination of restricted exchange regimes and increasing external public debt, the combination of opening the capital account and a pegged exchange rate in the short-run can have growth inducing effects which help to smooth the distributional conflict of democratization. This strategy is prone to failure, however, if fiscal policies and microeconomic regulation are not adapted to the new circumstances. Unfortunately, prudent regulation of the financial sector and fiscal adjustments limit the growth effect and tend to eliminate economic rents. Thus, while in emerging democracies with a high degree of political fragmentation, capital account opening might well obtain political support; the necessary 'secondary' policy measurements of microeconomic regulation and fiscal adjustment are more difficult to achieve. Consequently, the fact that some emerging democracies have been less affected by macroeconomic instability should be related to their low level of political fragmentation.

In order to fully develop my argument, the next section of this chapter concentrates on an attempt at linking the concept of economic time inconsistencies with the findings on financial crisis and the research on democratization. Hereafter, an empirical analysis of the 1982–97 period suggests that emerging democracies within this time span have been over-proportionally affected by the combination of banking and currency crises, and that the vulnerability of such financial turmoil in emerging democracies has been strongly correlated with the degree of political fragmentation. I will conclude by discussing some implications for global economic governance, as the presented findings point at a tension between the goals of fostering democratization and market driven integration into the world economy at the same time.

Time inconsistency, financial crisis and democratization

From the perspective of the collective choice approach in social sciences, macroeconomic stability is a collective good. Through predictable and stable prices, macroeconomic stability substantially reduces transaction costs of economic actors and makes resource allocation more efficient. Thus, for private actors and governments, cooperation aiming at macroeconomic stability should reflect a first best solution. Unfortunately, macroeconomic stability is not for free. While the long-term effects of macroeconomic stability are desirable to government and private actors alike, the distribution conflicts surrounding sound macroeconomic policies make the achievement of this collective good a difficult task. To establish and secure macroeconomic stability, governments have to impose policies, which can be politically costly. They have to avoid chronic and unsustainable overspending, be it by paying favours to special interest groups or by acting as a lender of last resort for bankrupt business. Furthermore, in order to avoid price destabilizing market failure, they have to implement policies of market regulation and corporate governance, which also will be confronted with opposition from particular interest groups. In this context, times of political uncertainty and low political legitimacy constrain governments' political manoeuvring space. Under such circumstances governments are often tempted to promise economic interest groups certain policy measurements in order to persuade them to behave according to the governments' interest. Such dynamic situations provoke time inconsistencies, where agents' *ex ante* and *ex post* incentives may differ and the actor 'in the short run has an incentive to renege on its longer term commitments' (Majone 2001: 62).[7] Consequently, governments should be more tempted to renege on their commitments if they are confronted with a low level of political legitimacy and prefer the short-term gains instead of welfare optimizing results of long term oriented policy making.[8]

As shown in Figure 3.1, financial crises in the course of capital account opening can be analyzed through the lenses of time inconsistency. In game 1 a government interested in foreign capital inflows pegs the exchange rate and promises that it will keep the exchange rate unchanged. As long as the government maintains policies oriented toward fiscal discipline or market friendly reforms, capital owners tend to believe the government and invest, be it through giving loans to the government or by pouring (portfolio) capital into the country's private sector. The situation changes however, if the government fails to implement measurements necessary to sustain the exchange rate regime. Declining fiscal discipline in combination with rising interest rates as a consequence of an overvalued currency might lead to increasing budget and current account deficits. In the case of capital account opening, the failure of a government to implement market sustaining and

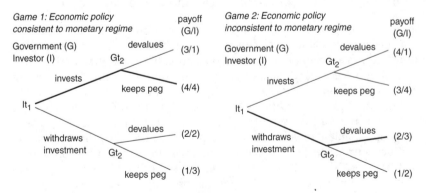

Figure 3.1 Time inconsistency and financial crises

transparency-increasing regulation, increases the number of bad loans and negatively affects overall productivity.[9] Consequently, investors' confidence about returns on investment will vanish as private bankruptcies connected with insufficient regulation emerge. If macroeconomic fundamentals with respect to the stability of the financial sector decline, the situation of game 1 is replaced by the interaction structure of game 2. The government keeps on promising to maintain its exchange rate policy, hoping that investors will not withdraw their investments and hoping to encounter a future 'window of opportunity' for devaluation with regard to the smooth implementation of market-friendly regulation. Yet, if investors are informed about the government's political incapacity to implement exchange rate sustaining policies, they become increasingly suspicious about the government's commitment. Instead of acting according to the government's interest, they rather will begin to withdraw their portfolio investment and start to speculate against the currency. In sum, investors will evaluate the probability of fiscal and regulatory reforms sustaining a fixed exchange rate according to a government's reform capacity. In a context of political instability and political fragmentation, they will be less willing to invest as the chances of consistent economic reforms decline. Mounting difficulties of a government to overcome particular interest groups and to implement policies compatible with the exchange rate regime thus make exchange rate commitments less credible, thereby increasing the probability of financial turmoil.

While the above argument is at least implicitly encountered in many analyses on the domestic causes of macroeconomic instability and financial crisis, it has not been systematically applied to the political context of emerging democracies. Reconsidering the economics of taking, autocratic regimes have vast opportunities to impose political market barriers, enabling autocratic coalitions to establish rent-generating mechanisms, thereby maximizing their political and economic profits (Olson 1993, 2000). Undoubtedly, rent-seeking mechanisms affect the economic development in liberal democracies, too. However, liberal democracies' institutional designs are oriented toward public competition through inclusive mechanisms of political participation (Dahl 1971) and a high level of protected individual property rights through the rule of law (Holmes 1995). In liberal democracies, competition regulates the temporary access to the natural monopoly of the executive, diminishing democratic governments' opportunities to impose a rent-seeking machinery. Compared to autocratic order, the principles of liberal democracy will improve overall economic conditions by allocating resources more efficiently. But again, and unfortunately, the establishment of liberal democracy creates collective action problems as it depends on a consensus of citizens on how to constrain the state. Therefore, the establishment of democratic participation and the rule of law is the result of a successful coordination process, as policing the sovereign by democratic means requires effective coordination of citizens (Przeworski 1991; Weingast 1997).

The successful solution of such coordination generally requires a long time and the pathway from autocratic rule to liberal democracy can be regarded as a time of institutional transformation. The implicit prospects of institutional change generate conflicts between members of the old autocratic coalition and formerly excluded interest groups. Formerly excluded interests, be they organized labour or newly emerging business, expect an economic pay-off from democratization. Equipped with political rights, they can mobilize social protest and have the opportunity to 'punish' the government with their vote. In contrast, members of the old autocratic coalition will try to use their remaining influence to maintain their economic privileges. Furthermore, the electoral constraints of democracy will make it increasingly difficult to shift the costs of macroeconomic adjustment to those formerly excluded, as democratization enhances their opportunities to articulate their economic interests. Yet, those who have profited from illiberal rule will not immediately lose their influence on economic policy making, as they often retain informal connection with bureaucracy. Furthermore, as profiteers of illiberal rule in general have become important capital owners, they can augment their political influence with the threat of capital flight or investment abstinence.[10]

In such an environment of economic conflict, two aspects undermine the achievement of macroeconomic stability. First, the endogenous distribution conflict of democratization increases the danger of political fragmentation. Fragile parties, fragmented party systems, electoral volatility, regional and ethnic divisions often end up augmenting the number of politic actors, who can block policy changes oriented towards macroeconomic stability (Haggard and Kaufmann 1995: 358). Under such circumstances, the executive's capacity to provide the collective good of macroeconomic stability diminishes, as the high number of veto positions makes sound economic reforms with redistributive consequences more difficult (Maxfield and Schneider 1997: 20). Second, if the distributional conflicts of democratization are not institutionally settled, uncertainty about the future course of economic policy increases and economic actors tend to prefer more short-term oriented goals. Both aspects make macroeconomic stability a relatively less valued good and increase tendencies for short-term profit maximizing. Consequently, the maintenance of macroeconomic stability, which depends on a government's capacity to resist short-term interests of societal pressure groups, will be difficult to achieve.

Perceiving democratization as a period of intense and under-institutionalized distribution conflicts, the linkage to the time inconsistency problem becomes obvious. In an environment of institutional uncertainty and political fragmentation, governments are tempted to pursuit short-term oriented economic goals to smooth distribution conflicts. External capital inflows, be it through increasing government debt or by opening up the capital account to international portfolio capital, can thus be interpreted as a means to increase the political legitimacy. The temptation of liberalizing the financial sector increases when international circumstances seem to be favourable. Furthermore, as democratization is mostly accompanied by the government's diminishing influence on the private sector, private firms call for access to relatively cheap international capital. These demands tend to grow stronger, if additional economic reforms such as deregulation and trade liberalization, increase the pressure on business to restructure and modernize production processes. Adding a fixed exchange rate to capital account liberalization too is, in the short run, a promising strategy. By pegging the exchange rate, governments try to make credible commitments to investors that their capital will neither be devalued by exchange rate devaluation nor by inflation. Furthermore, political systems with less transparency and a more fluid institutional environment, such as most emerging democracies prefer fixed exchange rates to Central Bank Independence or other autonomous regulation bodies, because fixed exchange rates are much easier to monitor by external agents (Broz 2002). Therefore, the 'primary contribution of exchange-rate pegs is to make it easier for the public to judge whether a policymaker has deviated from a previously announced commitment. In other words, they help reduce the information asymmetries between government and the public' (Keefer and Stasavage 2002: 752).

While, in the short-term, capital inflows can strengthen the legitimacy of the political regime through economic growth, this policy is not sustainable in the long run without fiscal discipline and prudent regulation of the financial sector. Yet, such policy measures have two consequences, making them less attractive and less achievable in emerging democracies affected by political fragmentation. First, those measurements would reduce the amount of capital inflows, at least in the short run, thereby reducing the short-term growth effect and thus the legitimacy gains expected by the government. Second and more important, the introduction of fiscal discipline and/or prudent financial regulation has the effect of making resource allocation more efficient, thereby eliminating economic rents. Introducing fiscal discipline and/or prudent regulation therefore has distributive consequences, and creates political opposition from negatively affected interest groups. Consequently, in a polity characterized by political fragmentation, such policies are hard to implement, making the commitment to sustain the exchange rate regime less credible, thereby increasing the probability of a twin crisis.

Empirical evidence

Since the outbreak of the Asian Crisis, many economists and political scientists have intensified their efforts to detect possible sources of financial crises. A summary of recent findings presented in Table 3.1 illustrates that the majority of macro-quantitative studies have identified domestic factors as the crucial causes of currency and banking crises. This is not to say that international

Table 3.1 Macro-quantitative research on financial crises, 1998–2002

Authors	Dependent variable	Cases	Variables of influence
Bernhard and Leblang 2000	Currency speculation	16 OECD countries, 1975–98	Budget deficits (+), inflation (+), unemployment (+), elections (+), left party governments (+)
Demirgüc-Kunt and Detragiache 1998, 2000	Banking crisis (BC)	65 countries (developing, OECD), 1980–95	Financial liberalization (+), corruption (+), rent-seeking(+)
Eichengreen and Rose 1998	BC	105 developing countries, 1975–92	International interest rate (+), low growth in OECD (+), short-term-debt (+)
Eichengreen and Arteta 2000	BC	65–105 countries (developing, OECD), 1975–97	Combination of expansive macroeconomic policies and private credit boom (+), financial liberalization (+)
Eichengreen 2000	BC	see Eichengreen and Rose, 1998 but 1975–98	Short-term-debt (+), financial liberalization (+)
Ghosh and Ghosh 2002	Currency crisis (CC)	40 countries (developing, OECD), 1987–99	'Bad' governance (+), 'bad' corporate governance (+), macroeconomic imbalances plus domestic credit boom (+)
Glick and Hutchinson 2000	CC	69 developing countries, 1975–97	Capital control mechanisms (+)
Glick and Rose 1999	CC/contagion	161 countries (developing, OECD)	Contagion correlated with similar foreign trade structures (+)

Hutchinson and McDill 1999	CC, BC	90 countries (developing, OECD), 1995–97	Corruption (+), inappropriate regulation (+)
Kaminsky and Reinhart 1999	CC, BC	24 countries (developing, OECD), 1970–97	Macroeconomic imbalances (+), domestic credit boom (+)
Kaminsky and Reinhart 2000	CC/contagion	80 currency crises (developing countries, OECD)	Contagion of currency crisis correlated with similar investment strategies and similar foreign trade structures (+)
Keefer 2001	BC	40 BC, 35 countries (developing, OECD)	Absence of political checks and balances (+)
Keefer and Knack 2002	Country credit worthiness	Developing and OECD countries	Socioeconomic fragmentation plus competitive elections (−)
Leblang 2002	Currency speculation	78 democracies in developing countries, 1975–98	Budget deficit (+), inflation (+), international interest rate (+), domestic credit boom (+), elections (+)
Lensik et al. 2000	Capital flight	65 developing countries, 1970–90	Political risk (+)
Rijckeghem and Weder 2001	CC/contagion	Mainly developing countries	Contagion of currency crisis correlated with similar investment strategies (+)
Weller 2001	BC	27 emerging markets, 1973–98	Financial liberalization plus inadequate financial regulation (+)

influences do not play an important role as triggering factors of financial turmoil. However, especially twin crises, defined as the parallel appearance of currency and banking crises, almost always occur in a context in which domestic factors cause increasing vulnerability towards external shocks such as speculation or contagion.

The combination of financial liberalization, imprudent regulation and strong evidence of corruption has been identified as an extremely danger-ous mixture, which strongly augments the probability of financial turmoil. Furthermore, elections and socio-economic fragmentation also tend to increase governments' difficulties in maintaining macroeconomic stability and international creditworthiness. In sum, most of the existing findings at least do not support those arguments, which makes the changing interna-tional context responsible for twin crises, even if international factors can still play an important role as triggering factors. Yet, despite those efforts demonstrating the importance of domestic factors, there have been very few and unsystematic attempts, that concentrate on the sources of financial crises in emerging democracies.[11] In order to fill this gap, a sample of 84 countries, for which data on banking and currency crises are available for the 1982–97 period has been divided according to each country's politi-cal regime. The identification of political regimes is based on data from Polity IV and Freedom House.[12] A country has been considered as an *autoc-racy* if its Polity IV value has been less than 1 on a scale that ranges from -10 to $+10$. If, according to the Polity IV dataset, a country obtains a value greater than 1, and if the average of political rights and civil liberties taken from the Freedom House data set is between 2.5 and 4.5, the country has been classified as an emerging democracy.[13] A country has been identified as a *consolidated democracy* if its Polity IV value exceeds 1 and if Freedom House has rated the country as a politically free country for more than 10 consecutive years. After having categorized countries according to their political regime, the probability of currency and banking crises in each regime type has been calculated. Data of banking crises and currency crises were taken from a study by Reuven Glick and Michael Hutchinson (2001). According to these authors, a currency crisis occurs when there are large changes of currency pressure, defined as the weighted average of (monthly) exchange rate changes and (monthly) reserve losses. To identify banking crises, these authors employ a combination of criteria such as forced closure, forced merger, strong government intervention, non-performing assets and problem loans. Based on these data, I have identified a twin crisis (CCBC), if a banking and a currency crisis have occurred in the same year, or if one type of crisis followed the other in the consecutive year. The results in Table 3.2 demonstrate that the probability of a twin crisis was substantially higher in emerging democracies than it was in consolidated democracies or in autocracies. Furthermore, currency and banking crises were also more prob-able in emerging democracies while those phenomena tended to occur

Table 3.2 Currency and banking crises in 84 countries, 1982–97

	Observations (years)	BC	BC/ years	CC	CC/ years	CCBC	CCBC/ years
Autocracies	505	113	0.22	89	0.18	24	0.05
Emerging democracies	410	109	0.27	85	0.21	40	0.10
Consolidated democracies	429	84	0.2	43	0.10	19	0.04

Sources: Glick and Hutchinson 2001; Freedom House, Polity IV.

much less in consolidated democracies than in the two other regime types. As especially twin crises are mainly caused by domestic circumstances, these findings are consistent with the argument that democratization as a period of institutional change increases governments' difficulties in providing the collective good of macroeconomic stability.

However, the overview presented in Table 3.2 does not provide evidence on the variance of crisis probability within the sub-sample of emerging democracies. It contains no information about why some emerging democracies like Chile or Taiwan have been confronted with less financial turmoil than others. To gain insights about the varying probability of twin crises in emerging democracies, I have analyzed those countries of the sample that can be considered as emerging democracies. According to my argument, those emerging democracies confronted with a higher degree of political fragmentation should have had more difficulties avoiding currency and banking crises as governments should have found it more difficult to gain the necessary autonomy to engage in long-term oriented policy making. To verify this hypothesis, I rely on the veto-player framework introduced by George Tsebelis, who defines veto-players as an 'individual or collective actor[s] whose agreement is required for a change in policy' (1995: 301).[14] If the proposed hypothesis about the influence of political fragmentation on macroeconomic time inconsistency is translated into the veto-player-framework, there should be a correlation between the constellation of veto-players and the average of financial crisis occurrence in emerging democracies. Stated more precisely, while probably every state submitted to the process of democratization is confronted with similar problems of maintaining macroeconomic stability and avoiding financial turmoil, polities with lesser and more convergent veto-players should cope better with those challenges than polities with a high number of veto-players with divergent political programmes.

To test this hypothesis, I have performed several cross section linear regression analyses, where the dependent variable (CCBC) is the average of twin crisis in a country considered as an emerging democracy. The CCBC variable is calculated as the sum of twin crises in a given period within the 1982–97 time span divided by the number of years of the period. Furthermore only those countries have been included in the sample that have been considered as emerging democracies for at least five consecutive years. This threshold is used as the independent variable is based on an average calculation, which can be distorted by very short time spans.[15] The degree of political fragmentation is measured by a variable taken from the Database of Political Institutions Version 3.0 (Beck *et al.* 2001). The variable FRAG is based on the *check3* variable of this data set, an index that tries to measure the number of veto-players and the programmatic distance between veto-players. FRAG is the average *check3* value for the period during which a country has been identified as an emerging democracy. To control the effect of political fragmentation, several other variables have been included: (1) the level of socioeconomic development at the beginning of the analyzed period, measured by the Human Development Index (HDI) regularly published by UNDP; (2) the total factor productivity growth (TFP) in the given period (Bosworth and Collins 1999); (3) the average of the legal structure and security of property right indicator (GOV) published by the Fraser Institute in its Annual Report on Economic Freedom (Gwartney *et al.* 2001); (4) the average degree of capital account openness (CAO) as measured by Menzie Chinn and Hiro Ito (2002), who construct an index of capital account openness from information available in the IMF's Annual Reports on Exchange Arrangements and Exchange Restrictions; (5) the number of years in which the country has been regarded as an emerging democracy (YEARS).

As the dependent variable is the probability of a crisis in a country during a given period, the resulting cross section regression analysis reduces the number of cases to 26–32 for which data are available. Therefore, several regression analyses with three and four independent variables are performed in order to test the 'robustness' of the FRAG variables' sign and strength. The results presented in Table 3.3 are consistent with the presented arguments. Within the given sample of emerging democracies, political fragmentation has a positive and highly significant influence on the average occurrence of twin crises. The signs of the control variables included in the analysis are also consistent with existing finding on the domestic sources of financial crises, but with the exception of the TFP variable are not significant. As already mentioned by Krugman (1994), low levels of TFP growth thus seem to indicate a higher possibility of macroeconomic instability, even if overall growth rates might be impressive. Furthermore, within the sample, a low degree of law and order and insecure property rights tended to increase the probability of financial crisis, as did capital account opening. Additionally, the negative correlation between the probability of a twin crisis and the number of years during which a country has been identified as an emerging democracy, further sustains the main argument. As the distribution conflicts surrounding the introduction of the rule of law and democratic participation tend to be stronger in the immediate period after a transition to democracy, so should be a government's difficulties in maintaining a policy mix that guarantees a high degree of monetary credibility and financial stability.

Table 3.3 Twin crises in emerging democracies, 1982–97

	Model 1	Model 2	Model 3	Model 4	Model 5
HDI	.107 (.092)	.112 (.103)	−.0819 (.127)	−.0328 (.115)	
FRAG	.02802 (.010)**	.03709 (.011)***	.04942 (.019)***	.04706 (.014)***	.03582 (.01)***
TFP	−.0211 (.007)***				−.0131 (.008)*
GOV		−.0130 (.011)			−.0251 (.012)**
CAO			.002502 (.002)		
YEARS				−.00616 (.004)	−.00514 (.003)
Constant	−.0687 (.063)	−.0421 (.086)	−.0463 (.096)	.0255 (.088)	.152 (.080)*
Adj. R2	.353***	.285***	.120	.239**	.413***
N	29	31	28	32	29

Countries: Argentina, Bangladesh, Bolivia, Brazil, Chile, Colombia, Dominican Republic, Ecuador, El Salvador, Guatemala, Guyana, Honduras, Hungary, India, Korea (Rep.), Madagascar, Malaysia, Mali, Nepal, Nicaragua, Paraguay, Peru, Philippines, Romania, South Africa, Spain, Taiwan, Thailand, Turkey, Uruguay, Zambia.

Conclusion: global governance and big bills on the sidewalk

> ... the familiar old joke about the assistant professor who, when walking with a full professor, suddenly reaches for the $100 bill he sees on the sidewalk; but he is held back by his senior colleague, who points out that, if the $100 bill were real, it would have been picked up already.
>
> Mancur Olson

In his eloquent critique of mainstream economics, Mancur Olson has questioned the assumption that big bills are necessarily taken straight away (Olson 1996). Because mainstream economics often makes no differentiation between the economics of making and the economics of taking, it underestimates the distorting effect of political influence. Yet, disregarding that 'inefficiency by design is commonly observed in politics' (Williamson 2000: 110), and assuming that resource allocation always tends to be socially efficient, ignores the vast coordination efforts necessary to pick up the big bills of our societies. If financial stability and liberal democracy are such big bills, the presented findings give further support to those arguments in the social sciences which highlight the enormous tensions between individual and collective rationality, as well as to the inherent conflicts of similarly promoting different collective goods. With respect to the national level, this analysis on financial turmoil in emerging democracies further sustains the divergence argument within the globalization debate. The offered empirical evidence demonstrated that the average of twin crises within the chosen country sample has varied according to the domestic configuration of veto-players. Even if the trend towards free finance poses similar challenges and provokes similar grand strategies of national policy makers, the concrete policy design and the subsequent impacts of increasing economic globalization strongly respond to domestic constellations. Within a large sample of countries, the average of twin crisis was substantially higher in emerging democracies than in autocratic regimes or in consolidated democracies. Within the sample of emerging democracies, the average of twin crises increased with the degree of political fragmentation. Thus, under the circumstances of strong distributional conflict and a fragmented polity, market reforms such as capital account liberalization tend to be oriented towards the fulfilment of short-term oriented political goals, thereby creating a tension between democratization and the introduction of market-friendly institutions.

Beyond having presented further evidence on the varying impact of economic globalization on national policies, the presented findings might also prove useful for the discussion on global governance. Disputes on global governance have long centred on the tension of creating effective governance mechanisms at the global level while at the same time building participatory structures that feed those mechanisms with democratic legitimacy. This tension reflects the old problem of democratic governance: how to create a government that is capable of granting effective rules to organize a given societal space but at the same time is not strong enough to exploit citizens by taking their political and economic rights? Besides this tension, however, there is another puzzle within the context of global governance that deals with the problem of parallel fostering democracy and economic liberalization. Following the presented arguments, the concentration on global governance mechanisms in the policy field of financial regulation may prove insufficient in dealing with the underlying political sources of financial crisis in emerging democracies. If fiscal imbalances and risky capital account opening have been at least partly a response to domestic political challenges resulting from political transformation, global governance mechanisms that only focus on economic liberalization and improving financial regulation might fall short of tackling the underlying problem of financial stability in emerging democracies. Failing to recognize that the domestic distribution conflicts of political change are crucial for the course of democratization and domestic economic management might even aggravate the problem of political legitimacy in emerging democracies. Therefore, reducing the probability of financial crisis by mechanisms of global governance should also imply the search of strategies to smooth emerging democracies' domestic distribution conflicts. Fostering the reduction of trade barriers in the OECD world could be an adequate strategy to stimulate growth in the developing world, thereby indirectly contributing to more consistent macroeconomic policies.

Notes

1 For empirical support of the divergence hypothesis, see, among others, Busch in this volume, Ch. 5; Mosley 2000, 2003; Verdier 1999.
2 See for example Frieden and Rogowski 1996, Goodman and Pauly 1993, Schirm 2002.
3 For differentiated interpretations of external and internal influences see for example the volumes edited by Armijo 1998, Kahler 1998, Noble and Ravenhill 2000; for a broad analysis of financial crisis see Eichengreen 2002.
4 See, for example, Huffschmid 2000.
5 A simple overview on twin crises during the 1990s reveals that a high percentage of crisis states were emerging democracies in the course of democratic consolidation. Among the most affected countries were emerging democracies such as Mexico, the Czech Republic, Thailand, South Korea, Russia, Brazil, Turkey and Argentina.
6 Democratization is defined as the transformation from autocratic order to liberal democracy. While *emerging democracies* can be considered as regimes, where democratic features prevail, they cannot be considered as liberal democracies. They still have to conclude democratic consolidation and thus are often characterized by persistent institutional deficiencies such as illiberal institutions (Collier and Levitsky 1997; Merkel and Croissant 2000; O'Donnell 1994).
7 For example, a government might promise investors tax cuts simply to confiscate properties after the investments have been made (Bates 1998). Governments might also promise organized labour tight monetary policy to persuade them to smooth loan negotiations just to renege afterwards on their commitment in order to boost growth and employment (Kydland and Prescott 1977).
8 As Mancur Olson (2000) has illustrated, even an autocratic ruler only tends to renege on macroeconomic promises when he is confronted with a shortening political time horizon. In democracies, macroeconomic time incosistencies especially appear during times of election and increasing distribution conflicts among economic interest groups (Bernard and Leblang 2000).
9 For a more detailed explanation, see, among others, McKinnon and Pill 1998; Obstfeld and Taylor 1998; Weller 2001.
10 On the political economy of democratization, see, among others, Przeworski 1991; Haggard and Kaufmann 1995; Faust 2001.
11 An interesting exception is the case study of Arvid Lukauskas (1997) on democratization and financial sector reform in Spain.
12 For the Polity data see Jaggers and Gurr 1995; Marshall *et al.* 2001.
13 The Freedom House *Survey* employs two series of checklists, one for questions regarding political rights and civil liberties, both categories ordered numerically within a range of 1 to 7. The political rights and civil liberties ratings are averaged in order to assign each country and territory to a status of 'Free' (1–2.5), 'Partly Free' (3–4) or 'Not Free' (4.5–7).
14 While institutional veto-players are defined by the constitution, 'the number of partisan veto players is specified endogenously by the party system and the government coalitions of each specific country' (Tsebelis 1995: 304). In essence,

'it differentiates political systems by the number of actors who can block or veto – a change in policy' (MacIntyre 2001: 86).

15 For example, Brazil has been considered as a young democracy for 13 years (1985–97) within the 1982–97 time span. According to the data of Glick and Hutchinson (1999), Brazil was confronted with two twin crises during this period, so the dependent variable in this case would be 2/13.

References

Armijo, L.E. (ed.) (1999) *Financial Globalization and Democracy in Emerging Markets*, New York: Palgrave, St. Martin's.

Bates, R. (1998) 'Institutions as investments', in Borner, S. and Paldam, M. (eds), *The Political Dimension of Growth*, New York: St. Martin's Press, 3–19.

Bates, R.H. (1997) *Open-Economy Politics: The Political Economy of the World Coffee Trade*, Princeton: Princeton University Press.

Beck, T., Clarke, G., Groff, A., Keefer, P. and Walsh, P. (2001) 'The database of political institutions', in *World Bank Economic Review*, 15(1), 165–76.

Bernhard, W. and Leblang, D. (2000) 'The politics of speculative attacks in industrial democracies', in *International Organization*, 54(2), 292–324.

Bosworth, B.P. and Collins, S.M. (1999) 'Capital flows to developing economies: Implications for saving and investment', Washington, DC, The Brookings Institution: Brookings Papers on Economic Activities: 1/1999.

Broz, L. (2002) 'Political system transparency and monetary commitment regimes', in *International Organization*, 56(4), 861–87.

Chinn, M. and Ito, H. (2002) 'Capital account liberalization, institutions and financial development: Cross country evidence', Washington, DC: NBER Working Paper no. 8967.

Collier, D. and Levitsky, S. (1997) 'Democracy with adjectives: Conceptual innovation in comparative research', in *World Politics*, 49, 430–51.

Dahl, R. (1971) *Polyarchy – Participation and Opposition*, New Haven and London: Yale University Press.

Demirgüc-Kunt, A. and Detragiache, E. (2000) 'Does deposit insurance increase banking system stability?', Washington, DC: IMF Working Paper WP/00/3.

Demirgüc-Kunt, A. and Detragiache, E. (1998) 'Financial liberalization and financial fragility', Washington, DC: IMF Working Paper WP/98/83.

Eichengreen, B. (2002) *Financial Crises – and What To Do About Them*, New York: Oxford University Press.

Eichengreen, B. (2001) 'Capital account liberalization: What do cross-country studies tell us?', in *World Bank Economic Review*, 15(3), 341–65.

Eichengreen, B. (2000) 'The EM in retrospect', Cambridge, MA: NBER Working Paper no. 8035.

Eichengreen, B. and Arteta, C. (2000) 'Banking crisis in emerging markets: Presumptions and evidence', Center for International and Development Economics Research, University of California, Berkeley, Working Paper Coo-115.

Eichengreen, B. and Rose, A. (1998) 'Staying afloat when the wind shifts: External factors and emerging-market banking crisis', Washington, DC: NBER Working Paper no. 6370.

Faust, J. (2001) 'Marktkonstruktion und politische Transformation. Politökonomische Ursachen defizitärer Demokratisierung (Market construction and political transformation – The political economic of defective democratization)', in Bendel, P.,

Croissant, A. and Rüb, F. (eds), *Zwischen Demokratie und Diktatur. Zur Konzeption und Empirie demokratischer Grauzonen*, Opladen: Leske and Budrich.

Freedom House: 'Annual Survey of Freedom Country Scores 1972–73 to 1999–2000', taken from *http://www.freedomhouse.org/*

Frieden, J. and Rogowski, R. (1996) 'The impact of the international economy on national policies: An analytical overview', in Keohane, R.O. and Milner, H.V. (eds), *Internationalization and Domestic Politics*, Cambridge: Cambridge University Press, 25–47.

Ghosh, S. and Ghosh, A. (2002) 'Structural vulnerabilities and currency crisis', Washington, DC: International Monetary Fund, Working Paper WP 02/9.

Glick, R. and Hutchinson, M. (2001) 'Banking and currency crises: How common are twins?', in Glick R., Moreno, R. and Spiegel, M. (eds), *Financial Crises in Emerging Markets*, New York: Cambridge University Press.

Glick, R. and Hutchinson, M. (2000) 'Capital controls and exchange rate stability in developing countries', Pacific Basin Working Paper Series No. PB00-05, Center for Pacific Basin Monetary and Economic Studies, Federal Reserve Bank of San Francisco.

Glick, R. and Hutchinson, M. (1999) 'Banking and currency crisis', San Francisco Reserve Bank, Pacific Basin Series PB 99-07.

Glick, R. and Rose, A. (1999) 'Contagion and trade: Why are currency crises regional?', in *Journal of International Money and Finance*, 18, 603–17.

Goodman, J.B. and Pauly, L.W. (1993) 'The obsolescence of capital controls? Economic management in an age of global markets', in *World Politics*, 46(1), 50–82.

Gwartney, J. and Lawson, R. with Walter Park and Charles Skipton (2001) 'Economic Freedom of the World', *Annual Report*, Vancouver: Fraser Institute, taken from *http://www.freetheworld.com*

Haggard, S. and Maxfield, S. (1996) 'The political economy of internationalization in the developing countries', in *International Organization*, 50(1), 35–68.

Haggard, S. and Kaufmann, R.R. (1995) *The Political Economy of Democratic Transitions*, Princeton: Princeton University Press.

Holmes, S. (1995) *Passions and Constraint – On the Theory of Liberal Democracy*, Chicago and London: University of Chicago Press.

Huffschmid, J. (2000) 'Das Verhältnis Metropolen-Peripherie unter dem Aspekt der Finanz- und Währungsbeziehungen', in Boris, D. (ed.), *Finanzkrisen im Übergang zum 21. Jahrhundert. Probleme der Peripherie oder globale Gefahr?*, Marburg: Metropolis, 43–64.

Hutchinson, M. and McDill, K. (1999) 'Are all banking crises alike? The Japanese experience in international comparison', *Journal of the Japanese and International Economies*, December.

Jaggers, K. and Gurr, T. (1995) 'Tracking democracy's third wave with Polity III data', in *Journal of Peace Research*, 32, 469–82.

Kahler, M. (ed.) (1998) *Capital Flows and Financial Crisis*, Manchester: Manchester University Press.

Kaminsky, G. and Reinhart, C.N. (2000) 'On crisis, contagion and confusion', in *Journal of International Economics*, 51, 145–68.

Kaminsky, G. and Reinhart, C. (1999) 'The twin crisis', in *American Economic Review*, 89(3), 473–500.

Kaminsky, G. and Reinhart, C.N. (1998) 'The twin crisis: The causes of banking and balance of payments problems', International Finance Discussion Paper no. 544, Board of Governors of the Federal Reserve System.

Keefer, P. (2001) 'Politics and the determinants of banking crisis: The effects of political checks and balances', Santiago de Chile: Central Bank of Chile Working Paper no. 119.

Keefer, P. and Knack, S. (2002) 'Social polarization, political institutions, and country creditworthiness', Washington, DC: World Bank Policy Research Working Paper 2920.

Keefer, P. and Stasavage, D. (2002) 'Checks and balances, private information and the credibility of monetary commitments', in *International Organization*, 56(4), 751–802.

Kydland, F. and Prescott, E.C. (1977) 'Rules rather than discretion: The inconsistency of optimal plans', in *Journal of Political Economy*, 85, 473–92.

Leblang, D.A. (2002) 'The political economy of speculative attacks in the developing world', in *International Studies Quarterly*, 46(1), 69–91.

Lensik, R., Hermes, N. and Murinde, V. (2000) 'Capital flight and political risk', in *Journal of International Money and Finance*, 19, 73–92.

Lijphart, A. (1977) *Democracy in Plural Societies*, New Haven: Yale University Press.

Mainwaring, S. (1999) *Rethinking Party Systems in the Third Wave of Democratization. The Case of Brazil*, Stanford: Stanford University Press.

MacIntyre, A. (2001) 'Institutions and investors: The politics of the economic crisis in Southeast Asia', in *International Organization*, 55(1), 81–123.

McKinnon, R. and Pill, H. (1998) 'International overborrowing: A decomposition of credit and currency risks', in *World Development*, 26(7), 1267–82.

Majone, G. (2001) 'Nonmajoritarian institutions and the limits of democratic governance: A political transaction-cost approach', in *Journal of Institutional and Theoretical Economics* (JITE), 157(4), 57–78.

Marshall, M., Jaggers, K. and Gurr, T. (2001) 'Polity IV project: Political regime characteristics and transitions, 1800–2000', *www.cidcm.umd.edu/inscr/polity/*

Maxfield S. and Schneider, B.R. (eds) (1997) *Business and the State in Developing Countries*, Ithaca, NY: Cornell University Press.

Merkel, W. and Croissant, A. (2000) 'Formale und informale Institution', in *Politische Vierteljahresschmift*, 41(1), 3–30.

Mosley, L. (2003) *Global Capital and National Governments*, Cambridge: Cambridge University Press.

Mosley, L. (2000) 'Room to move: International financial markets and national welfare states', in *International Organization*, 54(4), 737–73.

Noble, G.W. and Ravenhill, J. (eds) (2000) *The Asian Financial Crisis and the Architecture of Global Finance*, Cambridge: Cambridge University Press.

Obstfeld, M. and Taylor, A. (1998) 'The Great Depression as a watershed: International capital mobility over the long run', in Bordo, M., Goldin, C. and White, E. (eds), *The Defining Moment: The Great Depression and the American Economy in the Twentieth Century*, Chicago: University of Chicago Press, 353–402.

O'Donnell, G. (1994) 'Delegative democracy', in *Journal of Democracy*, 5(1), 55–69.

Olson, M. (2000) *Power and Prosperity. Outgrowing Communist and Capitalist Dictatorships*, New York: Basic Books.

Olson, M. (1996) 'Big bills left on the sidewalk: Why some nations are rich, and others poor', in *Journal of Economic Perspectives*, 10(2), 3–24.

Olson, M. (1993) 'Dictatorship, democracy and development', in *American Political Science Review (APSR)*, 87(3), 567–76.

Przeworski, A. (1991) *Democracy and the Market*, New York and Cambridge: Cambridge University Press.

Rijckeghem, C. van and Weder, B. (2001) 'Sources of contagion: Is it finance or trade?', in *Journal of International Economics*, 54, 293–308.

Scharpf, F. (1997) *Games Real Actors Play: Actor-Centered Institutionalism in Policy Research*, Boulder: Westview Press.

Schirm, S. (1999) *Globale Märkte, nationale Politik und regionale Kooperation in Europa und den Amerikas* (Global Markets, National Politics and Regional Cooperation in Europe and the Americas), Baden-Baden: Nomos.

Tsebelis, G. (1995) 'Decision making in political systems: Vetoplayers in presidentialism, parliamentarism, multi-cameralism and multi-partyism', in *British Journal of Political Science*, 25, 289–325.

Verdier, D. (1999) 'Domestic responses to free trade and free finance in OECD countries', in *Business and Politics*, 1(3), 279–317.

Weingast, B. (1997) 'The political foundations of democracy and the rule of law', in *American Political Science Review*, 91(2), 245–63.

Weller, C. (2001) 'Financial crisis after financial liberalisation: Exceptional circumstances or structural weakness?', in *Journal of Development Studies*, 38(1), 98–127.

Wibbels, E. (2000) 'Federalism and the politics of macroeconomic policy and performance', in *American Journal of Political Science*, 44(4), 687–702.

Williamson, O. (2000) 'Economic institutions and development: A view from the bottom', in Olson, M. and Kähkönen, S. (eds), *A Not-So-Dismal Science. A Broader View of Economies and Societies*, New York: Oxford University Press, 92–118.

Part II

States as Actors in Global Economic Governance

4
Governance by Negotiation: The EU, the United States and China's Integration into the World Trade System

Hubert Zimmermann

Introduction

When, in December 2001, the protocol stipulating the terms of China's accession to the World Trade Organization (WTO) was signed, a negotiating process came to an end which had lasted for more than fifteen years. It was a momentous event in the history of the attempt to create a truly global governance structure. China had not participated in the enormous expansion of world trade after World War II. Expectations were running high regarding the potential of an eventual opening of the China market, particularly in those industrialized countries which had been central in setting the parameters of China's integration into the global trade regime. By far the most important actors in this process were the European Union and the United States. Both define to a large extent the emergence of new governance structures in the international economic system. The case of China is, due to its political and economic importance, a good indicator for their respective strategies in this process. With a focus on the negotiations about China's accession to the WTO, this chapter tries to identify recurring patterns in the ways the EU and the United States manage the continuing expansion of globalization to new territories and sectors.

The major policy mode by which actors in the international system pursue their visions of global governance are negotiations. Therefore, this case study intends to contribute to theories about the characteristics and strategies of both actors in international negotiations. I argue that actor-centred theories are indispensable if we want to understand and explain the behaviour of actors such as the USA and the EU in the global economic system. The systemic theories which dominate research on international negotiations have to be supplemented by theories which, first, explain how actors respond to systemic effects and which, second, account for precisely those differences in these responses which systemic theories tend to neglect.

Global governance and international negotiations

Despite the emergence of an increasingly tight and legalized web of international institutions, negotiations will remain the central instruments of international governance. Increasing globalization and transnationalization reduces the room for unilateral policies that have no, or only a marginal, impact on other international actors. Hierarchical-authoritarian decisions or decisions taken under a 'shadow of hierarchy', which reduces in domestic systems the implementation problem (Scharpf 2000: 326), will in all likelihood not become decisive factors in obtaining international cooperation. Therefore, the acceptance of global norms has to be continuously negotiated. The extension of rule based regulation efforts to new sectors (services, international norms and so on) and the adaption of existing rules to changing political and economic conditions will be done via negotiations.

It is therefore rather surprising that the phenomenon of negotiations has not received the degree of attention in the scientific debate which its ubiquity would have warranted. Instead, the relative importance of systemic determinants of international relations and research about conditions and chances of international cooperation continue to dominate the discipline. How exactly cooperation is achieved, however, has been less studied. Maybe this is due to the fact that negotiations are a dynamic process. This poses specific challenges to a social science which is usually looking for regularities and continuities. The dominant way for explaining the preferences of state actors is to determine these either on the international (realism; regime theory), on the domestic (liberalism) or on an ideological (constructivism) level and thus to establish a stable set of preferences for the actors. Once identified, these systemic determinants, such as anarchy or international institutions or norms, tend to exert a 'harmonizing' influence on actors which shape their behaviour in similar and predictable ways. In the ideal world of realists and constructivists, negotiations are redundant. Either different power potentials or the common acceptance of norms resolve conflicts. However, in negotiations, change is intrinsic; for them to succeed, at least one party has to change its preferences. How this happens, under which conditions and on which terms is a question still in search of a theory.[1]

In a recent handbook article on international negotiations, Christer Jönsson (2002: 223) made a useful distinction between theories of negotiation which are issue-specific, situation-specific and actor-specific. Issue-specific theories are determined by the subject matter of the negotiations; for example, disarmament or trade negotiations. Situation-specific negotiation theory looks for specific constellations which determine the course of the negotiating process. Grounded mainly in game theory, they dominate the literature on international negotiations.[2] Actor-specific approaches concentrate on general characteristics of the actors in international negotiations. As will be argued below, negotiations can best be explained by looking at the characteristics of actors combined with some basic systemic insights. This approach encompasses all negotiating situations and, thus, there is no need for an issue-specific theory.

Given that systemic theory dominates the theoretical literature on negoti-ations, a few remarks are necessary to explain why, to my mind, it is not able to explain real-world negotiations. A whole school of theorists has tried to specify the conditions under which negotiations can be concluded success-fully or lead to optimal results.[3] The objective was, as in economics (in which most of this research is grounded), the search for situations under which negotiations were most likely to succeed with the greatest potential of gains for all parties involved. Since the actors are usually conceived as rational utility-maximizers, often the prospects for cooperation have been regarded as rather bleak. One way out of this dilemma of collective action are 'tit for tat' strategies in which actors rely on a 'shadow of the future' (that is, meet-ing again at future negotiations) and therefore behave cooperatively (Axelrod 1984). However, in an environment with many actors and uncertainty about one's own and the others' utility, 'tit for tat' strategies are not sufficient: par-ticularly since utility is not the only factor guiding the behaviour of actors in the international system (Holzinger 2001: 248). Furthermore, the ratification of negotiating results is often done by other actors than those who negoti-ated them. In the USA, for example, Congress ratifies international trade agreements. In the EU, this is done by the council of ministers. Tit-for-tat is therefore hardly imaginable if actors are conceived as corporate.

In fact, most game-theoretic models act on the basis of homogenous actors and develop theories for one level, the international system. However, as Wolf and Zangl (1996) have shown, it is not sufficient to develop models for the systemic level. International actors cooperate only if it is reasonably safe to assume that the results are implemented at the sub-systemic level. It is therefore necessary to model constellations of interests for both levels and link them (Zangl 1999). However, a major problem of this approach is that it skips over the fact that these constellations are subject to constant change during the negotiations. This becomes particularly clear if we split the nego-tiation process into three phases which are functionally different:

(1) the agenda setting phase, denoting the process of selecting the prefer-ences which are represented at the negotiating table;
(2) the negotiating phase, which is the actual interaction with the interna-tional counterpart; and
(3) the ratification phase, at the end of which lays the acceptance of the results by all actors which might topple the international agreement.

This way of splitting up the negotiating process is not particularly new but usually it is used to describe the temporal dimension of negotiations. However, the three phases can also be employed as analytical categories (see also: Nicolaïdis 1999). Proceeding from the assumption that negotiating enti-ties in the international system are corporate actors, a different institutional constellation is often at work in each phase. The result might be that in each phase and for each actor, a different set of preferences is privileged. The assumption of stable preferences all through the negotiating process, which is necessary to construct formal models of the negotiating process, neglects this factor. Furthermore, the preferences of actors are exogenously given in those models. The analysis of change during negotiations precludes, however, the assumption of fixed, exogenously given preferences. It is more useful to concentrate in the analysis of negotiations on those factors which systematically shape the *formation* of preferences and the behaviour of actors in different stages of negotiations.[4] A prime factor among those is the institutional system within which actors generate their preferences before and during international negotiations.

To illustrate its impact, one historical example might suffice. In 1934, the Reciprocal Trade Agreements Act (RTAA) involved a reform of the institutional framework of trade policy making in the United States, which changed the American negotiating behaviour and the formation of preferences completely. Before that, Congress had a pervasive influence in all matters of foreign trade which led to a dominance of protectionist demands. The RTAA, however, gave the presidency unprecedented autonomy to conduct trade negotiations. Accordingly, the preferences of the executive played a much more important role, and that made the creation of the postwar liberal trade system with its institutions and geopolitical background possible. In the 1970s, Congress tried to recapture lost influence. It succeeded, by acquiring important competencies in the agenda-setting and ratification stages. Once again, the basic American strategy changed, leading to a negotiating style which was both more erratic and less prone to compromise.

The central hypothesis of this chapter is that the characteristic features of the United States and the EU as negotiating powers are shaped by institutional factors which mediate between international and national objectives. It will be argued that these institutional dynamics systematically shape European and American policies in international negotiations. Of course, situative factors (economic and political interests) are central for the negotiating strategies of any conceivable actor in the global economic system at specific moments. However, the potential of an institutional approach lays in identifying the 'corridors' that delimit the range of possible policies and define the interests of the actors.[5] As quite stable determinants, they illuminate not only the emergence of actual preferences but also allow an estimate of future responses by both actors to new developments in global economic governance.

The analytical step of splitting the negotiating process also allows the fusion of classical IR theories with negotiation theories. Moravcsik has observed that liberal theories seem to be more useful for the explanation of the 'formation and interaction of state preferences' (that is, agenda setting), whereas realist theories explain the 'effects of the strategic environment on interstate bargaining'; that is, they are more useful for the negotiating phase

(Moravcsik 1992: 11, 15). This may indicate that different theoretical traditions might, in fact, not be incompatible regarding the explanation of international negotiations; they might as well have their strengths in different phases of the negotiating process, depending on the institutional set-up. For example, most democratic societies have isolated their chief negotiator (usually the executive) during the negotiating phase from societal interests in order to preserve his/her autonomy. Since an autonomous executive in international negotiations tends to privilege geopolitical or ideological motives, we might infer that realist theories are best in explaining the negotiating phase. Depending on the influence of societal actors (or ideas) during the agenda and ratification phases, other frameworks of research might be applicable. If, for example, certain interests have no access to decision making during the agenda setting, their concerns are likely to play no role during the negotiations themselves. This situation changes completely if these interests are involved in the ratification process.

In the following pages, I will try to apply this framework to the analysis of the strategies of the EU and the USA in the process of negotiating China into global trade institutions. Of course, given the limited space, the analysis remains preliminary. I will not go into any depth regarding the negotiations themselves. The main goal is to demonstrate the usefulness of the analytical framework for the explanation of the formation of, and eventual changes in, the preferences of state actors in international negotiations. A comprehensive test of contending IR theories along the lines indicated in the last paragraph is also not possible. However, I will provide at least a few indications in this respect.

The case study

The integration of China into the global economy was, and is still, an extremely complicated process, presenting a considerable challenge to the negotiating capabilities of the EU and the USA. The high hopes which were periodically entertained by the industrialized nations after periods of détente in the early 1970s, and the reforms introduced by the Chinese leader Deng Xiao Ping in 1978, had all come to naught. An impenetrable network of regulations and restrictions governing the access of foreign firms to the Chinese market impeded the integration of the country to the global trade system. The request for membership in the then GATT in 1986[6] signified that the Chinese leadership had realized that an opening of their economic system would be beneficial to their domestic development and enhance Beijing's international status. The complicated accession process began in the same year. Hampered by delays and setbacks, such as a two-year break after the massacre of Tiananmen Square in June 1989, the negotiations dragged on interminably. Not only inside the GATT/WTO structure, but also in multilateral settings, such as APEC and the Asia-Europe Meeting (ASEM), and in innumerable bilateral meetings, negotiations were going on about the terms of China's integration into the world economy. The by far most important questions had to be resolved in bilateral talks between China and the most important WTO members. That meant, that the USA and the EU were the decisive players.

The WTO accession negotiations are an excellent indicator for the characteristics of both the USA and the EU as negotiators in the global system. Both were confronted over a long period with quite similar problems. This allows a systematic comparison of similarities and differences in the way negotiating positions are formulated and preferences represented at the international level. To determine whether these negotiations are typical for the negotiating behaviour of the USA and the EU, the findings will be compared with accounts of other international trade negotiations. The core questions are: What characterizes the USA and the EU as negotiators in the global system, and what accounts for similarities and differences? Which preferences are privileged, and why, and which system is more efficient?

Hitherto, analyses of the external economic policies of the EU and the USA have focused either on specific economic problems, the empirical reconstruction of negotiating processes, such as the GATT rounds, or on the domestic process of formulating foreign economic strategies. Little work has been done on the characteristics and efficiency of the EU as external negotiator. The EU (which is represented in international trade negotiations by the Commission) is usually portrayed as a weak negotiating power, due to the dubious autonomy of the Commission during the negotiating process and the regular conflicts among the member states about common external positions (Hill 1993). Paemen and Bensch, in a voluminous study of EU policy making during the Uruguay Round, blame the lack of clout on the missing ability to apply to a electorate and on the transparency of European negotiating positions (1995: 109). Theoretically oriented studies, however, reach a somewhat different conclusion (see mainly the contributions by Meunier 1998, 2000; Meunier and Nicolaïdis 1999; Woolcock 2000). Based on a principal–agent model, they attribute to the EU as external negotiator more autonomy and efficiency than most of the more general literature on the EU's foreign policy does. However, they also decry the lack of democratic representation in foreign trade negotiations.

The USA also gets a mixed assessment. Realist and constructivist theories assume that it dominates international trade negotiations because of its sheer economic and political weight, and the extent to which the dominant free trade paradigm shapes the institutions of world trade. Liberal analyses of its trade policy focus on the interaction between the President and Congress. They offer a less sanguine picture, pointing to institutional veto points and the debilitating effects of disparate pressure by interest groups.[7] An early still influential analysis, for example, operated with the variable of 'state strength' and pointed to the weakness of the American state in coping with the challenge of negotiating in a heavily institutionalized environment (Krasner 1978). Lisa Martin, however, argues in a recent study that the presence of institutionalized conflict in American trade policy actually strengthens US external negotiating power since it enhances its ability to make credible commitments (Martin 2000). These differing assessments provide the background to the case study presented here. I will use a modified two-level game approach (Putnam 1988) to identify the features of American and European policies in international economic negotiations. However, in order to provide more complex answers than the ones offered by a simple domestic–international metaphor, the negotiating process will be split into three phases, which are functionally different: agenda setting, negotiation and ratification. The different extent to which societal actors, such as parliaments, or industrial and other lobbies, have access to and influence over the negotiating process in each phase, is crucial for the whole negotiating process and differences in the responses of both actors. At the same time, systemic factors, such as geopolitical constellations, international institutions, or norms, might have a different impact on actors in each phase.

Negotiating China's accession to the WTO: The EU

The institutional framework of EU policies in international trade negotiations

Since 1970, the European Commission has been formally responsible for all foreign trade negotiations and represents the Community in external negotiations. The legal base is Article 133 of the Amsterdam Treaty (revised Article 113 of the Maastricht Treaty). If the Commission wants to undertake negotiations with a foreign country, it presents recommendations on the objectives to be achieved to the Council via the so-called Article 133 Committee (which is composed of senior officials from the trade ministries of the member countries). When the Council endorses the initiative, it issues a mandate which works as a guideline for the Commission during the negotiating process. In general, the mandate is rather flexible and provides the Commission with considerable autonomy. This observation from the China/WTO negotiations is corroborated by a look at other EU negotiating mandates.[8] As soon as actual negotiations start, the Commission is required to report constantly to and consult with the Article 133 Committee. Neither the European parliament (EP) nor national parliaments have a particular influence on the mandate or the negotiations themselves, although the Commission informs the EP regularly. There is also no formal structure for consulting private interests (contrary to the USA). Once the negotiations are concluded, the Council reviews the results and ratifies them with qualified majority – in theory; in practice decisions are overwhelmingly taken unanimously (Meunier and Nicolaïdis 1999: 480). A subsequent ratification by parliaments in member states and the EP is not foreseen.

This institutional set-up suggests that the EU should have a negotiating strategy which is shaped by the geopolitical and ideological agenda of the executive and strong particular interests represented and pushed by the member states. Due to its limited autonomy in the negotiating phase, the EU should be a rather inflexible negotiator which frequently refers to the preferences of member states during the negotiations to justify its position. This means also that ratification usually presents no problem since the Commission has to stick to the mandate given by the Council and societal interests have little chances to interfere. The efficiency of the Commission, however, might be undermined by '*divide et impera*' strategies if the other side in the negotiations targets specific member states during the negotiations. Is this set of expectations confirmed by the case study?

Agenda setting phase

The perception that, during the 1980s, Europe was about to miss the opportunity to profit from the increasing economic boom in China, leaving the field to the competitors from Japan and the USA, was the core motivating factor behind the 'New Asia Strategy', announced by the German government in 1993. The EC's communication of 1995 built up on the German concept and urged European industry to catch up with their American and Japanese counterparts.[9] Trade Commissioner Leon Brittan rallied a group of industrialists and went to China, following the examples of Chancellor Kohl and French Prime Minister Balladur.[10] It is quite striking how much the member countries and the Commission pushed industry, and, thus, shaped the agenda for Europe's China policy. However, it soon became clear that a lasting success of this strategy could only be achieved if China was embedded in a legal structure which provided a framework for economic exchange. This framed with the basic EU policy mode. The core strategy was reflected in the guiding principles of the EU China policy which were pronounced in the communication 'Towards a new partnership with China'.[11] Emphasis was placed on integrating China into the global network of institutions by pursuing a policy of comprehensive and constructive engagement. Such comprehensive engagement was also seen as the best way to further human rights in China, reflecting a strong ideological commitment of the Commission (and the member states) to a policy of multilateral engagement. The WTO/China negotiations were a core project within this strategy. A similar reasoning lay behind the inauguration of the ASEM process in 1996, which tried to create a regular multilateral institutional forum for the meeting of European and Asian leaders (Dent 1999: 302).

Although the private sector was consulted during the agenda setting stage it was unable to dominate it, since this stage is closely co-managed by the Commission and the Article 133 Committee (see also Woolcock 2002: 380). Nor were single member state representatives able to place specific industrial interests of their home countries on the agenda against the will of the

Commission.[12] All in all, the agenda setting of the EU in international negotiations seems to be dominated to a greater degree by geopolitical concerns than by other preferences. Realist theories seem most relevant for the explanation of EU preferences in this phase. How do we explain that, nonetheless, the EU is often perceived to pursue very specific industry interests in international negotiations? The China/WTO negotiations show that this might be due to the specific institutional set-up and the way it works in practice during the negotiating phase.

Negotiating phase

The EU pursued its agenda with considerable consistency and it remained stable throughout the negotiations. The massacre of Tienanmen Square had only a very muted impact on the basic EU strategy to engage China by cooperative means. Very soon, European statesmen resumed economic negotiations and the Commission also emphasized its determination to press forward with the WTO negotiations. The reason for this limited impact of human rights issues on European trade negotiations with China is to be found mainly in the institutional disconnection of decision makers from potential societal protests. The consistency of the EU (which was much less prone than the USA to include new demands on the agenda during the negotiations) can also be explained by the relatively small influence of private sector groups in changing the basic strategy once it was set. Interviews with members of the EU negotiating team in the China/WTO process showed two remarkable results:

(1) The Commission was able to negotiate with relatively little interference by the member states. The state bureaucracies in the member states seem increasingly to lose the ability to follow the often extremely minute details of trade negotiations. The Article 133 Committee hardly ever intervened in the negotiations. The major reason for this is that the Commission simply stuck to the broad mandate, with a view to the necessary ratification of the results by the Council. Regarding the details, the Commission had a lot of freedom of manoeuvre. This points to the important role of information as a core factor in establishing the degree of autonomy of a given negotiator, and enabling it to manipulate the preferences of the principal. Last minute demands to China were tabled mainly by the Commission, not by the member states. The Commission seems to have squared the two apparently opposing objectives of autonomy and efficiency. In practice, it negotiates with great freedom of action due to its information advantage. However, it is still able to claim credibly that member states will not ratify any unreasonable demands. Thus, sporadic Chinese attempts to pursue a '*divide et impera*' strategy were unsuccessful.

(2) Contacts with private sector groups were extremely close during the negotiations. The EU negotiators were constantly consulting with

members of the industry in Brussels and on the spot, and this explains the information advantage.[13] The surprisingly great autonomy of the Commission during the negotiations themselves allowed it to draw on the industry's competence without getting captured by specific private sector interests. As gate keeper between the international and the domestic domain, it was well able to ward off particular lobbying efforts by the industry that might have endangered the basic strategy of comprehensive engagement, assuring Europe an equal position in the China market. There was no institution to which dissatisfied interest groups could turn with a reasonable chance of success in order to change the EU's negotiating objectives. The EU also negotiates under little public scrutiny. Human rights groups had no leverage to make their concerns heard at the negotiating table. All this allowed (or forced) the EU to negotiate in a style which was considerably less confrontational in its approach towards China than the USA (Eglin 1997: 495).

Ratification phase

Once the negotiations were concluded by the Commission and China, ratification presented no problem. The Council accepted the result without debate. The EP gave its opinion and criticized the absence of human rights considerations; however, this had no impact on final ratification and the EP knew this beforehand.[14] The smooth process of ratification stands in vivid contrast to the USA. The reason is that the EU institutional system is geared towards a uniformity of preferences of agent (Commission) and principal (Council) throughout the process. Only under exceptional circumstances does a split emerge that could lead to ratification problems. The major exception is the Uruguay Round.

Accounts of other cases of EU negotiations in international trade, by and large, confirm this picture.[15] Niemann studied the EU negotiating behaviour during the talks on the WTO agreement on Basic Telecommunications Services, and also identified a flexible mandate strongly influenced by geo-economic reasoning and a general free trade ideology on the part of the Commission. He demonstrates that member states that pursue a more hard-line approach in external negotiations than the EU find themselves in a very uncomfortable situation between the counterpart on the negotiating table and internal EU pressure (Niemann 2002: 33). Member state attempts were not able to capture the EU position. This was mainly due to another resource of the Commission; that is, the instrumentalization of pressure by the counterpart, in this case the US, to bring recalcitrant member states in line.[16] Thus, although the institutional set-up suggests the frequent occurrence of member state vetos in order to pursue specific interests (see, for example, Clark *et al.* 2000), the actual practice is rather different – even in cases when the exclusive competence of the EU is unclear and a unanimous vote is required to ratify the results. The member states are veto players which exercise their power only on rare occasions. Other potential veto-players have much less influence, as we have seen. One example is attempts by interest groups or the EP to influence the EU agenda prior to the Seattle Ministerial Conference in 1999, with little success (Elsig 2002: 174–5, 181).

All this makes '*divide et impera*' strategies by international counterparts more difficult than it appears at first sight (for an attempt by the USA, see: Meunier 2000: 128). Although further research on this conclusion is necessary, strong indications suggest that this is mainly due to the institutional isolation of the Commission in external negotiations and its information advantage. The fact that both the Council and the Commission in their trade policy are far from parliamentary and public scrutiny further helps to avoid a politicization of the negotiations. This greatly enhances the consistency of EU bargaining all through the three phases. All in all, the EU is a rather autonomous actor with a great ability to pursue its objectives in a consistent manner in international trade negotiations. This is due to the absence of easy institutional entry points for interests which disagree with the strategy set by the member states and the Commission beforehand. But, here is also the critical point of this policy for future negotiations: the results might suffer from a limited democratic legitimacy and this might endanger the implementation of internationally negotiated results.

Negotiating China's accession to the WTO: the USA

The institutional framework of US policies in international trade negotiations

US foreign trade policy has inspired a voluminous literature which has developed very diverse concepts for the explanation of this policy. Theories of hegemonic stability, for example, saw the position of the USA in the international system as the dominant factor shaping American foreign trade strategies. They explain protectionism (and, therefore, a tough negotiating strategy) with the decline of US power in the international system. The major part of the literature, however, concentrates on domestic determinants and analyses US trade policies as a pluralistic process. A wide variety of different influences has been identified by this literature.[17] A direct identification of American preferences in international negotiations with the positions of domestic interest groups is widely seen as misleading (see Bauer *et al.* 1972: ix). The political system interferes, and is quite able to pursue its own preferences, in foreign trade policy and trade negotiations. The extent to which it is able to do so, however, is still contested. As we have seen in the EU case, it depends very much on the institutional autonomy of the chief negotiator (or executive).

The literature usually identifies the relationship of executive and legislative, that is, of Congress and the president, as the core variable in US trade policy. The president is seen as much more open to demands from the international system and, due to his need for re-election, tries to devise a policy serving large groups, such as consumers (Shoch 2001: 20). He will therefore pursue a free trade oriented policy with a selected use of international institutions to further geopolitical goals.[18] Congress is more open to protectionist sentiments and geared towards the interests of a specific clientele. The same is, of course, true for the other major actors in the US system; that is, lobbying groups which include not only specific industries but also trade unions or human rights activists. How these different objectives are balanced is shaped by an institutional system which has evolved over a long period.

Article I, section 8 of the American constitution conveys upon Congress the power to regulate all matters of foreign trade. However, as discussed above, Congress was increasingly captured by conflicting demands of domestic interests and was unable to formulate a coherent foreign strategy. Thus, the RTAA of 1934 delegated the competence to conclude trade agreements with foreign countries to the executive. This (temporary) delegation allowed US presidents to conclude the multitude of bi- and multilateral trade agreements which constitute the core of the postwar trading system. The RTAA also gave the presidency the opportunity to utilize international institutions (Cold War institutions, WTO, IMF, treaties and so on.) to ward off protectionist demands by the Congress.[19] This might explain the continuing distance of the Congress towards these institutions. The American executive therefore has more difficulties than the Commission to invoke international norms in the effort to assure the ratification of international agreements. In the 1960s/1970s, the legislative started to recover lost influence in foreign trade policy. One important step was the installation of the US Trade Representative which is intended as link between the executive and the Congress, and now conducts trade negotiations instead of the State Department. The USTR consults very closely with members of Congress, particularly during the agenda phase, and often includes them in negotiating teams.

One goal of the institutional reforms in the US system was to preserve the autonomy of the executive during the negotiating phase in the interest of a coherent and strong representation of US positions in international negotiations. The introduction of the so-called fast track authority in the 1970s, a provision which authorizes the president to negotiate a package and gives Congress the right to vote it as a whole (without amendments), was an important step in this respect. It precluded excessive private sector influence during the ratification process, which could result in specific amendments leading to re-negotiations (Pfeil 2000). However, Congress achieved a much stronger say during the agenda setting and ratification phases. The trade act of 1974 enforced this, and requested the executive to inform Congress before the negotiations about their content and to include eventual demands by members of Congress. Private sector interests were institutionally embedded in the agenda setting process via so-called Advisory Committees (Twiggs 1987).

Of specific importance for this case study is the so-called Jackson Vanik Amendment, which strengthened the influence of Congress in the ratification phase. This amendment called for a yearly review of the Most-Favoured-Nation Status (MFN), later called Normal Trade Relations (NTR), for China by Congress. Almost every year, intense debate erupted on this issue. Since the WTO extends to all members as a principle the MFN, Congress had to grant Permanent NTR in order to make the provisions of an eventual WTO accession of China applicable to US–China trade. The debate about PNTR in 2000/1 equalled a ratification debate about the accession protocol negotiated by the USTR.

How might all this shape the negotiating behaviour of the USA? American presidents have been almost consistently advocates of engaging China. Presumably, the greater the autonomy of the president during the negotiations, the more he is ready to compromise. In this constellation, the executive might give up specific economic goals for geopolitical preferences and look for cooperative deals with the negotiating partner. An executive which is under pressure from the legislative and/or lobbying groups, however, will be much more demanding in its negotiating strategies. Otherwise, ratification is endangered (Putnam 1988). The latter case was the usual situation in the last two decades. In the WTO/China negotiations we might therefore expect a rather inconsistent policy. The general interest of the executive for engaging China and bringing the results to a conclusion has to be pursued very carefully to avoid damaging the chances for an eventual ratification of the agreement. The institutional set-up gives both Congress and private actors very good chances to influence the agenda setting as well as the ratification processes, and this should have a strong impact on actual negotiations. An important resource of the executive, however, is its information advantage, which it gains during the negotiating phase.

US agenda setting

The American China policy during the past 20 years strikes many observers as disjointed and incoherent (Lampton 2001; Mann 2002). Before the 1980s, it was dominated by geopolitical interests. The gradual opening of the China market and, later, the concerns about the human rights situation, put China in the centre of an increasingly vociferous domestic debate. Nonetheless, American presidents generally defined the objective of the talks, like the EU, in terms of constructive engagement which was motivated by geopolitical concerns and a general interest to secure a dominant position for the American industry in the China market.[20] This agenda, however, was often supplemented and dominated by highly visible, contentious side issues. One example is the conflict about violations of intellectual property rights by China. This led to a near complete blocade of the negotiations in the first half of the 1990s (Eglin 1997: 493). A further complicating factor was the human rights question which time and again interfered with the negotiations.

In 1993, for example, President Clinton linked the issue directly with the continuation of the MFN. Due to heavy industry protests, the link was soon abolished. The success of European delegations in acquiring contracts in China during that period also played an important role (Lampton 2001: 42f.). Thus, geopolitical concerns and the pressure of industry assured the continuation of negotiations. However, the US negotiating team had difficulties in presenting a consistent agenda, and Chinese negotiators complained all the time about constantly shifting demands by the USA (Eglin 1997). This is the result of an agenda setting process which is structured so as to guarantee a broad representation of those societal interests which might have a say in the ratification phase. US negotiators relied on systematic consultation with private sector interests during the agenda phase and afterwards.[21] This shaped the US negotiating style during the negotiation phase.

Negotiation phase

US negotiators generally pursued a tough strategy, bolstered by threats pointing to possible ratification hurdles in Congress. Such an assertive strategy is very credible, given the tendency of Congress to scrutinize trade agreements closely. Not only China, but almost every actor negotiating with the USA in the past thirty years saw itself confronted massively with this argument. Examples are Mexico and Canada during the NAFTA talks (Cameron and Tomlin 2000) or Japan during negotiations on semiconductors in 1988 (Odell 2000: 150). However, contrary to an often conveyed impression, the fact that the industry has no direct say in the ratification process results in its interests being not always reflected by the negotiating strategy. Often, different sectors of the industry have opposing objectives and counterbalance each other. Even the toughest lobbying efforts were not able to overcome President Clinton's resistance to conclude a deal when the Chinese Prime Minister Zhu Rongji offered groundbreaking concessions during his Washington visit in April 1999.[22] This failure led to a long stalemate. Only when the USTR was able to present a series of highly visible concessions which directly applied to the interests of districts by undecided Congress members (for example, on agriculture) did it dare to finalize the agreement. Thus, the autonomy of the American chief negotiator during the negotiations regarding the pursuit of his own objectives is severely limited. With an eye always towards the ratification hurdle, American trade negotiators often shift course and display little flexibility. They often fought strongly for highly visible, symbolic concessions. An element which is completely lacking in the EU is the politicization of many issues and often the whole negotiations, particularly in the case of divided government. This limits the autonomy of the executive even further and makes it very risk-averse.

Ratification

It took another long debate until Congress finally extended Permanent NTR in summer 2001 and thus, in effect, ratified the bilateral accession protocol.

Although an overwhelming industrial lobby supported ratification with unprecedented effort, it was a hard fight. A Congressional committee was set up that was to review the implementation of the agreements by China and report on a regular basis on the Chinese performance. That construction ensures that future presidents will have to continue listening to congressional concerns despite the conclusion of the negotiations.

Are the WTO/China negotiations typical of American negotiating behaviour in the international economic arena? The trend over the past twenty years – societal interests have an increasing influence on US negotiating behaviour – has been noted frequently. This leads, on occasion, to a situation in which a weak executive cannot pursue any consistent agenda during trade negotiations. One example is the Seattle Ministerial Conference during which the governments' objectives were undermined by statements of US senators on the spot (Elsig 2002: 185). In a study of the Canada–US free trade negotiations, Michael Hart notes that 'the US political decision-making process virtually guarantees imprecision and frequent changes in direction' (Hart 1994: 41). The veto-player Congress ensures that the US is a very effective negotiator but it effectively thwarts long-term strategies, as evidenced by EU–US negotiations in the past twenty years (Clark *et al.* 2000).

To sum up: the institutional framework of trade negotiations, which permits the easy politicization of trade issues, forces the executive to include as many interests as possible in the agenda phase and to pursue an aggressive strategy during the negotiations. The agenda is often redefined. Geopolitical interests play a relatively small role (despite the enormous US interest in the Pacific area). Only if a Congress with a majority from the president's party assures an easy ratification process, might these interests be pursued by the executive with more freedom during international trade negotiations. And only in this case, can realist theories be useful. Otherwise, a liberal theory of preference formation is necessary. The strong role of the Congress in the ratification phase neutralizes the autonomy of the executive during the negotiations and invalidates the information advantage.

The EU and the USA as international negotiators: some observations

The EU is a strong and efficient actor in international negotiations, if we define strength as the coherence and capability with which the Commission pursues its preferences at the international and domestic level, from the agenda phase all through the negotiations until the ratification phase. In the long run, it might have difficulties in implementing due to rather weak inclusion of societal interests in the negotiating process. This probably has no impact in the case discussed here, since the accession of China to the WTO has not sparked any significant opposition in the member states. However, regarding future negotiations in the Doha Round, this situation might change quite dramatically. Even already concluded agreements could be easily disregarded if, in some member states, the opposition to specific provisions becomes too strong. Based on this argument, Martin (2000) claims that the high level of democratic commitment as evidenced in American ratification debates gives eventual agreements greater credibility. This is only true to a certain extent. The effect of a leadership change might easily invalidate such a commitment as, for example, the recent history of the Climate protocol demonstrates.

On efficiency, an assessment of both actors shows a mixed result. The EU has clear advantages regarding the consistency of its negotiating strategy. However, the USA has a much higher credibility regarding the use of threats. A final judgement depends, therefore, on a normative understanding of efficiency. If it is defined as serving best the national interest, the USA is more efficient; if, however, the normative aim is a cooperative global governance structure, it is the EU which is in much better shape to sustain it via the multiple negotiating processes which will be necessary for its maintenance.

Notes

1 Detailed analyses of international negotiations usually are presented in the form of historical case studies. By eschewing theory, and thus avoiding the constraint of a generalized stable explanation, these can in fact cover the dynamics of specific negotiations. But the significance of these studies rarely goes beyond the case under research.
2 For a recent overview, Kremenyuk and Sjöstedt (2000), and numerous articles in the *Negotiation Journal* or the *Journal of Conflict Resolution*.
3 The best introduction for those who are not specialized in game theory is P. Terrence Hopmann (1996).
4 This approach corresponds to the liberal-constructivist approach which is advocated by Stefan Schirm in the introductory chapter of this volume.
5 This understanding of institutions fuses two of the three broad approaches which have, by and large, been accepted as framing institutionalist research: rational-choice institutionalism and historical institutionalism. The third approach, sociological institutionalism, has problems, for theoretical and methodological reasons, in analyzing international negotiations. For a readable introduction to institutionalist theories, see Peters 1999 and Scharpf 2000.
6 According to the Chinese interpretation, this was not an application but a request for re-entry since China had been a founding member of GATT. However, after its defeat in 1949 the National Chinese government decided to leave the organization and Communist China had not bothered to occupy the vacancy.
7 Recent examples are Gibson 2000, Martin 2000 and Pfeil 2000.
8 For the mandate on the Doha Round, see Woolcock 2002: 380; for the negotiations on the WTO Agreement on Basic Telecommunication Services, see Niemann 2002: 26. Conflicts often arise regarding the exclusive competence of the Commission to represent the member states in international negotiations. This derives from the suspicion on part of some of the member states that the Commission might overstep the mandate in a similar way as it did – allegedly – during the Uruguay Round. Usually, however, these conflicts are resolved with reference to member states' ability to make their voice heard during the negotiating stage.
9 The new Asia strategy is printed in *Europa-Archiv*, 6/1994: D 187–200. For the EU strategy, see 'Towards a New Asia Strategy', COM (94), 314 final.

10 European Report, 9 November, 1996.

11 EC-Commission, A long-term strategy for Europe–China relations, COM (95) 279 final, 5 July, 1995.

12 Interview with a long-term member of the Article 133 Committee. He said that even an alliance of two or three member states usually has no chance against a strongly held opinion of the Commission.

13 Interviews with members of the EU negotiating team.

14 Interview with a member of the EP.

15 The empirical evidence for this claim is rather thin. Apart from the well-analyzed Uruguay Round negotiations, empirical research on EU trade negotiations is rare. A compilation of major trade negotiations in which the EU participated would be of enormous use for future research.

16 The often cited exception is the case of France during the Uruguay Round. Another example is the blocking of Croatia's admission to the WTO by France in 1999. Those two examples, however, are not enough to claim that it is a frequent feature of EU negotiating behaviour that member states take the others hostage in international negotiations (for this claim, see Elsig 2002: 51f.).

17 Even a cursory review would lead too far. For an overview, see Destler 1995.

18 On this point, Democrat and Republican administrations display an ideological difference, with the former much more willing to take international institutions seriously.

19 The framework of this analysis also allows a differentiated look at the impact of international institutions on negotiating strategies. Due to limitations of space, this subject cannot be dealt with here. For a lead and an interesting perspective, see Checkel 1999.

20 See, for example, IHT, 'Clinton gives strong push to admitting China to WTO', 8 April, 1999.

21 For an impressive example in the case of NAFTA, see Cameron and Tomlin 2000: 55.

22 IHT, 'China's Lost Trade Horizon', 14 January, 1999.

References

Axelrod, R. (1984) *The Evolution of Cooperation*, New York: Basic Books.

Bauer, R.A., Pool, I. de Sola and Dexter, L.A. (1972) *American Business and Public Policy: The Politics of Foreign Trade*, Chicago: Aldine Atherton.

Cameron M.A. and Tomlin, B.W. (2000) 'Negotiating North American free trade', in *International Negotiation*, 5(1), 43–68.

Checkel, J.T. (1999) 'Norms, Institutions and National Identity in Contemporary Europe', in *International Studies Quarterly*, 43(1), 83–114.

Clark, W., Duchesne, E. and Meunier, S. (2000) 'Domestic and International Asymmetries in US–EU Negotiations', in *International Negotiation Journal*, 5(1), 69–95.

Dent, C.M. (1999) *The European Union and East Asia: An Economic Relationship*, London: Routledge.

Destler, I.M. (1995) *American Trade Politics*, 3rd edn, Washington, DC, and New York: Institute for International Economics.

Eglin, M. (1997) 'China's entry into the WTO with a little help from the EU', in *International Affairs*, 73(3), 489–508.

Elsig, M. (2002) 'The common commercial policy from Maastricht to Nice. Institutional debates and the Union's role in world trade', Dissertation, Zürich: Universität Zürich.

Gibson, M.L. (2000) *Conflict amid Consensus in American Trade Policy*, Washington, DC: Georgetown University Press.

Hart, M. (1994) *Decision at Midnight: Inside the Canada–US Free Trade Negotiations*, Vancouver: University of British Columbia Press.

Hill, C. (1993) 'The capability-expectations gap, or conceptualizing Europe's international role', in *Journal of Common Market Studies*, 31(3), 305–28.

Holzinger, K. (2001) 'Kommunikationsmodi und Handlungstypen in den internationalen Beziehungen. Anmerkungen zu irreführenden Dichotomien', in *Zeitschrift für internationale Beziehungen*, 8(2), 243–86.

Hopmann, P.T. (1996) *The Negotiation Process and the Resolution of International Conflicts*, Columbia: University of South Carolina Press.

Jönsson, C. (2002) 'Diplomacy, bargaining and negotiation', in Carlsnaes, W., Risse, T. and Simmons, B.A. (eds), *Handbook of International Relations*, London: Sage, 212–34.

Krasner, S.D. (1978) 'US commercial and monetary policy: Unravelling the paradox of external strength and internal weakness', in Katzenstein, P.J. (ed.), *Between Power and Plenty. Foreign Economic Policies of Advanced Industrial States*, Madison: University of Wisconsin Press, 51–88.

Kremenyuk, V.A. and Sjöstedt, G. (2000) *International Economic Negotiation: Models versus Reality*, Cheltenham: Edward Elgar.

Lampton, D.M. (2001) *Same Bed, Different Dreams: Managing US–China Relations, 1989–2000*, Berkeley: University of California Press.

Lardy, N.R. (2002) *Integrating China into the Global Economy*, Washington, DC: The Brookings Institution.

Mann, J.H. (2002) *About Face: A History of America's Curious Relationship with China, from Nixon to Clinton*, New York, NY: Vintage.

Martin, L. (2000) *Democratic Commitments: Legislatures and International Cooperation*, Princeton: Princeton University Press.

Meunier, S. (2000) 'What single voice? European institutions and EU–US trade negotiations', in *International Organization*, 54(1), 103–35.

Meunier, S. (1998) 'Divided but united: European trade policy integration and EC–US agricultural negotiations in the Uruguay Round', in Rhodes, C. (ed.), *The European Union in the World Community*, Boulder: Lynne Rienner Publishers, 193–211.

Meunier, S. and Nicolaïdis, K. (1999) 'Who speaks for Europe? The delegation of trade authority in the European Union', in *Journal of Common Market Studies*, 37(3), 477–501.

Moravcsik, A. (1992) 'Liberalism and international relations theory', Harvard Center for International Affairs, Working Paper No. 92–6.

Nicolaïdis, K. (1999) 'Minimizing agency costs in two-level games: Lessons from trade authority controversies in the United States and the EU', in Mnookin, R.H. and Susskind, L.E. (eds), *Negotiating on Behalf of Others*, Thousand Oaks: Sage, 87–126.

Niemann, A. (2002) 'Communicative action, the Article 113 Committee and the WTO agreement on basic telecommunications services', Dresden: Dresdner Arbeitspapiere Internationale Beziehungen Nr. 6.

Odell, J. (2000) *Negotiating the World Economy*. Ithaca, NY: Cornell University Press.

Paemen, H. and Bensch, A. (1995) *From the GATT to the WTO: The European Community and the Uruguay Round*, Leuven: Leuven University Press.

Peters, G.B. (1999) *Institutional Theory in Political Science. The 'New Institutionalism'*, London and New York: Pinter.

Pfeil, A. (2000) *Abschied von der 'schnellen Schiene'? NAFTA, GATT und die Ratifizierung von Handelsabkommen in den USA, 1974–1999*, Berlin: Dunker & Humblot.

Putnam, R.D. (1988) 'Diplomacy and domestic politics: The logic of two-level games', in *International Organization*, 42(3), 427–60.

Scharpf, F. (2000) *Interaktionsformen. Akteurzentrierter Institutionalismus in der Politikforschung*, Opladen: Leske und Budrich.

Shoch, J. (2001) *Trading Blows: Party Competition and U.S. Trade Policy in a Globalizing Era*, Chapel Hill, N.C.: University of North Carolina Press.

Twiggs, J.E. (1987) *The Tokyo Round of Multilateral Trade Negotiations. A Case Study in Building Domestic Support for Diplomacy*, Lanham, MD: University Press of America.

Wolf, D. and Zangl, B. (1996) 'The European Economic and Monetary Union: Two-level games and the formation of international institutions', in *European Journal of International Relations*, 2(3), 355–93.

Woolcock, S. (2002) 'European trade policy: Global pressures and domestic constraints', in Wallace, H. and Wallace, W. (eds), *Policy-Making in the European Union*, New York: Oxford University Press, 373–99.

Woolcock, S. (2000) 'European trade policy', in Wallace, H. and Wallace, W. (eds), *Policy-Making in the European Union*, 4th edn, Oxford: Oxford University Press, 373–99.

Zangl, B. (1999) *Interessen auf zwei Ebenen. Internationale Regime in der Agrarhandels, Währungs- und Walfangpolitik*, Baden-Baden: Nomos.

5
The Resilience of National Institutions: The Case of Banking Regulation

Andreas Busch

Introduction

The topic of globalization is one that cuts across sub-field lines in political science: both in International Relations (IR) and in Comparative Government (CG), the subject of globalization, its origins, definitions, characteristics and consequences have contributed to an academic growth industry in the last decade or so. But the subject sits uneasily in either of the two subdisciplines alone, it needs the combined contribution from both scholars of IR and CG, for the process of globalization changes both the workings of the international system and of national systems of government.

Globalization thus poses as much a challenge to the organization of scholarly discourse in political science as it does to systems of governance both on the national and international level. For, all too often, the two subdisciplines ignore each others' results and arguments. While in IR it was often taken for granted that new conditions had rendered the nation state's capacity to act impotent, and thus the focus was shifted to the necessity for strongly increased inter- and supranational cooperation in order to make up for that loss, scholars in CG have demonstrated in a variety of studies that this loss is by far not as extensive as often presumed. They themselves however remain largely pessimistic about increased cooperation above the level of the nation state and often ignorant of the empirical studies that have been conducted on this by scholars of IR.

While attempts have been made at various times to bridge this sub-disciplinary divide and turn the 'dialogue of the deaf' into a proper discourse – in the German literature see, for example, Busch and Plümper 1999 – this task is far from completed. This chapter seeks to contribute to and also further that dialogue. I aim to do this by questioning some deeply held beliefs about the consequences of globalization in an area often considered to be most strongly affected by that process; namely, the sphere of finance and, more precisely, banking regulation and supervision.

Globalization and the role of the state

In the last ten to fifteen years, the simultaneous processes of globalization and European integration have informed an ongoing debate about the issues of governance and the role of the nation state. The latter topic has been particularly prominent in political science. Here, it has been widely accepted that the role of the state has in reality become quite different from that put forward by political theory, which traditionally described the state as characterized by external independence and sovereignty within (Hintze 1970).

By the end of the twentieth century, this role has changed significantly. Internally, sovereignty has been challenged by the growing differentiation of societal subsystems as well as by pluralist and corporatist influences which successfully resist state attempts at hierarchical coordination; externally, sovereignty is penetrated by growing transnational links and supranational integration (Scharpf 1992).

But the debate about these developments is far from resolved. Indeed, participants in that debate draw quite different conclusions as far as the consequences for the nation state are concerned. Some speak of an 'erosion' (Cerny 1996), 'decline' (Schmidt 1995), 'crisis' (Dunn 1995), 'retreat' (Strange 1996) and even 'the end' (Ohmae 1995) of the nation state. They point to the impotence of state governance of the economy in a world largely without borders, and the futility of attempts at compensation through welfare state measures which will only serve to disadvantage the competitive position of domestic business. Ultimately, the cohesion of society and the legitimacy of the state are seen to be under threat, as the following quotation illustrates: '[T]he more economies of scale of dominant goods and assets diverge from the structural scale of the national state [...] the more the authority, legitimacy, policy-making capacity, and policy-implementing effectiveness of the state will be eroded and undermined both without and within' (Cerny 1995: 621).

On the other hand, there are authors who refute the hypothesis of the growing insignificance of the state and see not only a continuing significant task for the nation state, but one that may actually be growing. These authors talk about the 'revival of the nation state' (Lütz 1996) and of 'new tasks' for it (Sassen 1998). In this perspective, the hypothesis of the withering nation state is seen as a 'myth' (Weiss 1998): rather than losing importance, the nation state continues to be the crucial institution determining the conditions under which the process of economic globalization takes place. This is even the case in the seemingly so autonomous sphere of financial markets (Helleiner 1994, 1995; Kapstein 1994). Even for the future, prospects for continuing state capacity look good: 'It seems likely that as we move into the twenty-first century, the ability of nation-states to adapt to internationalization (so-called "globalization") will continue to heighten rather than diminish national differences in state capacity and the associated advantages of national economic coordination' (Weiss 1998: 212).

Why is it that this debate has spawned such wildly different views of the role of the nation state? Conditions for state action are changing – that is not only agreed in the academic debate, but also the result of voluminous studies from international organizations (United Nations Research Institute for Social Development 1995; World Bank 1997). But so far, the academic community has not been able to agree on a common view as to the direction of that change.

One reason for this, I would suggest, is that theoretical considerations offer two different perspectives and dynamics for an interpretation of that process, and consequently expect different outcomes: one sees an overwhelming pressure for policies to converge (and hence reduce the role of the individual nation state), the other expects exactly the opposite; namely, a continuing or even mounting divergence of policies (and thus a continuing or enhanced role for the individual state). In the remainder of this chapter, I will first briefly sketch out these two different views, and then confront their predictions with results from two recently concluded studies that deal with governance and state capacity in the financial sphere, the reason for that choice being that this is where 'pressure' from globalization is commonly perceived to be highest, making this policy area into an ideal and 'hard' test case for theories of convergence that presently dominate the discourse about globalization.[1]

Convergence or divergence?

Research about the state's capacity to act (and the potential change thereof) requires hypotheses that can be empirically tested. There are at least two strands of theory regarding the consequences of greater integration for advanced industrialized states that inform the analyses in the debate mentioned previously – even if these theoretical foundations are often not explicitly mentioned or acknowledged. One predicts greater convergence, the other constant or even increasing divergence.

Convergence

Theories that predict a trend towards political convergence can be traced back, on the one hand, in the economic theory of international trade, on the other to theories of intergovernmental or inter-jurisdictional competition.

The former is built on the *Heckscher-Ohlin theorem*, which sees comparative advantage as based on differences in relative factor endowments across countries and differences in relative factor intensities across industries. A country will thus tend to export such goods where it has a relative abundance of factor endowments, and import such goods where there is a comparative scarcity of production factor endowments. Building on such standard economic theory, Ronald Rogowski suggested a model – which makes rather simple assumptions about the domestic political process[2] – to explain the development of societal cleavages (Rogowski 1987, 1989). Later, this model was extended to accommodate the process of globalization and to explain the policy preferences of relevant domestic actors, the policies implemented and the development of domestic institutions (Frieden and Rogowski 1996). Thus, the authors postulate that the ability of interest groups to assert themselves co-varies with the mobility of their production factor: those who can most credibly threaten with *exit* will increase their negotiating power and prevail. It follows that a consequence of globalization will be the adaptation of government policy to the interests of capital (as the most mobile production factor), and since this will take place everywhere, a convergence of policies will be the result.

The second approach focuses on government action under conditions of competition and ultimately arrives at similar conclusions. The fundamental idea is that governments compete for mobile capital, seeking the highest net return. This leads to an international equalization of net yields and consequently to tax competition between countries seeking to offer the best conditions for business.[3] Competition, however, is not limited to taxation alone, but extended to labour markets, social and environmental regulations – which all have an effect on the expected return on capital – and leads to an equalization here as well.

To sum it up, these theories postulate that growing international integration will have implications for domestic policy – once indirectly through a change in the domestic distribution of political power, once directly through influence on government policy – and will lead to a convergence of policies and institutions.

Divergence

Another group of theories, however, expects completely different consequences from the same process. These approaches focus on the stability of specific national characteristics, such as differences in national policy styles, the stability of institutional arrangements and the importance of path dependence. Consequently, they predict constant or even increasing divergence in national policies and institutional structures.

These theoretical approaches – an early representative is Andrew Shonfield's (1965) study on 'Modern Capitalism' with its emphasis on the importance of specific historically derived assumptions of national actors – focus, for example, on differences in policy making and policy implementation, such as in the concept of 'policy styles' (Richardson 1982). These national policy styles show a great deal of resilience when challenged (Waarden 1995), which is not least due to institutional stability: '[T]o portray political institutions simply as an equilibrium solution to the conflicting interests of current actors is probably a mistake. Institutions are not simply reflections of current exogenous forces or micro-behaviour and motives. They embed historical experience into rules, routines, and forms that persist beyond the historical moment and condition' (March and Olsen 1989: 167f.).

As a consequence, even increasing international integration is not likely to lead to major changes, both in terms of institutions and policies.

The most general formulation of this perspective can be found in the concept of *path dependence* as pioneered above all by the institutional and transaction cost schools of economic theory (North 1990; Williamson 1994). In this view, positive returns to scale, network externalities and feedback effects can lead to equilibrium outcomes that are very stable (*lock-in*). Therefore, the costs of change are prohibitively high and consequently change is very rare.[4]

To sum this position up, one can expect that even growing international integration would not deflect states from their historically rooted trajectories, so that not convergence, but constant and perhaps even increasing divergence would be the result for policies and institutions.

We can conclude this section by saying that there are good theoretical grounds for both positions – that of convergence and that of divergence. This controversy is consequently one that can only be resolved by subjecting it to empirical research and checking which of the two schools of thought's predictions are more accurate and reflective of the developments in reality.

State regulation of the banking sector

As an empirical test case, this chapter chooses state regulation of the banking system in order to test the two competing sets of hypotheses outlined in the previous section. This policy area seems particularly suitable to the task at hand for a number of reasons.

On the one hand, the banking sector plays a special role in the economy. The reason for this is twofold:[5] the banking sector makes credit available to all the other sectors in the economy and to consumers; a well-functioning banking sector is thus a vital prerequisite for a well-functioning economy as a whole. Yet, at the same time, it is particularly vulnerable, for the failure of a bank can have distinctly different consequences from the failure of a business in another sector of the economy, and threaten the viability of the whole banking sector (*bank run*). States have therefore traditionally subjected the banking system to specific regulation. This regulation could take a variety of forms, such as:

- socialization of the whole or part of the banking system
- the issuing of detailed directives to allocate credit to specific purposes
- a legally enforced separation of activities between commercial banks and investment banks to limit risk
- state setting of interest rates for deposits and lending
- the creation of a mandatory system of deposit insurance.

As a result, national institutional configurations in this policy area have historically developed in widely differing ways, making it an ideal test case for the convergence hypothesis.

At the same time, globalization is particularly prominent in the financial sphere, which has so far come closest to the idea of an integrated world market that is working twenty-four hours a day. Add to that the rapid decrease of capital controls in most countries since the mid-1970s[6] and – at least partly resulting from that – a massive increase of cross-border bank lending in the same period, and it becomes clear that national regulators were faced with quite a challenge to maintain banking system stability in the last thirty or so years.

Indeed, many countries suffered substantial problems in their banking system in the period since the breakdown of the Bretton Woods system of fixed exchange rates in 1973 – no fewer than two-thirds of IMF member states reported problems in the period since 1980 (Lindgren *et al.* 1996). But the success or failure of the national regulatory systems is not the focus of this chapter.[7]

Rather, the country sample was chosen so as to reflect as much variety as possible in a small group. In choosing the United States, the United Kingdom, Germany and Switzerland, this was largely achieved: the group comprises different 'varieties of capitalism', having two members of the 'Anglo-Saxon' (USA, UK) and 'Rhenish' (GER, CH) type each; EU member states (GER, UK) and non-EU member states (USA, CH); and lastly representatives of the 'consensus' (CH, to a lesser degree GER) and majoritarian types of democracy. Table 5.1 summarizes the key indicators. Categorizing countries in this way provides a link to research that is concerned with institutional constraints on central state governments and, more generally, on the position of 'veto players' in the political system.[8] It will be interesting to see whether any systematic relationships between these indicators and the results of the present study can be established in the end.

Developments in these four countries in the field of banking regulation were researched through detailed case studies for the period 1974–99. A multiplicity of interviews with key actors in regulatory agencies, interest groups and legislative bodies as well as academic experts were conducted to gain insights into the motives, world views and problem definitions not accessible through the analysis of legislative and other policy documents alone.

Much variation to start with

While the detailed case studies of the four countries under consideration cannot be reproduced here in the breadth of their historical and institutional detail, some paragraphs can serve to summarize them in order to support the main claim to be made here; namely that there was very significant variation at the beginning of the time period under consideration.

Table 5.1 Summary of country characteristics

	USA	*UK*	*GER*	*CH*
Political system	Presidential	Parliamentary	Parliamentary	Presidential
Balance between parliamentary chambers	Symmetrical	Asymmetrical	Asymmetrical	Symmetrical
Judicial review	Yes	No	Yes	No
Territorial organization	Federal	Unitary	Federal	Federal
Dominant party in government, 1950–94 (Schmidt 1996)	Conservative	Conservative	Centrist	Liberal
Party system	Two-party system	Two-party system	Multi-party system	Multi-party system
EU member	No	Yes	Yes	No
Type of economy (Soskice 1999)	Liberal market economy (LME)	LME	Coordinated market economy (CME)	CME
Type of financial system (Cox 1986)	Capital market oriented	Capital market oriented	Credit oriented	Credit oriented
Type of banking system (Pohl 1994)	Specialized banking system (political regulation)	Specialized banking system (historical development)	Universal banking system	Universal banking system

The United States

Among the four cases considered here, the US banking system must be considered the most heavily regulated in the early 1970s. This was largely the legacy of the strict regulation imposed after the traumatic experiences of the Great Depression in the early 1930s and its massive banking crisis. After almost a quarter of all existing banks had failed, stringent controls were introduced in the 'most comprehensive attempt ever to restructure the American financial system' (Cerny 1994: 181). Extensive product, price and geographical regulations were introduced in order to curtail the 'excessive competition' that was viewed as the root cause of the problems.

Together with a multiplicity of regulatory agencies that had been set up since the middle of the nineteenth century, an extremely complicated system of various types of banks regulated by a multiplicity of agencies with often overlapping briefs was the result. Figure 5.1 attempts to depict the

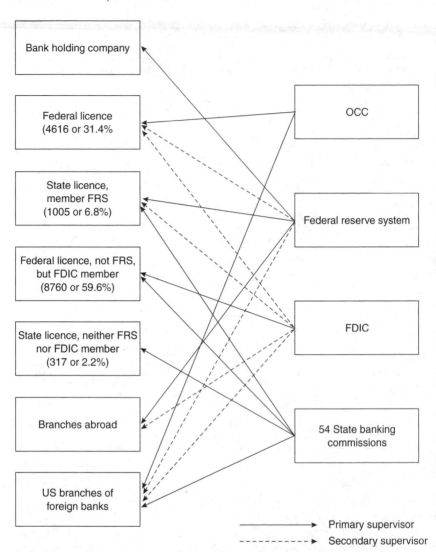

Figure 5.1 Overlapping regulatory competences in the US banking system
Source: Adapted from Busch (2003: 76).

relationship between types of banks (left), regulatory agencies (right) and primary (solid line) and secondary (dashed line) regulatory oversight.[9]

Evidently, this complicated system is unlikely to produce optimal results – an opinion widely shared by many observers since the 1950s. Many scholars and various commissions formed by Congress had called for wholesale reform of the system, simplification, and the abolition of the regulations introduced by the *Glass-Steagall Act*.[10]

The United Kingdom

If the US system had to be regarded as highly regulated in the early 1970s, that of the UK was the complete opposite, at least with respect to formal regulation. For no formal system of banking regulation and no agency empowered by law to deal with this area existed in the UK at all. Rather, a both geographically (the 'City') and, in terms of the number of banks, highly concentrated system had weathered even the crises of the 1930s remarkably well and was guided by advice from the Bank of England. The latter, for centuries a private bank and only nationalized in 1946, 'served as spokesman both for the City within the government and for the government within the City' (Vogel 1996: 98). Preferring the flexibility and informality traditionally associated with the 'club culture' of the City (and stressing the latter's cost efficiency), the Bank was not in favour of codifying its powers and preferred a system in which the 'raised eyebrows' of the Bank's Governor were the ultimate sanction.[11] Its success in avoiding major problems in the British banking system were a considerable resource in defending its position.

The Federal Republic of Germany

State regulation in Germany had reacted swiftly to the major banking crisis in the early 1930s by imposing an encompassing system of banking regulation and partly even of bank socialization, but the latter was quickly reversed until the end of the 1930s. In the Federal Republic, a relatively liberal approach to banking regulation was taken. Caps and ceilings on interest rates, introduced in the 1930s in an attempt to avoid 'destructive competition', were lifted in the mid-1960s. The Federal Republic was thus one of the first countries to liberalize this sector, and no attempts were ever made to use the banking system as a means of monetary policy (as in Britain) or for the allocation of credit (as, for example, in France or Sweden). Also, the whole topic was politically uncontentious, in marked contrast to the situation in the USA. There were, however, two specific topics that were recurrent during most of the twentieth century: on the one hand, a public debate about the 'power of banks' (deemed excessive by exponents of both the political left and right, albeit for different reasons), and worries about deposit insurance.

Switzerland

Lastly, the Swiss case. While it had introduced a system of banking supervision as a reaction to the banking system crisis of the 1930s, the Swiss state handled it in a very liberal way and never tried to impose wide ranging regulations through it. Also – and remarkably in so strongly federalized a state – this was a unitary supervision system which mainly operated through fiduciary agencies assessing the banks' accounts according to rules set up by a largely independent 'banking commission'. While the majority of Swiss political opinion was in favour of the traditionally liberal approach towards the banking sector (economically one of the most important sectors of the Swiss economy), a sizeable minority – the Social Democrats – demanded stricter regulations and were critical of the negative economic consequences of a strong banking sector, such as upward pressure on Swiss currency (induced by capital movements) and the ensuing problems for Swiss exports. After the breakdown of the system of fixed exchange rates and the switch-over to a system of currency floating in the early 1970s, these problems became particularly pressing.

Twenty-five years later: what are the results?

As the previous section has argued, the four countries under consideration exhibited considerable differences, both in terms of institutional setup and the extent and use of regulation in the early 1970s. They therefore entered the ensuing decades of growing economic integration and globalization from quite different positions.

Given the competing theoretical models outlined at the beginning of this chapter and the questions they raise, is there a clear result that allows us to endorse or refute one or the other position? Did globalization lead to a convergence of policies and institutions? And, if so, was that the result of democratically legitimate action and conscious political decisions, or did internationalized, anonymous markets force that development? Or did policies and institution follow the trajectory determined by past decisions and, if so, for reasons of conscious political choice or because of an inability to adapt to changing circumstances? Depending on how these questions are answered, four results are possible. They are summarized in Figure 5.2.

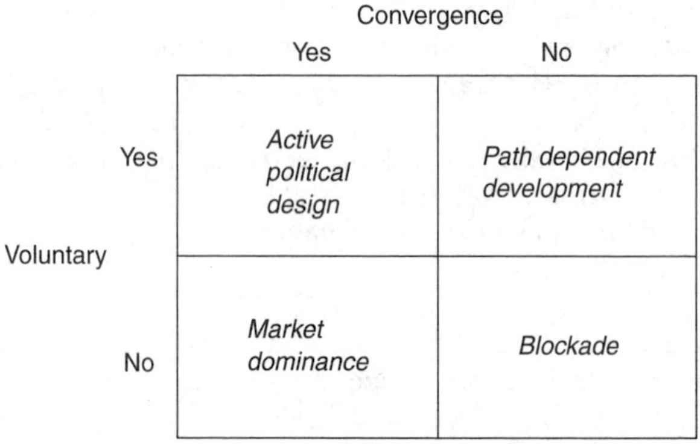

Figure 5.2 Typology of possible policy outcomes

Obviously, the different developments in each of the four countries cannot be summarized in the space available here.[12] Only some hints at main aspects of the various developments are possible in the remainder of the chapter. But even if one takes all the evidence into account, it is not possible to give a clear affirmative or negative answer to any of the above questions. However, a differentiation between the dimensions of *policy*, *politics* and *polity* – the content, processes and the institutional aspects concerning our topic – can help to make further distinctions and yield more insights.

Policy

Looking at the content of regulation, it becomes evident that here much convergence has taken place in the last twenty-five years. Compared to the situation in the mid-1970s, there has been a clear trend towards both codification and liberalization in the field of banking regulation. While the UK did not have a formalized system of banking regulation at the start of the period, it developed both an institutional structure and legal regulations by the end of the 1970s, catching up with the other countries that had developed such institutions already in the 1930s. Both a national banking crisis and the development of European integration played a role in the British case. Liberalization was also an international trend, even if in this sample only the heavily regulated US banking market was affected, and the result was less than successful, being characterized by abject policy failure (the crisis of the *Savings & Loan* system in the 1980s and early 1990s) and an endless series of attempts at repealing the *New Deal* regulations of the 1930s that heavily restricted the banking system. Blockade in Congress resulted ultimately in both courts and regulatory agencies taking the lead in deregulation.

These trends, however, produced nothing like perfect convergence in terms of policy. While international cooperation in the *Basle Process* has helped to coordinate regulations by focusing on agreed parameters, such as banks' own capital ratios, implementation of these measures varies widely across countries. Not least, the fact that a new round of negotiations (the *Basle II Process*) was started in 1999 demonstrates continuing differences in the content of regulations – but also the desire to overcome them. So far, top international bankers keep complaining about the different treatment their banks receive in different countries, and even within the European Union and its single market, different national implementations of the respective directives as well as opt-out clauses and effects of the tax system have led to some continued divergence. Thus, while there is a strong overall tendency towards convergence, there still remain significant differences between the countries considered here.

Politics

In the politics dimension, however, there is practically no convergence whatsoever at play. The hypotheses assuming that growing international economic integration will lead to more power and influence for the capital side and result in 'convergence towards an agenda set by investors' (Cohen 1996: 288), find no support in the case studies. Rather, a more complex picture emerges: attempts at liberalization can, for example, fail because of the resistance of sub-groups of the capital side (as in the USA), or they can be forced through even against the express wishes of the capital side – as was the case with the abolishment of bank cartels in Switzerland in the early 1990s.[13] In the view of this evidence, any assumptions often made about homogenous interests within this rather divergent group of sectors and companies must seem highly questionable.

Above all, the case studies demonstrate that the national systems of interest intermediation and the various policy networks work in very different ways, and demonstrate great stability over time. The more consensual systems of Germany and Switzerland are here contrasted with the more adversarial systems of the UK and the USA.[14] Change, if it takes place at all, is only marginal. This can partly be explained by the stability of the institutional frameworks within which these processes take place (see below), but also by the fact that in each country a multiplicity of issues compete for influence on the national political agenda. The assumed 'pressure' from globalization – a comparatively long-term and slow process – must be judged as relatively small and unimposing. Only in cases of acute crisis, the issue of banking regulation gains universal attention, as the episodes in all four country studies demonstrate. Otherwise, this issue is characterized by *low politics* and a relatively high degree of expert influence and technicality, which is unlikely to arouse political passions and create media headlines.

Polity

Similarly, convergence seems largely absent from the institutional dimension. The components of the national policy networks in banking regulation appear, in their clear majority, very stable and highly resistant to change. This is particularly evident in the case of the USA, where repeated attempts to reduce the number of regulatory agencies and/or reform their respective tasks (and assign them in a more logical way) failed. Both in the German and Swiss cases, there were no attempts at institutional reform.[15] The only exception from the rule is the case of the UK, where a major institutional reform took place after 1997. It not only stripped the *Bank of England* of its supervisory role, transferring that task to a new *Financial Services Authority* (FSA), but also transferred all areas of financial market supervision to that new institution – once more, proof that if a Westminster type political system has made up its mind, there is literally nothing that can stop it. But the characteristics of the FSA do not resemble the institutional structures of any of the other countries' regulatory systems – so, clearly, there is no tendency towards convergence on a common institutional model, or even the emergence of a 'reference model'.[16]

In addition, it must be emphasized that the reform in Britain was triggered by two national failures of the existing system of banking regulation (*BCCI* in 1991 and *Barings Bank* in 1995) and not by the pressures emanating from international developments of globalization. And both the blockade of institutional reform in the USA and the implementation thereof in the UK can best be explained by characteristics of the national political institutions; namely the tendency of Congress for stalemate in dealing with contested measures in the maze of committees and sub-committees on the one hand, and unchecked centralization of power in the case of the British Westminster system on the other.

A convergence of institutional systems in the foreseeable future thus seems rather unlikely. And since different institutions react differently to identical challenges, namely according to their 'logic of appropriateness' (March and Olsen 1989), even complete convergence in the content of regulations (the policy dimension) would still likely yield different national reactions to similar crises.

The sources of change and their national filters

Looking at the, if varying, changes that have taken place in the national systems described in this chapter, it is interesting to ask whether common sources exist for these changes.

Among such potential common sources, the 'Basle Committee' stands out. Following disturbances in foreign exchange markets after the end of the system of fixed exchange rates, it was set up in December 1974 by the G10 countries and operated under the auspices of the *Bank for International Settlements*. It is within this institutional context that international cooperation in the field of banking regulation has been conducted since. However, the Basle Committee's agreements are not legally binding – they are merely 'gentlemen's agreements' which are voluntarily followed by the participating parties, as well as many other countries. Since there is a large degree of overlap between the memberships of the Basle Committee and the European Union,[17] the recommendations of the former are usually transformed into EU directives. This was the case with the First Banking Directive of 1977, which included the principle of home country control as well as the commitment to further supervisory cooperation. As the idea of a common European banking law failed because of member states' resistance, the 1980s saw the application of the principle of mutual recognition of national practices enshrined into the Second Banking Directive of 1989. Banks from EU member states thus only needed a 'single passport'; that is, to be licensed in one member state allowed operation in all member states.

The regulations emanating from the 'common sources' are not very detailed. They leave room for national manouevre and different implementation – a necessary condition given the varying characters of national financial systems.

But more importantly, these recommendations and regulations do not constitute an external imposition for nation states, but are the result of international negotiations that have been voluntarily accepted.[18] But what happens with these regulations in the national systems? Here, the 'stimuli' that emanate from the international regulatory sphere meet very different domestic circumstances which act as national filters. Two examples may serve to illustrate that point.

In the United States, for example, the national environment in this policy area is characterized by a high degree of politicization, a multiplicity of policy actors[19] and a policy style that is confrontational and legalistic. As a result, adaptation of the existing regulatory system through changes of the laws governing it failed for many years – repeated attempts at reform failed to overcome the high consensus requirements in the maze of committees and subcommittees on Capitol Hill in the brief time span of a congressional period of session.[20] Given the blockade of the legislative system, however, the necessary changes were provided by other parts of the system which acted, one can argue, as 'safety valves', preventing lasting damage. Court decisions and changes of long-standing interpretations on the part of the regulatory agencies introduced the flexibility into the process that the legislative system could not provide. Ultimately, in 1999, after several decades of failed attempts, a law was passed that only ratified the changes courts and regulatory agencies had already imposed.

In contrast, the system in Germany is characterized by low politicization and a high degree of corporatist cooperation which takes place both between the industry associations and the state, and between the sectoral peak associations of the three main banking sectors. This system, in which consultation of industry is mandatory before any changes are introduced, has provided the state with relatively low costs (as the associations take on a large part of the supervisory work themselves), and has given the industry a high degree of flexibility. Within this system, the shift from a system largely determined on the national level to one largely determined on the European level has been implemented without any great disruptions.[21] Apart from the two directives mentioned above, seven more directives have been incorporated into national law between 1983 and 1995 (Busch 2003: 128ff.).

The different domestic environments, it is therefore argued, work as national filters, preventing convergence and producing continuing difference among both banking systems and regulatory systems. These, in turn, produce different interests in regulatory matters on the national level. As international institutions like the Basle Committee, however, are made up of national representatives, these different national interests are being brought into the international negotiation process. As a consequence of such cycles, one would expect negotiations in the Basle Committee to become more time-consuming and politicized, and this is indeed what seems to be the case. The more detailed Basle regulations become (and the more they matter under conditions of increasingly integrated financial markets), the more governments get involved. What used to be primarily technical negotiations now become more and more politicized. This is certainly a completely different situation from that of the Basle Committee's first meeting, where 'supervisors sat around a table, quiet and suspicious of each other'.[22] Nowadays, national representatives no longer have such problems. They seek to further their national interests and advantages – and the fact that it took fourteen years (from 1974 to 1988) to reach an agreement on standards of own capital shows just how difficult these negotiations are.

This is also the reason why the Basle Committee cannot be adequately described as an epistemic community, for the modus of negotiations is clearly one of bargaining rather than arguing. World views and interests differ substantially among this group of experts, which constitutes a clear difference over the existence of a shared belief system that unites the community of central bankers and has made policy coordination in that area so much easier (Haas 1992). In banking supervision, however, the role and influence of ideational factors is quite limited, which is not least due to the highly technical nature of the field and the absence of the reference point of a 'best practice' model (Busch 2004).

The changes in the preferred instruments of banking supervision (from no common instruments at all in the 1970s, to a focus on fixed capital ratios in the 1980s, to the use of flexible risk-adjusted models in the 1990s) do not therefore reflect the pursuit of a coherent vision of banking regulation, but rather the increased experience with the workings of financial markets, the development of ever more sophisticated financial instruments and the influence of powerful interests that push for the adoption of instruments that save them money[23] or suit the interests of their national banking system.[24]

While the Basle Committee, being the focus of international cooperation in questions of banking regulation, may thus be a common *source* of change, it cannot be considered the *cause* of these changes. Mancur Olson has advocated that distinction, and (criticizing his fellow economists' explanations of economic growth) stated that 'they trace the water in the river to the streams and lakes from which it comes, but they do not explain the rain' (Olson 1982: 4).

In a similar fashion, looking at the Basle Committee tells us a lot about the way standards in banking regulation were invented and implemented, but it does not explain why the need for them was felt. After all, systems had worked for decades without such common standards. If we want to explain why this situation changed, looking at the development of and negotiations in the Basle Committee will not get us very far. Rather, we will have to take into account more basic underlying factors such as technological development (computer and IT revolution, the invention of ever more sophisticated financial instruments), but above all the experience of crises. For it is both on the national level (see below) and the international level that crises led to the perception of the need for change: the Basle Committee was set up as a reaction to the failure of the German *Herstatt Bank*; its *Concordat* was revised as a reaction to the Latin American debt crisis and the collapse of *Banco Ambrosiano* in the early 1980s and again in the 1990s as a reaction to the *BCCI* case.

Conclusion

Looking back on the arguments presented in this chapter, what is the conclusion? It was demonstrated that evidence from the policy area of banking regulation does not support the more sweeping claims at (policy and institutional) convergence often found in the literature on globalization. While there is substantial (but imperfect) convergence in terms of regulatory content and policy, there is none in terms of the political processes and the institutional dimension. Policy discourses in the field are only to a small degree characterized by the *frame* (Rein and Schön 1993) of international competitiveness, while more often national specific issues dominate the day-to-day legislative debates – for example, in the Swiss case the issue of money laundering, in the UK the details of the several high-profile banking failures that each triggered changes in banking legislation, and in Germany the debate about the right of access to bank accounts for everybody.

But does that mean that there is more support for the theories of divergence and path dependence? Again, some relevant qualifications have to be made. When faced with the momentous changes in the policy field in the mid-1970s, countries did not primarily embark on the search for national specific solutions, but tried to coordinate their actions through the Basle Committee. Even if these negotiations took fourteen years to reach a first agreement, they resulted in a common regulatory framework that often required substantial changes in national regulation.

With respect to the dimensions of politics and polity, however, the latter theoretical approaches are much better suited to explain the absence of change and the continuing divergence. Nationally specific institutional configurations, historically developed, produced incentives which favoured certain patterns of action and inaction, and thus influenced the strategic choices of political and economic actors. Routines and patterns of interaction were developed and in turn created stability and lowered transaction costs.

If there was any change, it was in all four cases triggered through *national* crises, not international developments, and different national contexts led to very different reactions:

- in Germany, the *Herstatt* crisis led to substantial self-regulation, if only after the threat of massive state intervention
- in Switzerland, the *Chiasso* scandal also led to increased self-regulation, but as an influential party (the Social Democrats) was not satisfied with the result, continuing politicization was the result

- in Britain, reactions to crises came exclusively from the side of the state or the regulator, the *Bank of England*. Banks and associations never proposed any reforms of their own, which they did not regard as their task
- and in the United States, not even the *Savings & Loan* crisis with its enormous costs could stop the long-standing trench warfare about liberalization. Also, there were no reform proposals from associations here either, but that was more probably due to their competitive relationship with each other than with their perceived role in the policy process.

Coming back to the question of institutional constraints and veto players mentioned in the section 'State regulation of the banking sector', we can now make a qualified assessment. Attempts at quantification of these constraints have arrived at a clear message: while the UK score is very low – indicating few, if any, constraints on central government – the USA, Germany and Switzerland score very high in this respect and are located at the top of the distribution of the OECD countries.[25] The present study supports the view that there are few constraints on central state policy making in the UK. It has also demonstrated, however, that things progressed quite differently in the USA on the one hand, and Germany and Switzerland on the other: while the former system tended towards blockade, the latter were primarily characterized by cooperation in spite of a high number of veto players. This shows that just adding up the number of 'hurdles' does not give a complete picture. Rather, factors like politicization of a policy area and underlying traditions of consensual or adversarial practice have to be taken into account to understand if and why institutional factors influence the dynamics in a given policy situation.[26]

National institutions, we can sum up, function in a way as 'filters' of globalization. The case studies presented here show that they deal with similar or even the same problems in their own specific ways, thereby producing different policy outcomes and dynamics in the various countries. In terms of the possible outcomes of Figure 5.2, we can say that these vary between 'active political design', 'path dependent development' and 'blockade'. That the position of 'non-voluntary convergence' or 'market dominance' could not be observed should, not least, be good news for reasons of democratic legitimacy of national policy making. Whether similar results can be demonstrated in other policy areas, remains a task for further research.

Notes

1 The comments in this chapter draw for empirical information primarily on the results of a study by the author on the subject of 'State and Globalisation: Banking regulation in comparative perspective', which focuses not only on state capacity under conditions of globalization (Busch 2003), but also on the results of the finance section of the project on 'Success and Failure in Public Governance', for which the author acted as sectoral editor (Bovens *et al.* 2001).

2 There are only two assumptions (Rogowski 1987: 1123):
   (1) Those who stand to profit from a change will promote it, while those who stand to lose will try to prevent or delay it;
   (2) Those whose welfare is presently or will in the future be enhanced will derive an increase in political influence.
3 A survey of the respective economic literature can be found in, for example, Schulze and Ursprung 1999.
4 For a recent application of the concept of path dependence to the study of politics, see Pierson 2000.
5 See Busch 2001: ch. 2, for a more detailed exposition of this argument.
6 Cf. the data presented in Simmons 1999: 42.
7 A detailed analysis of this can be found in the case studies in Bovens *et al.* 2001, and particularly in the sectoral introduction (Busch 2001).
8 Examples of these are Manfred Schmidt's indicator of 'institutional constraints' (Schmidt 1996: 172f.) and Tsebelis 2002.
9 The numbers given are for 1978–79.
10 See, as two examples among many, the FINE study (Pierce 1977) and Task Group on Regulation of Financial Services 1984.
11 A good overview of the system can be found in the contributions to Gardener 1986.
12 For that, see chs 4 to 7 of Busch 2003.
13 For similar developments in Spain see Pérez 2001.
14 Which, however, differ substantially in terms of state capacity! See more below.
15 It should be mentioned, however, that an institutional change did take place in Germany, but after the period under investigation here, namely in 2001. An integrated regulator, the *BAFin*, was set up. The main motive behind this, however, was the introduction of EMU and the changed role of the Bundesbank as a consequence of this and not pressure from globalization.
16 For example, in the way an independent central bank has become the international 'reference model' or 'best practice' for central banks during the last decade.
17 Eight of the twelve members of the Basle Committee are also members of the European Union.
18 This is true in the strict sense only for the states that participate in the Basle Committee.
19 See Figure 5.1 above.
20 See Reinicke 1995 for a detailed description of the process.
21 The German *Kreditwesengesetz* is today considered as 'largely determined by EU directives' (see Boos *et al.* 2000: V).
22 This is how one of the participants describes it (Kapstein 1994: 45).
23 This is, for example, the case with big international banks and the introduction of risk adjusted measures of core capital.
24 As is the case with the exceptions from the system of risk adjusted measures won by small banks.
25 See the data for the indices of Colomer and Schmidt in Schmidt 1996: 172f. An amended and updated version can be found in Schmidt 2000: 352f.
26 Also going beyond only the number of veto players, Tsebelis (2002) points out the importance of the ideological distance between them and (in case of collective veto players) the importance of their internal cohesion.

References

Boos, K.-H., Fischer, R. and Schulte-Matler, H. (eds) (2000) *Kreditwesengesetz. Kommentar zu KWG und Ausführungsvorschriften*, München: Beck.
Bovens, M., Hart, P. and Peters, B.G. (eds) (2001) *Success and Failure in Public Governance: A Comparative Analysis*, Cheltenham: Edward Elgar.
Busch, A. (2004) 'National filters: Europeanisation, institutions, and discourse in the case of banking regulation', in *West European Politics* 27(Forthcoming), (special issue: Opening the black box: Europeanisation, discourse, and policy change, Schmidt, V.A. and Radaelli, C.M. (eds)).
Busch, A. (2003) *Staat und Globalisierung. Das Politikfeld Bankenregulierung im internationalen Vergleich*, Wiesbaden: Westdentscher Verlag.
Busch, A. (2001) 'Managing innovation: Regulating the banking sector in a rapidly changing environment', in Bovens *et al.*, *Success and Failure in Public Governance: A Comparative Analysis*, 311–25.
Busch, A. and Plümper, T. (eds) (1999) *Nationaler Staat und internationale Wirtschaft. Anmerkungen zum Thema Globalisierung*, Baden-Baden: Nomos.
Cerny, P.G. (1996) 'International finance and the erosion of state policy capacity', in Gummett, P. (ed.), *'Globalization and Public Policy*, Cheltenham: Elgar, 83–104.
Cerny, P.G. (1995) 'Globalization and the changing logic of collective action', in *International Organization*, 49(4), 595–625.
Cerny, P.G. (1994) 'Money and power: The American financial system from free banking to global competition', in Thompson, G. (ed.), *Markets*, London: Hodder & Stoughton in association with the Open University, vol. 2 of *The United States in the Twentieth Century*, 175–213.
Cohen, B.J. (1996) 'Phoenix risen: The resurrection of global finance', in *World Politics*, 48(1), 268–96.
Cox, A. (1986) *State, Finance and Industry. A Comparative Analysis of Post-War Trends in Six Advanced Industrial Economies*, Brighton: Wheatsheaf.
Dunn, J. (ed.) (1995) *Contemporary Crisis of the Nation State?*, Oxford: Blackwell.
Frieden, J.A. and Rogowski, R. (1996) 'The impact of the international economy on national policies: An analytical overview', in Keohane, R.O. and Milner, H.V. (eds), *Internationalization and Domestic Politics*, New York and Cambridge: Cambridge University Press, 25–47.
Gardener, E.P.M. (ed.) (1986) *UK Banking Supervision: Evolution, Practice and Issues*, London: Allen & Unwin.
Haas, P.M. (1992) 'Introduction: Epistemic communities and international policy coordination', in *International Organization*, 46(1), 1–35.
Helleiner, E. (1995) 'Explaining the globalization of financial markets: Bringing states back in', in *Review of International Political Economy*, 2(2), 315–41.
Helleiner, E. (1994) *States and the Reemergence of Global Finance: From Bretton Woods to the 1990s*, Ithaca, NY: Cornell University Press.
Hintze, O. (1970) *Wesen und Wandlung des modernen Staats*, in Hintze, O., *Staat und Verfassung. Gesammelte Abhandlungen zur allgemeinen Verfassungsgeschichte*, Göttingen: Vandenhoeck & Ruprecht, 3rd edn, 470–96.
Kapstein, E.B. (1994) *Governing the Global Economy. International Finance and the State*, Cambridge, MA and London: Harvard University Press.
Kitschelt, H., Lange, P., Marks, G. and Stephens, J.D. (eds) (1999) *Continuity and Change in Contemporary Capitalism*, Cambridge: Cambridge University Press.
Lindgren, C.-J., Garcia, G. and Saal, M.I. (1996) *Bank Soundness and Macroeconomic Policy*, Washington, DC: International Monetary Fund.

106   *The Resilience of National Institutions*

Lütz, S. (1996) 'The revival of the nation-state? Stock exchange regulation in an era of internationalized financial markets', vol. 96(9) of MPIfG Discussion Papers, Köln: Max-Planck-Institut für Gesellschaftsforschung.

March, J.G. and Olsen, J.P. (1989) *Rediscovering Institutions: The Organizational Basis of Politics*, New York: Free Press.

Molyneux, P. (1996) 'Banking and financial services', in Kassim, H. and Menon, A. (eds), *The European Union and National Industrial Policy*, London and New York: Routledge, 247–66.

North, D.C. (1990) *Institutions, Institutional Change and Economic Performance*, Cambridge and New York: Cambridge University Press.

Ohmae, K. (1995) *The End of the Nation State: The Rise of Regional Economics*, London: HarperCollins.

Olson, M. (1982) *The Rise and Decline of Nations. Economic Growth, Stagflation, and Social Rigidities*, New Haven and London: Yale University Press.

Pérez, S.A. (2001) 'The liberalization of finance in Spain: From interventionism to the market', in Bovens *et al.*, *Success and Failure in Public Governance: A Comparative Study*, 383–400.

Pierce, J.L. (1977) 'The FINE study', in *Journal of Money, Credit and Banking*, 9(4), 605–18.

Pierson, P. (2000) 'Increasing returns, path dependence, and the study of politics', in *American Political Science Review*, 94(2), 251–67.

Pohl, M. (ed.) (1994) *Handbook on the History of European Banks*, Aldershot: Elgar.

Rein, M. and Schön, D.A. (1993) 'Reframing policy discourse', in Fischer, J. and Forester, F. (eds), *The Argumentative Turn in Policy Analysis and Planning*, Durham and London: Duke University Press 145–66.

Reinicke, W. (1995) *Banking, Politics and Global Finance. American Commercial Banks and Regulatory Change 1980–1990*, Aldershot: Elgar.

Richardson, J.J. (ed.) (1982) *Policy Styles in Western Europe*, Boston: Allen and Unwin.

Rogowski, R. (1989) *Commerce and Coalitions: How Trade Affects Domestic Political Alignments*, Princeton: Princeton University Press.

Rogowski, R. (1987) 'Political cleavages and changing exposure to trade', in *American Political Science Review*, 81(4), 1121–37.

Sassen, S. (1998) 'Zur Einbettung des Globalisierungsprozesses: Der Nationalstaat vor neuen Aufgaben', in *Berliner Journal für Soziologie* 8(3), 345–57.

Scharpf, F.W. (1992) 'Die Handlungsfähigkeit des Staates am Ende des Zwanzigsten Jahrhunderts', in Beate Kohler-Koch (ed.), 'Staat und Demokratie in Europa', 18. Wissenschaftlicher Kongreß der Deutschen Vereinigung für Politische Wissenschaft, Opladen: Leske & Budrich, 93–115.

Schmidt, M.G. (2000) *Demokratietheorien. Eine Einführung*, 3rd edn, Opladen: Leske & Budrich.

Schmidt, M.G. (1996) 'When parties matter: A review of the possibilities and limits of partisan influence on public policy', in *European Journal of Political Research*, 30, 155–83.

Schmidt, V.A. (1995) 'The New World Order, Incorporated. The rise of business and the decline of the nation state', in *Daedalus*, 124(2), 75ff.

Schulze, G.G. and Ursprung, H.W. (1999) 'Globalisierung contra Nationalstaat? Ein Überblick über die empirische Evidenz', in Busch and Plümper (eds), *Nationaler Staat und internationale Wirtschaft. Anmerkungen zum Thema Globalisierung*, 41–89.

Shonfield, A. (1965) *Modern Capitalism. The Changing Balance of Public and Private Power*, London, New York, Toronto: Oxford University Press.

Simmons, B. (1999) 'The internationalization of capital', in Kitschelt *et al.*, *Continuity and Change in Contemporary Capitalism*, 36–69.

Soskice, D. (1999) 'Divergent production regimes: Coordinated and uncoordinated market economies in the 1980s and 1990s', in Kitschelt *et al., Continuity and Change in Contemporary Capitalism*, 101–34.

Strange, S. (1996) *The Retreat of the State: The Diffusion of Power in the World Economy*, Cambridge: Cambridge University Press.

Task Group on Regulation of Financial Services (1984) *Report: Blueprint for Reform*, Washington, DC: US Government Printing Office.

Tsebelis, G. (2002) *Veto Players: How Political Institutions Work*, Princeton, NJ: Princeton University Press.

United Nations Research Institute for Social Development (1995) *States of disarray: The social effects of globalization*, Genf: UNRISD.

Vogel, S.K. (1996) *Freer Markets, More Rules: Regulatory Reform in Advanced Industrial Countries*, Ithaca, NY: Cornell University Press.

Waarden, F. van (1995) 'Persistence of national policy styles: A study of their institutional foundations', in Unger, B. and Waarden, F. van (eds), *Convergence or Diversity? Internationalization and Economic Policy Response*, Aldershot: Ashgate, 333–72.

Weiss, L. (1998) *The Myth of the Powerless State*, Ithaca, NY: Cornell University Press.

Williamson, O.E. (1994) 'Transaction cost economics and organization theory', in Smelser, R. and Swedberg, N.J. (eds), *The Handbook of Economic Sociology*, Princeton: Princeton University Press, 76–107.

World Bank (1997) *World Development Report (1997): The State in a Changing World*, New York: Oxford University Press.

6
Global Governance: From Fordist Trilateralism to Neoliberal Constitutionalism

Christoph Scherrer

Introduction

The United States government has been, without doubt, the decisive force in establishing and shaping the main multilateral institutions of the world market since the Second World War. It has consistently pursued the opening of other nations' markets. This leadership in liberalizing international trade has been mainly achieved by lowering access barriers to the American market. Given the mercantilist history of US foreign economic policy and the injury inflicted on many American industries by lowering tariffs, this leadership is quite an extraordinary achievement. This is all the more true, as trade deficits and, more recently, the end of the Cold War have undermined the original foundations of the American commitment to a liberal world market order: economic superiority and anti-communism.

For an explanation of the US postwar commitment to a liberal world market, I will turn to the so-called neo-Gramscian approach. This concept picks up on key insights from the prison writings of the Italian communist leader, Antonio Gramsci. In particular, Gramsci's specific interpretation of hegemony and his focus on class promise a better understanding of power asymmetries in international relations. In the following, I will argue that the ability of the US government to exert hegemony in world markets continues to rest on the hegemony of a group of 'corporate internationalists' within the USA. There is thus a 'double hegemony' at play: a nation state and a class-based hegemony.

In dealing with this 'double hegemony', my main focus will lie on the domestic side of US hegemony. Only in passing will I concern myself with the quality of American leadership in the world market, whether this leadership passes as hegemony in a Gramscian sense.

Theoretical approaches to American foreign economic policy making

In the immediate postwar era, interest-group 'pluralists' and 'realists' in the field of international relations were at ease in explaining the dominance of so-called free-traders within the US polity (Bauer *et al.* 1972; Keohane 1980). Most industries displayed a foreign trade surplus and the USA reigned supreme among Western nations. After 1970, when the trade surplus turned into a huge deficit and when the US international predominance eroded, however, the US government not only continued to espouse a free trade rhetoric but also pursued actively further multinational negotiations for trade liberalization. The executive's interest in maintaining the commitment to a liberal world market order (shared by Congress, though to a lesser degree) has so far lent no support to the gloomy predictions of economists and public choice scholars using models of a 'market for protection' (Bhagwati 1988; Magee and Young 1987).

Authors in the tradition of Max Weber find the reason for this contradiction in the independent status of policy makers. For example, Stephen Krasner has argued that state actors try to represent national interests. When confronted by a choice of interests, state actors would usually give priority to broader foreign policy concerns over more narrow economic interests, such as the inexpensive supply of raw materials (Krasner 1978).

Similarly, Judith Goldstein has argued that 'continued support for the liberal economic regime is a function of the acceptance by the policymaking community of a set of rules and norms' (Goldstein 1986: 180).

This ideological consensus among decision makers rests on the belief that free trade is beneficial as long as all participants respect the rules. The increase in exceptions to the free trade rule while the rule is, in principle, upheld fits well with these statist arguments. However, the mechanisms for maintaining the ideological consensus among state actors have yet to be conclusively identified. To suppose a greater sensitivity to international obligations among state actors may be justified, but since the content of these obligations is open to interpretation, and not all of them have been honoured in recent years, this sensitivity may not be sufficient for maintaining ideological consensus. Furthermore, the assumed coherence and internal cohesiveness of the state bureaucracy in this Weberian tradition contradicts the institutional structure of the US state, commonly described as decentralized, fragmented, and relatively responsive to social forces. Even in the area of foreign policy, where Krasner believes a 'strong state' exists, numerous state agencies and actors compete vigorously for policy authority. All attempts to create an effective, centralized trade ministry have failed thus far.

The belief that capitalist elites instrumentalize the state for their foreign economic interests dominates the heterodox political science tradition (Mills 1956; Shoup 1980). The free trade ideology of the state actors would therefore be the result of their dependence on dominant capital fractions. While the influence of resourceful capital groups must be considered in any explanation, the power elite theory falls short for at least three reasons. First, as with pluralist approaches, it does not question state capacity. Second, it neglects the unintended consequences of actions as well as the unravelling of economic 'logic'. Third, the state remains a 'black box': this approach does not explore the relationship between society, on the one side, and the structure and functions of the state on the other side.

This critique applies less to studies inspired by a reading of Gramsci's work. These studies can account for the role of ideas, for the mechanisms producing consent, and for the impact of economic 'logics'.

Neo-Gramscian approaches[1]

The point of departure of Antonio Gramsci's analysis of power relations is that capitalist society cannot ensure its own reproduction. The 'dull compulsion of the production relations', based on the separation of producers from their means of production, is insufficient for keeping the working class in its dependent position forever. But even the use of coercion is not adequate for this purpose; other, non-'coercive' strategies are required. To analyze these strategies, which aim at creating active consent among the subordinate classes, Gramsci developed several concepts: hegemony, organic intellectual, common sense, and historic bloc. Of primary interest here is the concept of hegemony.

Hegemony refers to an entrenched form of rule that resorts to coercion only in exceptional cases. A ruling class is hegemonic and not just dominant if it succeeds in winning approval to its authority among the members of other societal classes. The more this authority is not merely passively tolerated but actively supported, the more secure the hegemony is. The degree of approval generally rests on how far the ruling institutions address the respective interests of the other classes. The congruence of interests can be achieved, first, by taking into account the interests of other classes in the formative stage of the institutions. Second, attempts can be made to mould these interests so that they become equated with the institution itself. A hegemonic order will try to embrace both variants because a simple adaptation to the interests of other classes carries the risk that its own interests will be ignored and thus hegemony cannot be exercised. On the other hand, aligning the interests of other classes with one's own can only be achieved by cunning or extreme 'coercive' measures. Whenever hegemony relies essentially on cunning and coercion, as Gramsci believed the ruling middle class did after successfully removing the yoke of feudal power, then it lacks ethical legitimacy. One particularly effective form of hegemony by deception, Gramsci argued, is the cooption of the leadership of subordinate classes, so-called transformism. The ethical side of hegemony – leading other groups to the pinnacle of knowledge, technology, and culture – pertains only to allied classes, not to rival, 'ruled' classes.

The prerequisites for the hegemony of a class, Gramsci maintained, are, first, that the class effectively organizes the production of goods; second, that it be capable of taking into account the interests of other groups; and third, that it has cultural leadership. The hegemonic class typically passes through three phases that correspond with its division of society into a socio-economic structure, a civil society, and a political society. In the economic-corporative phase, the members of a class discover their sets of interests based on their status in production and begin to organize themselves accordingly. In this stage, their demands are short-sighted and fixated on their own economic interests. Only when they are in a position to develop strategies for 'universalizing' their interests – which presupposes abandoning short-term interests – do they reach the next, ethico-political phase. The final, hegemonic or state phase is attained if the members of a class can give their political agenda the nature of a state and thus 'armour' their hegemony in civil society with state coercion. Even though Gramsci saw hegemony as rooted in the production sphere, the so-called base, he nonetheless under-stood the so-called superstructure – henceforth differentiated by Gramsci as 'bourgeois-civil' and 'political-statist' society – as more than a mere reflex of the base. On the one hand, dominance of a class in the social relations of production does not automatically translate into its dominance in the super-structure; on the other, power relations, institutions, and ideologies in the superstructure have an impact on the production sphere.

Gramsci believed that the ruling middle class does not rely solely on the state in the narrower sense but finds its support in civil society. This point is worthy of further investigation in a field characterized by the absence of a central 'coercive power'. In contrast to the neo-realism theory of interna-tional relations, which sees the state as the sole actor on the international stage and reduces power relations to quantifiable resources, neo-Gramscians introduce the parallel dimension of class and develop a concept of power that primarily rests on the ability to 'universalize' the particular interests of a group.

The first approach to using Gramsci's work for understanding international relations is found in an essay by Robert Cox on US relations with the International Labour Organization (ILO).[2] Cox shed light on the quality of American hegemony within international organizations as well as on the neo-corporatist integration of US unions into the hegemonic project of the USA. In his critical contribution to the debate on Kindleberger's hegemonic stabil-ity thesis, Cox presented Gramsci's concepts as an alternative method of ana-lyzing the international relations of capitalist nations. Cox demonstrated the empirical implications of this instrument in a comprehensive study on the social structure of the capitalist accumulation process and the emergence of international historic blocs since the beginning of the industrial age.

Kees van der Pijl, still strongly influenced by structural-deterministic Marxism, studied processes of transatlantic class formation in the postwar era, laying the groundwork for the central research field of the neo-Gramscians: formation processes of an international bourgeoisie. 'Cox student' Stephen Gill in particular was instrumental in propagating the neo-Gramscian approach. The textbook he co-authored with David Law on international political economy contrasted the theoretical bases, methodology, and empirical application of the approach with those of the leading paradigms of the discipline. What followed was an empirical study of the Trilateral Commission (see below), which underpinned Gill's previous thesis about an 'ethical hegemony' of the USA over the Western industrial nations (Cafruny 1990; Gill 1986, 1990; Gill and Law 1988).

From the neo-Gramscian viewpoint, the liberal world market order of the postwar era may be interpreted as a project of internationally oriented capital fractions in the USA (notably New York banks and law practices as well as transnational corporations from the various sectors). These fractions succeeded in hegemonically integrating into their project important groups in the USA on the one hand, and – through the resources of the US government – the other capitalist industrial nations on the other. Contact with the allied nations was organized not only at government level but also at private forums that served the capital fractions in terms of promoting the congruence of interests. The American actors were hegemonic in the sense that they took into account the interests of allied nations/capital fractions in the pursuit of their own long-term goals (Cafruny 1990; Gill 1990).

Criticism of the now voluminous works by neo-Gramscians commenced in the 1990s. Within the broad and diversified Marxist scholarship, critics of Gramsci and neo-Gramscians can be divided into two camps: orthodox and post-positivist. They differ primarily in their understanding of the reproduction mechanism of the capitalistic means of production. In the orthodox view, once the major institutions of capitalism have come into existence, then the capitalist means of production will perpetually create their own conditions for reproduction owing to an immanent capital logic. By contrast, from the post-positivist perspective, this reproduction process is never secure but is constantly in a position of peril. Rather, the contingent and open-ended nature of all societal institutions is assumed.

The orthodox literature accuses Gramscianism primarily of politicism or voluntarism. Their main charge is that the Gramscian tradition neglects capitalist structural constraints, thus overestimating the possibilities for conscious and strategic action and at the same time overemphasizing the necessity of such action for the reproduction of capitalist society. According to Burnham (Burnham 1991), market mechanisms of competition are what ensure the reproduction of bourgeois domination, political coordination in civil society being merely of secondary importance. Economic laws, particularly the law of value, govern international relations. Burnham cites as empirical evidence how the pace and manner of world market integration of Great Britain in the immediate postwar period were dictated by its balance of payments.

The accusation of politicism has a long tradition (Riechers 1970). It is based on Gramsci's break with the then predominant theory of the Communist movement, economic reductionism, which challenged not the primacy of the economic base in capitalism *per se* but the notion that society is fully determined by its base and that economic trends have the quality of laws of nature (Gramsci 1991: Gef 4, §38). Yet Gramsci only just touches on concrete economic laws, though regulation-theoretical works show that his political insights are compatible with an economic base (as long as the latter is not awarded ontological status). Likewise, the challenge to the laws of societal development in Gramsci's writings should not be taken as an undervaluation of the restrictive effect of structures. Although as party leader he tried to overcome structural constraints, and in prison he held on to the party primacy by taking a positive stance toward Jacobinism (Buci-Glucksmann 1981: 61ff.; Gramsci 1991: Gef 1, §44), his reflections on defeat as preserved in his prison writings are characterized by an analysis of structural conditions.

The charge of politicism is more appropriate concerning Gramsci's followers. Though Cox, Gill, and Law never fail to stress that hegemonic relations are entrenched in production, they do not consider how much economic functional interdependence (for example, balance of payments) influence the action of political players. Gill and Law, in particular, credit the elite with a surprisingly high degree of freedom of action (Gill and Law 1988). Rupert's analysis of the connection between US hegemony and labour disputes in the mass production industries shows, however, that Gill's voluntarism is not immanent in the Gramscian approach (Rupert 1995). Moreover, Rupert stresses one important element of the post-positivist approach: that (economic) interests are not fix, but instead develop and are therefore changeable and subject to influence by actors (see ibid. 56). Sadly, world market mediated effects are underrated by Rupert as well.

Thus, while orthodox criticism only partially applies to Gramsci, there remain some problematic orthodox remnants in Gramscianism. Ernesto Laclau and Chantal Mouffe convincingly argued that it has not consistently distanced itself from the essential apriorisms of traditional Marxist theory (Laclau and Mouffe 1991). Among these essentialisms is primarily classism, the idea that the working class represents the privileged actor of social change. In taking this criticism seriously, my approach differs from previous neo-Gramscian inspired studies of the USA and the world market by not privileging the world market oriented capital fractions *a priori* in my analysis. Instead, first, all relevant society and state actors and their positions on foreign economic policy are identified. Then the factors contributing to the defence or shifting of these positions will be defined. Only then did I study the relations of dominance in the free trade camp. Additionally, I look for open situations where the option of preventing further, or backtracking from previous, liberalization steps would have been possible. In so doing,

I endeavour to reconstruct the context of the decisions taken in terms of opportunities for action and structural constraints.

Project world market: the liberalization of US foreign economic policy

As mentioned earlier, the US government exercised its economic hegemony notably by opening its own market. In accordance with the standard of reciprocity of the world trade regime, the US government eased access to its own market in return for every tariff reduction and for every lifting of a non-tariff trade barrier (for example, technical standards). Access to this huge market was, and remains, coveted. The success of companies from Germany, Japan, South Korea, and now China on the US market has been responsible for the dynamic strength of their respective economies. At the same time, this success has bolstered the export oriented forces in these countries.

Although the opening of the US market is a key prerequisite for globalization processes, it cannot be taken as a matter of course. Even less so, considering that US reliance on an international division of labour has been comparatively small.[3] Until the Second World War, US foreign economic policy was shaped by an ideology of economic nationalism, which took the form of a high tariff policy for industrial products. Ever since, the key players in foreign economic policy making have been guided by the free trade gospel of dismantling trade barriers of all kinds. Yet polls show that, over the entire postwar period, a majority of Americans have viewed the opening of the US market with a great deal of scepticism, if they have not outright opposed it. The question arises how foreign economic policy could have been liberalized when there was neither obvious economic necessity nor unequivocal democratic legitimization.

The liberalization of US foreign economic policy from 1936 on found wide consensus among the elite, the approval being strongest among representatives of government, banks, corporations, and the media as well as among economic experts. Their interests in a liberal foreign economic policy can only be partly explained by economic self-interest and the preservation of institutional power. In the various international and foreign economic policy organizations (for example, Council on Foreign Relations), consensus on the advantages of a liberal foreign economic policy was driven by other political goals, particularly the containment, first, of German and then of Soviet influence.

The emphasis here on the discursive formation of free trade consensus should however not lead to the assumption that this consensus came about purely intentionally. Tendencies toward internationalization are immanent in the capitalist economic order. And the internationalization of economic activities cannot be reversed at the drop of the hat. The greater the integration of global markets, the higher the adjustment costs when trying to seal off the national economic arena. The irreversibility of internationalization is secured through international agreements. The renationalization of economic activities either violates contractual obligations or entails an arduous renegotiation with a multiplicity of nation states. Yet, as the transition to the flexible exchange rate regime (1971–73) showed, the USA as world economic hegemonic power could flout agreements with impunity (see below).

Although in the postwar period the world-market-oriented corporate elite needed the support of the White House, the media, and experts for formulating and implementing their trade policy interests, they wielded the greatest power in the free trade camp. Their authority is underpinned chiefly by money. Thus, they have formidable influence in the selection of candidates for political offices, including the Presidency. The fact that the media are privately owned is a boon for them, as over 40 per cent of campaign budgets is spent on radio and television advertisements.

Thus, the world market oriented capital fractions can be characterized as hegemonic because they could give their political agenda a statist form; that is, their agenda was institutionally incorporated into the government. Moreover, they succeeded in shaping the discursive terrain of foreign economic policy making. In contrast to the period prior to the Second World War, the demand for product specific protection no longer has the status of a universally valued principle but is now handled as a specific exception to a general principle of free trade. This reversal from the principle to the exception, which occurred in the immediate postwar era, facilitated the institutional channelling of protectionist demands and prevented companies threatened by imports from closing ranks.

Although the public was not convinced by the principle of free trade, it was open to the idea of fair trade, understanding fair to mean basically the reciprocal opening of the respective national markets. This distinction was never forgotten by the key players in foreign economic policy liberalization. They reached bi- and multilateral agreements on liberalization, propagated the content of such accords as reciprocal measures, and, after the Kennedy Round of GATT, they held out the prospect of compensatory payments for jobs lost due to import competition. There was another reason why the public's trade policy fears found little resonance in public discourse: It had no political representation. Until the late 1970s, both the unions and the pro-labour wing of the Democratic Party advocated the liberalization policy mainly out of consideration for the Western Alliance.

Beginning in the mid-1970s, however, some of the central assumptions underpinning the liberal foreign economic policy were successively called into question. First, the system of fixed exchange rates proved to be less and less compatible with America's global political ambitions and full employment goal. High expenditures for international military deployment (the Vietnam War), the growing demand for foreign products, and increasing direct investments in foreign countries led to a deficit in the balance of payments, which could be corrected only by official sales of gold or the inflationary printing of dollars. Presidents Kennedy and Johnson (1961–68) thus were confronted with the choice of scaling back their military engagement, rescinding the liberalization of the movement of goods, slowing down capital drain, or deflating the domestic economy. They decided to restrict the formerly unimpeded cross-border capital movements.

As long as the capital controls were merely temporary measures, the societal protagonists of the free trade project, notably the New York financial world, accepted these restrictions of their power of disposition and profit-making opportunities. From 1965, however, as the cross-border activities of more and more companies came under state supervision, the search began for ways of reconciling free trade and free capital movements. One remedy, propagated especially by monetarist economist Milton Friedman (Friedman 1963) was the transition to flexible exchange rates.

The rejection of capital controls marked a shift of the interests in the world market. Where earlier anti-communism united the free trade coalition, with the world market as the means for integrating both the allied nations and the working public into a Fordist production coalition, now the unifying interest was to use the world market in order to reject workers' demands. The unions' departure from the free trade coalition accelerated this shift of interests. The 'Burke–Hartke' bill launched by the unions in 1971, which called for extensive state regulation of transnational corporations, sent the domestic market oriented corporations and the remaining newspapers with protectionist stances into the camp of the free traders. 'Burke–Hartke' turned foreign economic policy into a class question: nearly all business associations were pitted against nearly all unions.

Trilateralism: a response to Nixon's unilateralism

In the Nixon administration, the internationalists had to share power with groups of a more domestic market orientation. This became painfully clear when, in 1971 – the year of the first trade deficit since the turn of the century – President Nixon abandoned the Bretton-Woods Monetary Order and unilaterally imposed a 10 per cent import surcharge. The latter policy alarmed the internationalists since unilateral US protectionist action would have seriously undermined the credibility of the free trade gospel. Several transnational liberals resigned their posts within the administration and joined the efforts of David Rockefeller to found the Trilateral Commission. The Commission set daunting tasks for itself; namely, 'to oppose a return to the mercantilist policies of the 1930s; to integrate Japan into the core of the American alliance system; and to change the orientations of the foreign and domestic policies of the major capitalist powers so that they might become congruent with a globally integrated economic structure' (Gill 1990: 143), The Commission explicitly included CEOs and political consultants from

Western Europe and Japan. Its credo was to overcome the nation state: 'The public and leaders of most countries continue to live in a mental universe which no longer exists – a world of separate nations – and have great difficulties thinking in terms of global perspectives and interdependence.'[4] The objectives of the Trilateralists went further than criticizing Nixon for a lack of concern for the liberal world market order. Those Commission members affiliated with the Democratic Party were trying to regain domestic consent to and international legitimation for US international activism, which had been lost owing to the Vietnam war and the cynical use Nixon and Kissinger made of 'Realpolitik'.

Their solution was most forcefully articulated by Zbigniew Brzezinski (the Trilateral Commission's first director): Engage in a human rights campaign, share power with the Western allies, and respond to Third World aspirations 'within a framework of generally cooperative relations'.[5]

The Trilateralists were successful at first. The import surcharge was rescinded. With the demise of Nixon, the access of the Trilateralists to the executive was greatly improved. At the end of 1975, President Ford realized the idea of closer coordination among the Western powers by attending the first summit of the seven most powerful Western nations held at Rambouillet. The apex of the Trilateralists' triumph was reached when their fellow member Jimmy Carter became president. Carter recruited most of his foreign policy staff from within the Commission and started in earnest the experiment to manage the world market (and world politics) in close collaboration with the most important allies.

Seen from outside the USA, the policy success of the Trilateralists was an attempt to reinvigorate US hegemony in a Gramscian sense; that is, by taking into account the interests of allies. To accomplish this renewal of hegemony, the corporate internationalists had to renew their own hegemony within the USA. They succeeded by developing an intellectually cohesive programme and by establishing a new organizational vehicle to lend institutional support for this programme. They benefited greatly from the obvious failures of 'Realpolitik'.

The limits of trilateralism

At the end of Carter's tenure, the Trilateralists considered their own project a failure. The revolution in Iran and the Soviet intervention in Afghanistan were both interpreted as resulting from a lack of Western determination. A decision making structure built on consensus, they argued, could not adequately avert the challenges to the capitalist world order. The allies also displayed little willingness to share in the costs of maintaining the *Pax Americana*. West Germany's chancellor, Helmut Schmidt, showed little inclination to support the Carter administration's policies of economic expansion. He refused to defend the US dollar. The dollar's subsequent precipitous decline in 1979 encouraged Carter to impose budget austerity and the Federal Reserve to increase interest rates. The world of nation states, which supposedly had already been overcome, had reared its ugly head.

These foreign developments did not simply challenge the idea of trilateralism. They also posed an immediate threat to the interests of the Commission's corporate members. Third World assertiveness translated into higher prices for raw materials, threatened their steady supply, and, at times, led to the expropriation of assets. The weakness of the US dollar imperiled the privileged role of American banks in the world capital markets.

The critique of trilateralism on an international scale coincided with the rejection of tripartism in the domestic arena. The Carter administration had developed the concept of tripartite re-industrialization to manage the impact of growing foreign competition. This was to be jointly conceived and implemented by representatives of capital, labour, and the state. From management's perspective, however, tripartism perpetuated precisely what was perceived to be the main cause of their lack of competitiveness: the accommodation of labour's interests. In contrast, political action 'against' the state held the promise of improving industry's conditions of accumulation at the state's expense. It would also give firms the freedom to pursue strategies to weaken labour or, if these failed, to move out of production altogether. The managers of industries in distress, with the exception of Chrysler, rejected Carter's offers for tripartite crisis management (Scherrer 1992: 200–9).

In response to the international challenges and the new domestic agenda, many internationalists abandoned trilateralist 'accommodationism' and turned to the unilateralist position espoused by the supporters of Ronald Reagan (Gill 1990: 223–6). US interests were to be furthered by the 'free play' of market forces. International cooperation was no longer considered necessary. Complaints of other countries that the US budget deficit and high dollar were distorting the international monetary and financial system, went unanswered.

Instead, it was hoped that the unilateral actions would force other countries to pursue 'structural (that is, microeconomic) policy reforms to bring down inflation and free-up labour, capital, and product markets' (Nau 1990: 216). Thus, Reagan's unilateralism was not a rerun of Nixon's 'domesticism' but a conscious attempt to project America's structural economic power abroad and set the conditions of its economic relations with other states. Internationalism was not abandoned. Rather, it was stripped of its 'cosmopolitan' rhetoric and became firmly rooted in 'national interests'.

Yet, the limits of unilateralism became apparent shortly after its adoption. When Mexico threatened to default on its loans, the liquidity crisis threatened US banks. In response, the Reagan administration negotiated a common debt crisis strategy with other creditor nations. Moreover, the policy of strengthening the dollar had made imports ever more cheaper and ubiquitous. Hard-pressed domestic industries cried for protectionism. The administration deflected these calls with a devaluation strategy. But this presupposed cooperation with the other central banks, for unilateral action would have risked an uncontrollable flight out of the dollar. Thus, by the mid-1980s, the USA returned to cooperation (cooperation here should not be confused with harmony of interests).

Despite these obvious limits of unilateralism, the return to a more cooperative strategy at least toward the Western allies, was made possible precisely because unilateralism had achieved its main objective: to avert the challenges to capitalist rule. The power of labour, both inside and outside the USA, had been weakened. The terms of trade for raw materials deteriorated and the debt crisis forced many countries in the periphery to adopt a more 'welcoming' attitude to foreign enterprises. Furthermore, American unilateralism did enjoy support from abroad. Basically all those groups who wanted to break loose from the Christian/Social Democratic class compromise welcomed the policy shift under Reagan, foremost the British Tories under Prime Minister Margaret Thatcher.

The new trilateralism as global constitutionalism

A further consequence of the high interest rate and high dollar policy of the early Reagan years could be used against the allied industrial nations; namely, the meteoric rise in trade deficits. Contemporary trends in foreign economic theory provided arguments for a 'strategic trade policy', which would force other nations to open their markets by threatening to close the US one. In addition to companies from the high technology sector, suppliers of sophisticated services and owners of copyrights joined the group of open market strategists. Together with various think tanks and supported by large internationally oriented foundations, they popularized the notion that services could be rendered transnationally, that national regulations of the respective sectors prevented this, and that consequently the dismantling of these barriers must be negotiated in the framework of GATT. This idea was received enthusiastically by the Reagan administration because it afforded the possibility of channelling commercial pressure toward free trade.

Paradoxically, the trade deficit gave the USA bargaining power. Foreign countries were much more dependent on access to the US market than the American economy was on access to foreign markets. Thus, the Washington government could function as a battering ram against the national self-interests of transnational corporations in other countries. The threat of imposing sanctions – occasionally enforced – compelled not only Japan to lower non-tariff trade barriers and to deregulate its economy, but Western Europe as well. Again, the US demands were welcomed in both regions by many economists, the top leadership of business groups, and parts of the ministerial bureaucracies.

The unilateral measures proved to be helpful in concluding bilateral free trade and investment protection agreements as well as in establishing the

World Trade Organization (WTO). The Canadian government's decision to crown its neoliberal policy change of the mid-1980s with a free trade zone with the USA was driven by a growing wariness of increased protectionist measures on the part of the US government. Moreover, the conservative Mulroney administration saw a free trade agreement with its neighbour (enacted in 1988) and the concomitant concessions to the US government as a catalyst for further neoliberal reforms in Canada.

Similar motives underlay the Mexican government's interest in the North American Free Trade Agreement (NAFTA). Among the NAFTA boosters in the United States, who, like David Rockefeller before them, had pushed for a continental free trade zone since the 1960s, support for NAFTA took on virtually counter-revolutionary dimensions. The motive of contractually exorcising the spectre of an independent Latin American course was divulged in manifold ways in the statements of NAFTA advocates. In six out of ten New York Times editorials on NAFTA, the lock-in of neoliberal reforms in Mexico was mentioned as one of the specific advantages of the agreement. This motive conspicuously resurfaced in the discussions on the peso crisis after NAFTA came into effect. Appearing before a Senate committee, development expert Rudiger Dornbusch raised the spectre of bolstering the 'retrograde camp' in Mexico if 'our model' there were not safeguarded by the monetary rescue package (Herman 1995: 37).

Moreover, negotiations on a free trade zone with Canada aimed at influencing the GATT round, as the first time inclusion of services in a free trade agreement should serve as a model for GATT rules. The investment and copyright protection provided for in NAFTA should, in turn, serve as the basis for multilateral agreements with developing countries and emerging economies.

At the close of the Uruguay Round of the GATT, the developing countries were willing to make hefty concessions toward opening their markets in the hope that a more powerful dispute settlement process in the framework of the World Trade Organization would hinder Washington from taking unilateral trade actions. In contrast to its stance toward the International Court of Justice, the United States has thus far abided by the decisions of the WTO.

The restrictions to state 'tyranny' – notably toward foreign investors – brought about through debt crises, NAFTA, and the WTO would be broadened and cemented in the 1998 Multilateral Agreement on Investments (MAI), which would initially apply only to OECD member states. This agreement would guarantee the protection of international investors from expropriation and from discrimination that favours locally based companies. Investors would even be given the right to sue a government in an International Court of Justice. The implications of this agreement were aptly described by the former Director General of the WTO, Renato Ruggiero: 'We are writing the constitution of the united world economy' (Wallach 1998: 16). At first, opposition by France and determined mobilization, particularly by the American consumer organization, Public Citizen, blocked the signing of the MAI. But this initial failure did not discourage the diverse national and international corporate alliances (including Business Investment Network, Transatlantic Business Dialog, European Roundtable, as well as the Trilateral Commission). Together with the finance and economics ministries of most industrial nations, they pursued this 'bill of rights' of capitalism primarily through bilateral agreements between their state spearhead, the US government, and other countries.

Since its beginnings in the early 1970s, the trilateral project has moved from securing a liberal world market order by accommodating labour and Third World interests to a global constitutionalism where private assets are protected from state interference and restrictions.

The success of the internationalists rested not only in their ability to transform nationalist impulses into strategies for opening up other nations' markets. They used their privileged position in society and the state for effective discursive strategies.

On the one hand, they swayed public opinion through numerous strategies: by appealing to and invoking common sense, by restricting the field of public discourse, through selective publication and interpretation of poll results, by playing down the significance of a given subject in the public's eye. They used canvassing methods to develop their discursive strategies; that is, they conducted surveys to test the persuasiveness of individual foreign trade policy arguments. This revealed the effectiveness not so much of economic arguments, but of portraying liberalization measures as a way of honouring the US right to leadership (Scherrer 1999: 145–55). Nor did the administration, the media and the experts shy away from consciously deceiving the public on a number of occasions (Scherrer 1999: 347–8).

On the other hand, they succeeded in preventing the still largely critical attitude of the public from affecting policy. In particular, their ability to build consensus among the elite enabled them to hinder, until the late 1960s, the public's free trade scepticism from finding political representation. Later, the free trade consensus of the elite (which was especially strong among the media) helped marginalize those persons and organizations who tried to exploit the public's protectionist tendencies for campaign purposes, or to mobilize against further liberalization measures (Scherrer 1999: 240–6). In some cases, most recently during the implementation legislation for the Uruguay Round of GATT, the administration and congressional leadership delayed controversial votes until the risk of not being reelected was at a minimum (Scherrer 1999: 304).

Moreover, each administration knew how to play on the foreign trade fears of the public. Although often no more than symbolic gestures, the president and Congress insisted on reciprocity, stipulated special protectionist clauses, and granted financial compensation.

Meanwhile the critics of liberal foreign trade policies contributed to their own marginalization. The trade union federation AFL–CIO was incapable of closing ranks with critics of other aspects of the prevailing foreign policy, nor did it show itself adept at using academic expertise or attracting experts for its positions. In important foreign trade policy decisions (for example the Bretton-Woods monetary crisis, the dollar crisis under President Carter), it therefore lacked convincing alternatives. The analysis of public opinion polls further demonstrates that the AFL–CIO did not grasp how to turn its foreign trade policy positions into a foreign policy programme palatable to the public (Scherrer 1999: 97–104, 284–300). Thus proving the critical relationship between the quality of a political project and its power to influence policy. Quality means not only a solid academic basis for the arguments, but primarily the ability to incorporate the interests of important societal actors as well as to take into account structural effects of practices that are either unquestioned or well-defended. Naturally, this insight applies also to projects of the elite networks.

Symbolic politics: social clauses[6]

The disputes over social clauses in the World Trade Organization are instructive for a discussion on the double nature of the US hegemony because they disclose the following paradox: the opposing forces are the hegemonic internationally oriented economic circles in the USA, whereas the Washington government was one of the most staunch supporters of social clauses.

For many years the International Confederation of Free Trade Unions has called for the incorporation of core workers' rights into trade agreements as social clauses. The trade privileges granted in these agreements would be made contingent on the respect for the following core rights: freedom of association, collective bargaining, prohibition of child labour and forced labour, banning discrimination in work and career as well as the elimination of gender-based wage discrimination. A joint advisory body of the WTO and the International Labour Organization would monitor compliance of the clauses. In the event of non-compliance, technical and financial assistance would be provided in an effort to support the relevant country in achieving compliance. The ILO could recommend further measures – including trade sanctions – only in cases of flagrant or persistent violations and government intransigence.

A good case can be made for claiming that internationally binding social standards not only guarantee respect for human rights, but can also enhance a country's opportunities for economic development.

Yet this viewpoint is shared neither by most governments of developing and threshold countries, nor by economists and managers. All the major trade associations in the USA reject social clauses. Why then did the Clinton administration become their champion? Past experience might help to answer this question. In 1984, human rights groups were able to push through the social clause in the US General System of Preferences (GSP) against the will of President Reagan at the time. They succeeded because of a particularly favourable political situation. Apart from President Reagan, only a handful of active supporters advocated the renewal of the GSP programme; namely, those exporters, multinational corporations, and US importers trading in goods that would have incurred high or very high tariffs without GSP. In addition, Reagan stood behind the demand of business to link the granting of GSP to the protection of intellectual property. In view of this breach of the GSP principle of non-reciprocity, Reagan as well as Congress could not refuse social conditionalization. Opposition to these clauses was indeed minimal, not least because the President was afforded ample power of discretion. The enforcement history of the social clauses confirms the Reagan administration's calculation that it could get by with symbolic politics for the most part. Preferences were withdrawn only from politically outcast countries.

The 1994 North American Agreement on Labor Cooperation marked the first time within the framework of an international trade agreement, NAFTA, that a Commission for Labor Cooperation was set up to monitor compliance with national social standards. This agreement came about because many Americans did not share the enthusiasm for NAFTA felt by the leaders of diverse political-societal institutions. Candidate Clinton tried to dispel criticism by promising renegotiations. As president, he promptly honoured his promise, and in March 1993 negotiations began with the Mexican and Canadian governments over side agreements on workers' and environmental issues. In light of Mexico's intransigence, private sector opposition in America, and the conservative Canadian government's apathy, the outcome of the negotiations was quite paltry. Although the unions and environmental groups remained steadfast in their opposition to NAFTA, the side agreement facilitated its passage.

The Labor Side Agreement provides little leeway for imposing sanctions, which is then an involved procedure. Mainly moral suasion or diplomatic pressure is exercised. No noteworthy progress has been made in any of the cases thus far.

The Clinton administration's demand for social clauses in the framework of a continental free trade zone (Free Trade Area of the Americas, FTAA) or the WTO would have performed the same function; namely, to supply the president with a congressional mandate to conduct negotiations. Yet he was denied this mandate after the ratification of NAFTA in 1993 and GATT in 1994. The Republicans, who reached a majority in Congress in 1994, were reluctant to give the Democrat president an opportunity for success in trade policy, which would have further loosened the purse strings of corporate donors. At the same time, though, they were eager to show the business community which party had its trade interests at heart. The Republicans succeeded at this balancing act over the issue of social and environmental clauses: by making the argument on behalf of the business community for free trade and against social and environmental conditions, they laid the blame for the mandate bill's failure at the President's door. Once the latter was ready to abandon the social and environmental conditions, the Republicans attempted to discredit as protectionists the House Democrats who were still committed to those clauses. These Democrats in turn maintained that it was the Republicans' unwillingness to compromise on the issue of the social and ecological conditionalization of world trade that led to the bill's demise.

This manoeuvring was possible only because the point of the negotiating mandate – the creation of a continental free trade zone – was less urgent than NAFTA, even among FTAA supporters. For US corporations, the planned WTO Millennium Round was less important than China's negotiations for membership in the World Trade Organization and the fight against trade sanctions being used as a foreign policy tool.

The minor significance the business community attached to an FTAA is conspicuous in the hard line it took on the issue of social and environmental clauses. The prevention of another precedence case linking workers' rights and environmental standards with the trade regime was a higher priority than a continental free trade zone. Corporations and corporate alliances even founded a new organization, the Coalition for a Sound Trade Policy, to fight social and environmental clauses. In the run-up to the third ministerial conferences in Seattle, leading free trade theorists including Jagdish Bhagwati advised against a WTO Millennium Round as long as there was still the danger of such a precedence case.

This opposition also explains why the Clinton administration came out strongly in support of social clauses in Seattle in December 1999 but was not willing to make concessions in other areas to the countries involved. In view of the strong reservations of the business community, Clinton could not possibly link the demand for social clauses with concessions to developing countries.

In conclusion, the apparent contradiction between the American government's supposed function as a state 'battering ram' to open markets worldwide and its actual position on social clauses becomes unravelled upon closer analysis of the actions of the economic internationalists. First, the internationalists could usually count on the opposition of the governments involved (see the ministerial conferences of the WTO). Second, because of this opposition, they could use the demand for social clauses as leverage for achieving other demands. At the second ministerial conference in Singapore in 1996, suspicion was rife that the USA had come out so staunchly in support of social clauses in order to achieve its real goal: the liberalization of the world market for information technologies. This measure was initially rejected by many countries of the South, but not as vehemently as was the demand for social clauses. In exchange for dropping the latter, the agreement on information technologies found easier ratification. Third, whenever societal opposition to their liberalization plans threatened to obtain a congressional majority, the internationalists succeeded in reducing the content of the social clauses to an almost purely symbolic dimension (see GSP social clauses and the NAFTA side agreement). Fourth, they have recently had other opportunities for achieving their goals (read debt crisis); thus they could afford to postpone further negotiations on opening markets, as long as the negotiating mandate for these could only be acquired at the cost of a stronger conditionalization of trade (see FTAA and the WTO Millennium Round). Fifth, there is an alternative to social clauses: voluntary codes of conduct.

The 'complex interdependence' of 'double hegemony'

Does Gramsci's conceptualization of the term hegemony deliver a better understanding of the power relationships in world markets? One will recall that Gramsci defined hegemony as the ability of a group to 'universalize' its particular interests. Hegemony is achieved primarily by 'non-coercive' means (for example, by offering a framework for the solution of other groups' problems) though not without coercion as a backdrop.

On the international level, US interest in securing a liberal world market and in containing communism matched well with Western Europe's and Japan's interest in military protection and in rebuilding their war-torn economies. Access to American markets proved to these allies extremely valuable. This access was made possible by a reversal of previous protectionist policies and by US support for a fixed exchange rate regime.

American hegemony eroded, however, when the US government attempted to shift the increasing costs of hegemony onto its allies. A transition period followed that was marked by failed attempts to regain hegemony under President Carter. Interestingly, the assertion of self-interest and the use of more 'coercive', unilateral means led to a renewed hegemony under President Reagan. However, coercion was by far not the only and dominant means. Intellectual efforts toward shaping a new, decidedly more market oriented vision were well received among the allies. While achieved mostly in a unilateral fashion, Western allies benefited from the restoration of a regime of secure and inexpensive raw materials and from the strengthening of property rights in general.

The interests in strengthening the right to manage, however, was not shared by all political groups and reveals a class bias in the renewed hegemony: it moved from a Fordist (Christian-Social Democratic) project, which included workers and their representatives, to a neoliberal constitutionalist project.

This bias became apparent within the domestic US context when economic internationalism lost support among the representatives of workers. In fact, the internationalists have never succeeded in obtaining the active consent of a majority of Americans to their policy of easing access to the American market. However, the internationalists have displayed an extraordinary capacity for instrumentalizing domestic nationalist challenges for their own purposes. They have transformed nationalist impulses into strategies for opening up other nations' markets.

This transition period from Fordist to neoliberal hegemony highlights three valuable Gramscian insights. First, it shows that economic strength may be a necessary precondition for hegemony but not a sufficient one. Economic or military strength does not automatically translate into hegemony. Rather, hegemony has to be discursively and strategically maintained. Second, international hegemony and domestic hegemony are interdependent. On the one hand, a nation's hegemony is consolidated only when its hegemonic forces support its outward strategies of 'universalizing' its national interests by accommodating foreign ones. Once this support waned in the US case, US hegemony became fragile. On the other hand, challenges to international hegemony threaten domestic hegemony. The increasing costs of the Fordist hegemony undermined the position of internationalists in the US domestic arena. The internationalists had to reinvigorate their hegemony by forging new domestic alliances and by discursively readjusting their objectives. This, in turn, allowed them to further their project of liberalizing the world market. In breaking down barriers to market access abroad, they made effective use of American power. Third, the common focus on hegemony in international relations as a characteristic of a nation state is far too narrow. The international space is divided not only by national boundaries but also by class and other categories of identity. American hegemony was successfully renewed because its market oriented message fell on the receptive ears of owners and managers of firms worldwide.

Perspective

Future research will explore to what extent the neoliberal constitutionalist project of global governance is at risk by recent shifts in the balance of power in favour of the US state and US financial institutions vis-à-vis their European and Japanese counterparts and, especially after the terrorist attacks of 9-11 (11 September, 2001), within the US state in favour of the military-industrial complex vis-à-vis multilateralist proponents of international law. On the one hand, both shifts may help along neoliberal constitutionalism by the greater willingness to exert pressure in bilateral negotiations with recalcitrant countries to move to more market friendly government policies. On the other hand, greater exertion of discretionary state power runs counter to the general credo of the constitutionalist project of minimal state intervention and undermines the foundations of global governance; for example, the rule of law as well as shared values of mutual respect and of restraints on the use of force.

Notes

1 See Antonio Gramsci 1991: *Gefängnishefte*, Gef 2, H3 §119; Gef 3, H4 §38; Gef 4, H6 §88, Hamburg: Argument-Verlag.
2 For a succinct introduction to the work of Cox, see Sinclair 1996. The same volume contains a brief autobiography by Cox. See also Cox 1977, 1987, 1993. See also, in this context, Keohane 1984.
3 For the postwar domestic growth path, see Scherrer 1992.
4 Trilateral Commission Task Force Report, 'Toward a Renovated International System', January 1977, quoted in *NACLA Report*, 'From Hemispheric Police to Global Managers', July/August (1981), 6.
5 Fred Bergsten, quoted in Holly Sklar, 'Trilateralism: Managing Dependence and Democracy', *Trilateralism. The Trilateral Commission and Elite Planning for World Management*, Holly Sklar (ed.) (Boston, MA: South End Press, 1980): 1–58; 25.
6 For an extensive discussion of social clauses, see Christoph Scherrer and Thomas Greven, *Global Rules* (Münster: Verlag Westfälisches Dampfboot, 2000).

References

Bauer, R.A., Pool, I. de Sola and Dexter, L.A. (1972) *American Business and Public Policy. The Politics of Foreign Trade*, 2nd edn, Chicago, IL: Aldine Altherton.
Bhagwati, J. (1988) *Protectionism*, Cambridge, MA: MIT Press.
Buci-Glucksmann, C. (1981) *Gramsci und der Staat. Für eine materialistische Theorie der Philosophie*, Köln: Pahl-Rugenstein.
Burnham, P. (1991) 'Neo-Gramscian hegemony and the international order', in *Capital & Class*, 45, 73–93.
Cafruny, A.W. (1990) 'A Gramscian concept of declining hegemony: Stages of US power and the evolution of international economic relations', in Rapkin, D.P. (ed.), *World Leadership and Hegemony*, Boulder, CO: Lynne Rienner, 97–118.
Cohen, B.J. (ed.) (1968) *American Foreign Economic Policy*, New York: Harper & Row.
Cox, R.W. (1993) 'Gramsci, hegemony and international relations: An essay in method', in Gill, S. (ed.), *Historical Materialism and International Relations*, Cambridge: Cambridge University Press, 49–66.
Cox, R.W. (1987) *Power, Production, and World Order*, New York: Columbia University Press.
Cox, R.W. (1977) 'Labor and hegemony', in *International Organization*, 31(3), 187–223.
Cox, R.W. and Sinclair, T.J. (eds) *Approaches to World Order*, Cambridge: Cambridge University Press.
Friedman, M. (1963) 'Using the free market to resolve the balance-of-payments problem', Statement in hearing before Joint Economic Committee of the Congress, reprinted in Cohen, B.J. (1968) (ed.), *American Foreign Economic Policy*, New York: Harper & Row, 87–98.
Gill, S. (1990) *American Hegemony and the Trilateral Commission*, New York: Cambridge University Press.
Gill, S. (1986) 'US hegemony: Its limits and prospects in the Reagan era', in *Millennium*, 15, 311–36.
Gill, S. and Law, D. (1988) *The Global Political Economy. Perspectives, Problems, and Policies*, Baltimore, MD: John Hopkins University Press.
Goldstein, J. (1986) 'Political economy of trade: Institutions of protection', in *American Political Science Review*, 80(1), 161–84.
Gramsci, A. (1991) Antonio Gramsci, Gefängnishefte: Gef 1, §44; Gef 2, H3 §119; Gef 3, H4 §38; Gef 4, H6 §88, Hamburg: Argument-Verlag.

Herman, E. (1995) 'Mexican meltdown; NAFTA and the propaganda system', in *Z Magazine*, 8(9), 36–42.

Holsti, O., Siverson, R.M. and George, A.L. (eds) (1980) *Change in the International System*, Boulder, CO: Westview.

Katzenstein, P.J. (ed.) (1978) *Between Power and Plenty: Foreign Economic Policies of Advanced Industrial States*, Madison, WI: University of Wisconsin Press.

Keohane, R.O. (1984) *After Hegemony: Cooperation and Discord in the World Political Economy*, Princeton, NJ: Princeton University Press.

Keohane, R.O. (1980) 'The theory of hegemonic stability and changes in international economic regimes, 1967–1977', in Holsti, O., Siverson, R.M. and George, A.L. (eds), *Change in the International System*, Boulder, CO: Westview, 131–62.

Krasner, S.D. (1978) 'United States commercial and monetary policy: Unravelling the paradox of external strength and internal weakness', in Katzenstein, P.J. (ed.), *Between Power and Plenty: Foreign Economic Policies of Advanced Industrial States*, Madison, WI: University of Wisconsin Press, 51–87.

Laclau, E. and Mouffe, C. (1991) *Hegemonie und radikale Demokratie*, Wien: Passagen Verlag.

Magee, S.P. and Young, L. (1987) 'Endogenous protection in the United States, 1900–1984', in Stern, R.M. (ed.), *U.S. Trade Policies in a Changing World Economy*, Cambridge, MA: MIT Press, 1987, 145–95.

Mills, C. Wright (1956) *The Power Elite*, New York: Oxford University Press.

Nau, H.R. (1990) *The Myth of America's Decline. Leading the World Economy into the 1990s*, New York: Oxford University Press.

Riechers, C. (1970) *Antonio Gramsci – Marxismus in Italien*, Frankfurt am Main: Europäische Verlagsanstalt.

Rupert, M.E. (1995) *Producing Hegemony: The Politics of Mass Production and American Global-Power*, Cambridge: Cambridge University Press.

Scherrer, C. (1999) *Globalisierung wider Willen? Die Durchsetzung liberaler Außenwirtschaftspolitik in den USA*, Berlin: edition sigma.

Scherrer, C. (1992) *Im Bann des Fordismus. Der Konkurrenzkampf der Auto- und Stahlindustrie in den USA*, Berlin: edition sigma.

Scherrer, C. and Greven, T. (2000) *Global Rules*, Münster: Verlag Westfälisches Dampfboot.

Shoup, L.H. (1980) *The Carter Presidency and Beyond. Power and Politics in the 1980s*, Palo Alto, CA: Ramparts Press.

Sinclair, T. (1996) 'Beyond international relations theory: Robert W. Cox and approaches to world order', in Cox, R.W. and Sinclair, T.J. (eds), *Approaches to World Order*, Cambridge: Cambridge University Press, 3–18.

Sklar, H. (ed.) (1980a) *Trilateralism: The Trilateral Commission and Elite Planning for World Management*, Boston, MA: South End Press.

Sklar, H. (1980b) 'Trilateralism: Managing dependence and democracy', in Sklar, H. (ed.), *Trilateralism: The Trilateral Commission and Elite Planning for World Management*, Boston, MA: South End Press, 1–58.

Stern, R.M. (ed.) (1987) *U.S. Trade Policies in a Changing World Economy*, Cambridge, MA: MIT Press.

Trilateral Commission Task Force Report (1977), 'Toward a renovated international system', January, in *NACLA Report 1981: From Hemispheric Police to Global Managers*, July/August.

Wallach, L. (1998) 'Das neue internationale kapitalistische Manifest', in *Le Monde Diplomatique*, German edn, February.

Part III

Private Business as an Actor in Global Economic Governance

7
The Role of Business in Global Governance

Doris A. Fuchs

Introduction

The core idea of the global governance debate is that political and economic changes associated with globalization have led to shifts in political capacity. Specifically, scholars argue that the state has been losing political capacity to non-state and supra-state actors (Messner and Nuscheler 1996). Among these, business plays a special role. In the view of many observers, business (in particular large transnational corporations) is among the primary bene-ficiaries if not causes of the 'decline of the state' (Fuchs 2002).[1] Yet, there is little systematic analysis of the political role of business in this globalizing world. Two debates attempt to shed some light on different facets of this role. What is missing so far, however, is a systematic integration of their findings as well as an embedding of arguments and evidence in a sound theoretical framework.

The first debate relevant for the role of business in global governance dis-cusses 'new' forms of political activities by business. This literature focuses on self-regulation, public private partnerships, and the role of specific busi-ness actors such as rating agencies in establishing binding rules for business actors and society alike. Moreover, the literature delineates examples of an increasing privatization of the public sphere, for instance in the security arena, as representative of the new political role of business. The evaluation of these new forms of political activity by business generally is controver-sial. Some scholars and practitioners see the respective business activities as a desirable if not necessary complement to the 'decreasing' capacity of the state. In contrast, others perceive a non-avoidable conflict of interest between commercial and public objectives, and deem an increasing involve-ment of business in political decision making undesirable by definition.

The second debate stresses the question of the extent and meaning of the (political) power of business in a globalizing world. It is motivated by reports of a continuing growth in power, in particular of TNCs, and a correspond-ing divergence in resources between business actors on the one side and the state and civil society on the other. This discussion is as controversial as the one on the forms of political activities by business. Numerous authors have voiced concerns that TNCs constitute a *de facto* world government. At the same time, a significant number of authors criticizes such accounts as overestimating the ability of business to decide unilaterally and enforce political decisions, and highlights the continuing dependence of business on the state's provision of a legal framework for business activities.

In order to provide the framework for a systematic integration and analysis of the debates on the forms of political activity by business and on its power, this chapter relates these two facets of the role of business in global governance to each other. Specifically, the chapter asks what we can learn from the perspective of an analysis of business power about the various forms of its political activities. At the same time, the chapter inquires how an analysis of the power of business through the lens of the various forms of its political activities contributes to our understanding of its role in global governance. On the basis of this exercise, the chapter demonstrates that – in our fascination with the newness of global governance – we should not ignore 'old' forms of political activity by business. These play a crucial complementary role in the current political game. In addition, the chapter draws our attention to signs of a noticeable growth in business power in the higher dimensions of power.

The chapter is structured in three sections. The first section will briefly review the 'new' forms of political activities by business identified in the literature, and introduce the main discussions regarding the role and meaning of these activities. The second section will lay out the nature of and motivation for a multi-dimensional analysis of the power of business in detail, drawing on the relevant theoretical and empirical literature. The third section will integrate the forms of activities from the first section with the dimensions of power from the second section to sketch current developments in business power in politics.

Forms of the 'new' political role of business

As pointed out above, the various forms of the new political role of business are the focus of one of the debates on the role of business in global governance. The activities discussed in this context range from self-regulation and quasi-regulation, to public–private partnerships and regimes, and the privatization of the public realm.[2] In each of the categories, in turn, a variety of forms of practice can be identified.

Examples of self-regulation exist in great multitude and in a large variety of forms. They range from loose and informal to formal and institutionalized arrangements, from binding and mandatory rules and regulations to voluntary and non-binding agreements. Self-regulatory arrangements are developed by business actors for their own sake, for purposes of preventing governmental regulation, or on behest of government. They include the regulation of the internet as well as the international environmental management standard ISO 14000, for example. Among the many benefits of self-regulatory arrangements by business are their potential efficiency, the availability of the necessary expertise, their likely support by the business community itself, and the potential legitimacy they may draw from 'regulation by one's peers'.

The potential drawbacks of self-regulation by business are just as many. The most fundamental concerns relate to the frequently voluntary nature of arrangements and the lack of public influence on the contents of standards and procedures. The voluntary nature of arrangements means, of course, that the worst offenders may just decide not participate. The lack of public influence on the contents of standards and procedures means that the latter may miss the teeth required actually to achieve the desired goals.[3]

Examples of quasi-regulation frequently discussed in the global governance literature focus on the roles rating agencies, consultancies, and transnational financial corporations play in evaluating the politics and policies of countries, and in imposing the preferences of transnational investors on societies. The most prominent example in this case is rating agencies, which determine the credit worthiness of countries, and thereby the ability of countries to attract capital (Sinclair 1999). The justification for calling this type of activity 'quasi regulation' is that these rating agencies have the potential power to enforce a relatively stringent standard of acceptability and inacceptability of political objectives and measures on countries. The economic justification for their activities is easy to understand, of course. From the perspective of investors, the services provided by independent rating agencies in evaluating the safety of and likely return on one's investments are extremely valuable. The potential drawbacks are just as clear, however. The ability of one rating agency to decide the economic and social fate of a country and to determine the range of acceptable policies is highly problematic from the perspective of democratic ideals.

Public–private partnerships and regimes are an additional form of the new political activities by business. Here, business actors officially cooperate with governmental actors in the pursuit of common policy objectives. The most prominent example of a respective public–private partnership is the Global Compact of the United Nations (Kell and Ruggie 2001). Under this programme, corporations sign on to nine broad principles of corporate social and environmental conduct with a particular emphasis on human rights. Moreover, individual companies create projects to pursue specific environmental, social, or human rights objectives at one or more of their facilities, and promote the projects with the support of the United Nations. Again, the potential benefit of the programme is provided by the incentives it provides to business actors to create the respective projects and its ability to utilize business resources in the pursuit of public objectives. Among the potential costs are the misuse of the name and credibility of the United Nations by business actors in efforts to obtain legitimacy and commercial as well as political advantages without the achievement of substantial improvements in the targeted environmental, social, or human rights conditions.

Finally, the (re-)commodification of the public sphere presents an example of the new political role of business frequently explored in the literature as well (for example, Drache 2001). This form of the political role of business differs from those just discussed in that not just the legitimate provider of regulation changes, but also the legitimacy of rules and regulations as such. Examples of such privatization trends can be found in infrastructure such as telecommunications, transport, and energy and water supplies (Finger and Allouche 2002). The most startling example in this context is probably the privatization of security, one of the core areas traditionally considered the sole task of the state. After all, the monopoly over the legitimate use of force used to be seen as one of the defining characteristics of the state. A private security market, however, now exists worldwide.

Assessing power

The second debate on the role of business in global governance concentrates on the question of power rather than the forms of the political activities of business. Both in the popular and academic literature, we find references to this power frequently framed in terms of comparisons in resources between TNCs and other actors, in particular countries with small economies, the cornering of important global markets by a few companies, or the large share of international trade that is intrafirm (Ferguson and Mansbach 1999; Thomas 2000). Based on such numbers, critical observers have been calling for a global analysis of the power of business and of the ways in which this power is exercised (Bonefield and Holloway 1995; Gill and Law 1993).

Analyzing the power of business or the ways in which it is exercised is not an easy task, however. After all, while power is one of the core concepts in political science, it is also one of the most controversial ones. The following discussion identifies the major perspectives on power that dominate the scholarly debate today.

Instrumentalist approaches[4]

Instrumentalist approaches are attached to the idea of a functional, unilinear causality. They utilize an instrumental and relational concept of power based on the idea of individual voluntary action and focus on the direct influence of political actors on political/policy output; that is, the 'first face of power'. Such approaches have their origins in the 'realistic' concepts of power that became increasingly important in Renaissance Europe as a growing interest in strategic questions regarding power replaced concepts of an *a priori* determined political and social order. Instead of the *bonum commune*, analyses started to focus on the acquisition and maintenance of power for its own sake.

The triumph of the assumption of causality, in turn, originated in the increasing success of the natural science perspective. Due to these developments, power came to be seen as a political actor's ability to achieve results. Instrumentalist approaches to power still are very prominent today. Studying pluralism, democracy, and decision making, scholars utilize Weber's actor oriented concept of power and stringently apply the assumption of instrumental rationality in the use of power to political actors. Not surprisingly, Weber's concept of power still shines through Dahl's familiar definition: 'A has power over B to the extent that he can get B to do something that B would not otherwise do' (Dahl 1957: 201f.). The emphasis here is on concrete and observable behaviour, with power and influence often being used interchangeably. Instrumentalist approaches to power can also be found in traditional power theories in international relations, where scholars focus on the use of power by states in pursuit of national interests (Morgenthau 1948; Waltz 1979).

The strength of instrumentalist approaches is that they provide a framework for assessing the direct influence of interests on political output. Instrumentalist concepts of power also have a number of shortcomings, however, revealing their insufficiency in capturing the overall power of an actor. Among the core weaknesses are the assumptions of mechanistic causality and of the autonomy of actors' choices of actions arising from the neglect of structural and discursive sources of power.

Structuralist approaches

Structuralist concepts of power argue that the power structures underlying behavioural options need to be analyzed to achieve a comprehensive assessment of the distribution and exercise of power. They are based on the observation that some issues never reach the agenda and some proposals are never made, because the relevant actors know that these proposals would never have a chance of being adopted. In contrast to instrumentalist approaches, structuralist approaches focus on the input side of policy and politics, arguing that it is not sufficient to look at the decisions made but that non-decisions require attention as well.

In pursuit of this objective, structuralist assessments of power relations examine the broader context and identify the factors that make alternatives more or less acceptable before the actual and observable bargaining starts; that is, the 'second face of power'. As Bachrach and Baratz (1970) point out:

> Power is exercised when A participates in the making of decisions that affect B. Power is also exercised when A devotes his energies to creating or reinforcing social and political values and institutional practices that limit the scope of the political process to public consideration of only those issues which are comparatively innocuous to A. To the extent that A succeeds in doing this, B is prevented, for all practical purposes, from

bringing to the fore any issues that might in their resolution be seriously detrimental to A's set of preferences (7).

A two-dimensional view of power, therefore, combines analyses of decision making and non-decision making, actual and potential political issues, and influences on political output as well as input, thereby widening of the scope of 'politics' to be analyzed.

In political science, the concept of the second face of power took hold particularly in analyses of policy inputs and agenda setting. Moreover, in international relations (IR), there is some tradition of a focus on structural force (Galtung 1969). Structuralist approaches have received the most attention, however, in International Political Economy (IPE), specifically in research utilizing Marxist approaches (Cox 1987). Especially, studies of MNCs in the 1970s and 1980s frequently highlighted the structural dependence of state elites on private sector profitability, and the structural power of corporations promising jobs and income to countries.[5]

Even a two-dimensional analysis of power, however, falls short of getting the whole picture. Critics charge that structuralist approaches remain stuck in actor-centric conceptions of power as even non-decisions and structural forces are linked back to the power of actors. In other words, the 'second face of power' is still too individualistic. Due to a mistaken understanding of the way in which actors manage to keep issues from the agenda, an analysis based on this perspective focuses only on observable conflicts of interest. Such an approach 'confines itself to studying situations where the mobilization of bias can be attributed to individuals' decisions that have the effect of preventing currently observable grievances ... from becoming issues within the political process' (Lukes 1974: 37).

In other words, a two-dimensional concept of power still ignores the systemic conditions of power located before decisions and non-decisions by actors.

Discursive approaches

Discursive approaches to power adopt a sociological perspective on power relations in society, de-individualizing and in some cases de-substantializing the concept. According to this view, power is not only a characteristic of individuals and groups but also of a social system as such. This 'third face of power' exercises itself through norms, ideas, and societal institutions. It is reflected in culture and discourse, in communicative practices, and in procedures for problem solving and conflict resolution (Koller 1991). Two major implications for analyses of power arise from these insights. First, the 'third face of power' is closely tied to notions of legitimacy, and thereby authority, and is thus to be distinguished from mere influence. Second, this kind of power does not simply pursue interests but creates them.

A number of scholars have highlighted the relationship between power and authority and/or legitimacy. Arendt (1970) ties power to authority by contrasting it with force, the use of which according to her is an indication of a lack of power. Parsons (1967), likewise, links power to authority and excludes illegitimate uses of force. These scholars and others come to the conclusion that power is particularly big when nobody questions it.

The idea that power precedes interests also has been developed by various scholars. This perspective highlights the importance of social institutions in constituting political identities and interests.[6] Critical and Gramscian approaches emphasize the power over norms and ideas in this context. Lukes (1974), for instance, postulates that perceived needs and interests themselves are the result of the 'third face of power'. He argues that this power can be used by actors in pursuit of their perceived interests. Lukes applies this understanding of power to an analysis of the presence and exercise of power in the absence of observable conflicts of interests. He argues that such a conceptualization of power allows a more comprehensive explanation of how political systems prevent demands from becoming political issues. Specifically, he emphasizes that an exercise of power may not just prevent conflicts of interest to show up on the agenda. Rather, they will not even be perceived as such due to the influence of 'soft types of power' (Galbraith 1983) such as authority, manipulation, positive reinforcement, or social conditioning. Thus, an analysis of the 'third face of power' would consider the socialization of politicians and the public into accepting 'truths' about desirable policies and political developments (Lukes 1974).[7]

Within the IR literature, a number of authors have worked with the notion of discursive power as well. Joseph Nye (1991, 2002), in particular, is famous for drawing attention to the third face of power. According to Nye, 'soft power' (that is, the power to persuade and coopt other actors rather than coerce them), which originates in the perception of the legitimacy of one's aims by others, is a pivotal third source of power next to military and economic power. Based on this concept of soft power, Nye explains why some countries in the international system, such as the Netherlands, the Scandinavian countries, or Canada, have more influence than their military and economic power would allow. Moreover, he highlights the role information management, public relations, as well as education and cultural programmes play in determining the distribution of power in the international system. Likewise, Milner (1991) has tied authority to legitimacy, arguing that beliefs in the validity of an order support the stability of that order and the position of the dominant powers in the international system. Unfortunately, these analyses primarily consider state power. Strange (1988, 1996), as the one who most determinedly went beyond the focus on state actors, unfortunately fails to clearly differentiate the second and third faces of power in her concept of structural power, as pointed out above.

A three-dimensional analysis of the power of an actor, then, would pay attention to its influence on policy output and input, as well as on (its) hegemony over ideas, norms, and discourse, and, importantly, the interaction between them. Moreover, such an analysis would allow a differentiated assessment of developments in the individual dimensions of an actor's power. If a hierarchy of dimensions of power can be determined, then, developments in the higher dimensions of power would be particularly important; and indeed, most scholars would agree on such a hierarchy of power. Lukes (1974) and others, for instance, argue that the ability to persuade rather than to force, the power over norms and ideas, is the supreme form of power. Likewise, scholars postulate that rule making power (that is, agenda setting power and control over policy input) is a more effective channel of influence than the 'mere' influence on policy output. In consequence, a comprehensive analysis of power needs to consider the three faces of power, and to pay particular attention to changes in the higher dimensions of an actor's power.

The three-dimensional analysis of the power of business in global governance

Linking the different forms of political activities by business identified in the global governance literature to the three dimensions of power discussed above, we arrive at an interesting picture. Looking at the forms of political activities by business through the lens of dimensions of power, we notice a major omission in much of the general global governance literature dealing with the role of private actors. Looking at the dimensions of business power through the lens of the different forms of political activities, we notice signs of interesting and significant changes in business power, in particular in its higher dimensions.

The political activities of business from the perspective of power

Starting with the first question (the assessment of the forms of political activities by business from the perspective of dimensions of its power), we can identify rather clear linkages between self-regulation, quasi-regulation, and public–private partnerships, on the one side, and privatization trends on the other, with structural and discursive power respectively. Self-regulation, quasi-regulation, and to a large extent public–private partnerships, strongly reflect the exercise of structural power by business; that is, agenda setting power. These forms of formal or informal regulatory arrangements frequently allow business actors directly to influence policy input, to determine agenda setting by making some policy proposals more acceptable than others from the outset. Environmental and social standards developed by business carry the content business rather than the public desires and, in addition, may prevent further public regulation in this area. Rating agencies threaten with the global financial market withdrawing or not providing capital to a country that adopts undesirable policies. In sum, self-regulation, quasi-regulation, and public–private partnerships serve to strengthen the structural power of business.

The privatization of the public realm, in turn, is closely linked to the third face of power, the possession of discursive power and the acquisition of authority by business. The acceptance of the privatization of public tasks and services previously considered too sensitive to be left to the market by the public as well as political decision makers clearly demonstrates the increasing perception of private actors as superior and, most importantly, legitimate decision makers and the hegemony of the corresponding norms and ideas: 'The public at large has come to accept that certain private sector actors not only rule particular issues, but that they should do so' (Cutler *et al.* 1999: 22). The hegemony of norms and ideas sympathetic to business interests is reflected in the triumph of the competition state and the prioritization of efficiency and economic rationality in policy design and objectives, for example. In the eyes of observers, the result of this discursive power is a new constitutionalism enshrining the rights of business over states (Gill 1995).

Establishing linkages between self-regulation, quasi-regulation, and public–private partnerships and structural power, and between privatization and discursive power, brings up the question of the instrumental power of business. Interestingly, the dominant type of political activity through which business traditionally exercises its instrumental power, lobbying, does not appear in our global governance framed focus.[8] It does receive attention in specific issue focused analyses, such as studies of the role of private actors in the climate change negotiations. General assessments on the role of business in global governance as such, however, tend to ignore this area of traditional political activity by business.

Lobbying is still an extremely important political activity of business, especially as a complement to its structural and discursive power. Studying lobbying activity by business reveals that the traditional notion of pluralist competition (or corporatist cooperation) at the national level needs to be supplemented with a focus on the strong influence of lobbying by transnational business actors on national politics and the influence of lobbying by national and transnational business actors on supra-national politics. Empirically, an instrumentalist approach to forms of political activity by business in global governance would highlight, for instance, the role of business lobbying in influencing international agreements. Such an approach would identify the strong influence of TNCs on the TRIPS (trade related aspects of intellectual property) agreement through the Intellectual Property Committee, a lobbying group composed of twelve US based TNCs, for example (Sell 2000). Likewise, such an approach would draw the attention to the Global Climate Coalition's extensive lobbying efforts on behalf of their interests in the context of negotiations for an agreement on climate change (Levy and Egan 2000). A comprehensive analysis of the role of business in global governance, then, clearly needs to pay attention to all three dimensions of power and their interaction with old and new forms of political activity.

The overall picture of interaction between forms of political activity by business and dimensions of power is more messy than the simple one to one relationships delineated above, of course. Each form of political activity draws on or strengthens other dimensions of power besides the respective dominant ones identified. Lobbying, for instance, draws on structural power as well. The communication of business interests is likely to be much more successful if it is 'backed up' by the potential threat of a relocation of investment and jobs. Likewise, lobbying can be used to foster the development of structural and discursive power; for instance, in terms of lobbying against capital controls, for self-regulatory arrangements, and for the privatization of infrastructure and other service sectors. Likewise, self-/quasi-regulation and public–private partnerships do not only represent exercises of structural power, but benefit from the exercise of discursive power to the extent that they draw on notions of legitimacy and from the exercise of instrumental power, as pointed out above. At the same time, these arrangements can foster or decrease the possession of discursive power by business in so far as these regulatory arrangements are perceived as successes or failures. Finally, the privatization of the public realm is linked to instrumental and structural power as well. As described above, lobbying the public in particular can foster the development of notions of the appropriateness of moving the provision of certain goods and services into the market. In turn, discursive power can strengthen both instrumental and structural power; for instance, by making the lobbying activities of business or self-regulatory arrangements appear more 'legitimate'.

The power of business from the perspective of its forms of political activity

Turning to an analysis of changes in the power of business through the lens of forms of political activities, we arrive at additional important insights. While some controversy regarding the power of business remains, findings of a major share of the literature point to the likelihood of a general expansion in the power of business in all three dimensions. More importantly, such a trend is particularly widely reported for the 'higher' dimensions of power.

Lobbying and trends in the instrumental power of business

In terms of the instrumental power of business, studies of lobbying activities at the national level and case studies on a range of issues at the international level suggest both an increase in the quantity of lobbying activity by business and a qualitative expansion to transnational and supranational targets and strategies. While a few voices pointing out that business activity and influence via lobbying remain below expectations can be heard (Ansolabehere *et al.* 2003), the majority of evidence appears to point towards an increase in the instrumental power of business.

At the national level, studies suggest a dramatic rise in business activity in lobbying and a corresponding increase in influence since the 1970s. Responding to the challenge of broad environmental and social regulation introduced in many industrialized democracies in the late 1960s and early 1970s, business responded with a massive political mobilization (Getz 1997; Wilson 1990). Trends to establish corporate offices in the capital, the filling of staff positions with political tasks with top management, direct contacts between CEOs and top level management and relevant politicians, and single-issue maximizing, that started in the US in the 1970s, today can be noticed in all of the major capitals (Grande 2001; Kohler-Koch 2000; Shaiko 1998; Verba and Orren 1985). At the same time, government dependence on business input, both in the form of information and funding, has grown due to the increasing complexity of regulation on the one side, and the mediatization of politics and rise of the swing voter and associated rise in campaign costs on the other (Dalton and Wattenberg 2000; Naßmacher 2001; Römmele 2002).[9] With the influence of labour, the traditional opponent of business, on the decline in most industrialized countries (Beck 2002), business benefits from a strong preponderance in resources vis-à-vis its competitors (Sklair 1998), and scholars argue that the main threat to business influence via lobbying is business itself (Berry 1997).

The expansion of lobbying activities to transnational and supra-national levels, in turn, indicates a qualitatively new character of instrumental power by business. Transnational lobbying strategies allow business to target multiple governments at the same time (Hummel 2001). Moreover, business increasingly directs lobbying activities at supra-national institutions such as the European Union or other IGOs (Finger and Allouche 2002; Fischer 1997; Greenwood 1998).

Business, and especially corporate influence via lobbying, clearly is not unlimited. Scholars argue that on highly visible and controversial issues, the public still tends to win against business interests. However, empirical studies also point out that the majority of corporate political activity and influence can be found in areas with little visibility (Clawson *et al.* 1992; Helpman and Persson 2001; Smith 2000). Moreover, corporate strategies in controversial issues increasingly include the creation of a 'public' on their side through the creation of NGOs and 'astroturf organizing' (Lord 2000). In addition, the increasing instrumental power of business also results from the ability to choose between or combine different lobbying strategies (Levy and Egan 2000).

Self-regulation and trends in the structural power of business

A focus on the structural power of business in global governance from the perspective of its political activities, in turn, highlights the additional channels for an exercise of such power acquired by business. Today, the ability of business to influence agenda setting goes beyond its capacity to move capital. The traditional source of structural power by business, the ability of TNCs to divide the world into national states, competing on the basis of taxes as well as social, environmental, and moral standards, continues to exist, of course, and has, if anything increased (Beck 2002; Gill and Law 1993; Kobrin 1997).

Importantly, however, the rise in self-regulation, quasi-regulation, and public–private partnerships offers business new avenues for controlling agenda setting, determining the contents of regulation, and participating in global decentralized law making processes (Cashore 2002; Cutler *et al.* 1999; Teubner 1997). Scholars highlight the dramatic increase in the number and range of self-regulatory arrangements, especially in the form of standards and codes of conduct, either on the basis of delegation of public authority or voluntary efforts (Haufler 2001; Ronit and Schneider 1999). Such standards and codes of conduct now exist at the level of individual companies such as Levi-Strauss or Karstadt, at the sectoral level such as the Responsible Care Programme of the Chemical Industry, as well as at the global level such as ISO 14000 environmental management systems or the social accountability standard (SA 8000) (ILO 2002; Nadvi and Wältring 2002). Private actors now play a pivotal role in defining regulation across policy fields, including environmental issues (Clapp 2001), human rights (Kolk and Tulder 2002), or the international financial and monetary system (Underhill 2001).

Self-regulatory arrangements have not only increased in quantity, however, their qualitative role has changed as well. On the economic side, such systems play a pivotal role in structuring global value chains and determining the access of actors to global markets (Messner 2002). On the political side, these sources of structural power frequently are official, formalized, and perceived as legitimate (Brühl *et al.* 2001; Cutler *et al.* 1999; Haufler 2001; Higgott *et al.* 2000). Even legal scholars are focusing on corporations as authentic sources of global law (Robé 1997). Moreover, scholars point out that governments are beginning to adjust national policies in response to new self-regulatory arrangements (Altvater and Mahnkopf 2002; Nadvi and Wältring 2002).[10] The latter phenomena are particularly noteworthy, as they seem unassailable to existing evidence of significant weaknesses of voluntary codes of conduct as regulatory mechanisms.[11] In sum, the 'second face of power' of business deserves renewed attention.

Privatization and trends in the discursive power of business

An analysis of the discursive power of business in global governance via the lens of forms of political activity, finally, highlights the expansion of this power as well. The first indicator of this increase in discursive power is the movement of the privatization trend and the hegemony of neoliberal ideas[12] through different policy areas, from environmental policy and infra-structure to the areas of health and education, and finally to security. Observers report a 'renaissance of the market economy as the dominant socio-institutional system of resource allocation' (Dunning 1997: 1). There are hardly any policy areas remaining in Western and Eastern Europe, as well as North America and Oceania, that are not shaped by privatization and liberalization trends today (see, for instance, Grande and Eberlein 1999 on Western and Eastern Europe).[13] In the majority of the European welfare states, infrastructure, for instance, has been largely privatized at this point. In the wake of a General Agreement on Trade in Services, similar trends in education and health care are to be expected.

The most fundamental area of state responsibility, security, is currently being privatized around the world as well (Eppler 2002; Lock 2001). Since the 1990s, a global market in security, military and police functions has emerged with mercenaries and private security firms being hired by govern-ments and private actors alike (Leander 2001). Even in countries in which the market has traditionally been a more dominant social organizing mech-anism than in the European welfare states, such as the USA, this privatiza-tion of security represents a major change.

This privatization trend is associated with the hegemony of neoliberal ideas and an increasing reduction of the public realm (Drache 2001). Objectives such as social justice, participation, or public access, which in the past were at the root of government intervention on behalf of the provision of public goods (Grayson 2001; Kaul 2001), have been pushed back relative to economic growth and efficiency objectives (Kurbjuweit 2003).[14] With respect to the latter, business traditionally is perceived as more competent than government. However, one of the primary achievements of the hege-mony of neoliberal ideas is that the market is not just seen as the best provider of efficiency, but also as a superior provider of other social objec-tives. This perception is at the foundation of the increasing acquisition of authority by business; that is, legitimacy as a political actor (Cutler *et al.* 1999). The latter trend, in turn, can be observed at the national and inter-national level (Higgott *et al.* 2000). However, the discursive power of private actors is particularly noteworthy in the heterarchical governance structures of regional and global governance (Neyer 2002).

The discursive hegemony of neoliberal ideas and norms is especially visi-ble in the context of the general political debates on the role of the state at the national level or also in the context of the EU (Grande 2001). The com-petitiveness debate (Mazey and Richardson 1997), and the focus on the *Angebotsstaat* (Sturm *et al.* 2000) or competition state (Garrett 1998; Hirsch 1995), clearly signal a corresponding shift in the definition of the appropri-ate role of public and private actors. The 'new' task of the state is to create a climate favourable for business investment, which, in turn, is supposed to guarantee welfare for the general population, rather than the state.

An analysis of the discursive power of business via the lens of its political activities also highlights the employment of various forms of political activity by business in attempts to expand this power. Thus, business actors engage in efforts to lobby the public in order to increase perceptions of the legitimacy of their position on issues if not their legitimacy as political actors, thereby not only expanding the pressure on government but also attempting to expand its discursive hegemony (Berry 1997). Likewise, business increasingly pursues the building of coalitions and the melting of its identity with civil society actors; for instance, to increase its legitimacy. In cases, where such partners for coalitions cannot be found, business even creates its own NGOs (Levy and Newell 2002). Moreover, corporate philanthropy frequently pursues similar objectives (Himmelstein 1997).

Finally, however, an analysis of the discursive power of business would also show that the increase in this power is not unchallenged and that this source of business power, in particular, is far from invulnerable. Legitimacy as a political actor is not just something that business has acquired, but also something that it now chronically needs in order to continue in this role (Beck 2002). The failure of the MAI most noticeably demonstrated that the legitimacy of business is not uncontested (Walter 2001).

Conclusion

What can we learn from this three-dimensional analysis of the power of business in global governance and the relationships of the different dimensions of power to the various forms of political activities pursued by business? The above analysis has highlighted two pivotal points. First, research on the role of business in global governance cannot ignore the 'old' political activity by business. Lobbying is still extremely important, even for developments in the contexts of higher dimensions of power. Second, scholars studying the role of business in global governance need to pay particular attention to these higher dimensions of the power of business. It is here that important changes appear to be taking place, and these changes are also the source of much of the concern about a potentially disproportionate influence of business in global governance and the general fate of democracy.

In general, an analysis of the role of business in global governance shows that business exercises its power through micro-level processes of bargaining as well as the constraints imposed by macro-level structures of socio-economic and discursive relations. These different means of power provide the basis for an interplay of material, discursive, and organizational resources and allow business to pursue a 'contingent, multi-dimensional strategy relative to the national state and international institutions' (Levy and Egan 2000: 139). This ability to combine and choose between different strategies applies to the form of activity and dimension of power used. Thus, business can rely on 'voice' rather than 'exit', for example, if its structural power is weak. Likewise, business can attempt to foster the diffusion of ideas and norms supporting its interests, thereby reducing the need for lobbying as well as for threatening relocation. The same ability to combine or choose from a range of strategies applies to the level of target. Business actors can decide which level of governance to engage, or even engage several levels simultaneously through the targeting of the national level in combination with an up-shifting and/or down-shifting of power.

There is one downside to a three-dimensional study of the power of business in global governance, however. Such an analysis runs into problems with respect to empirical 'proofs'. Instrumental power already is difficult to prove, due to the incompleteness of data and the simultaneous presence of a variety of influences. To prove the exercise of structural power arising from the ability to move capital is relatively impossible, in the absence of explicit threats of companies to move investment if their demands are not met. Frequently, such threats are not and need not be made explicitly. And how would one measure the structural power inherent in self-regulatory arrangements, quasi-regulation, or public–private partnerships? Similarly, the existence and exercise of discursive power is extremely difficult to prove. Lukes (1974) has suggested the use of counterfactuals in identifying the exercise of this power, a focus on the absence of conflicts of interests where one would expect them. In order to assess the discursive hegemony of certain ideas, perceptions of legitimacy and authority, large scale surveys or contents analyses of extensive samples of discourse could also go some way. Linking authoritative ideas and norms back to agency, however, is tremendously difficult again. Finally, the evaluation of the impact of one dimension of power relative to another is almost impossible, as the various dimensions support and condition each other.

Difficulties in proving the exercise of power and its effects have damaged the research programme on the political influence of business in the past again and again. Critics of pluralists' claims of a benign balance in competition between interests failed to win the respective debates, due to their inability to prove a disproportionate influence of business. Research on MNCs in IR could not hold on to a core position in the field, which it appeared to be gaining in the 1980s, due to the same difficulties. The inability to prove the exercise of one or another dimension of power in a given situation, however, does not mean that this power does not exist and has not been actively used in the context. Moreover, the question is just too important to ignore just because the available data do not allow foolproof statistical analyses. In the absence of the ability to prove the exercise of such power, then, 'plausibilizing' respective power relationships on the basis of anecdotal evidence will have to suffice. Clearly, however, any such empirical analysis will have to be conducted in the context of a very specific issue area in order to be manageable.

Notes

1   The predominant focus in the general discussion on the role of business in global governance is on TNCs and business associations. The same is true for this chapter. Obviously, it is much more difficult for the owner of a small dye shop in India to participate in global governance than for CitiCorp. Even within business associations, corporate actors tend to speak with louder voices than small and medium-sized businesses. Moreover, while this chapter speaks about the power of business in general, it does not assume that business is a unitary actor. In fact, 'the greatest restraint on business may not be its critics, but the divisions within and between industries' (Berry 1997: 43). However, while powerful business interests may be on various sides on a number of issues, in terms of broad political directions and objectives, corporate actors often agree (Smith 2000). Moreover, Beck (2002) has delineated the power of politics as a by-product of uncoordinated actions of corporations, which does not require that business organizes itself as a political actor.

2   None of these activities is completely new; that is, without historical precedence. However, they are new in their extent as well as in terms of the acquisition of political authority by business.

3   In the case of ISO 14000 standards, for instance, a frequent complaint is that they lack actual environmental performance requirements and mainly require improvements in communication about environmental issues within companies and with stakeholders (Clapp 1998).

4   Scholars frequently use different terminologies in categorizing the various dimensions of power (Arts 2003; Caporaso and Haggard 1989; Levy and Newell 2002). Thus, instrumental power is sometimes called decisional power, while discursive power has been called locational power by some scholars.

5   The use of the terminology of 'structuralist approaches' and 'structural power' here should not be confused with Strange's (1988, 1996) concept of 'structural power'. Strange uses the label quite differently from the earlier and much of the later MNC literature. Specifically, Strange defines structural power as 'the power to shape and determine the structures of the global political economy within which other states, their political institutions, their economic enterprises and (not least) their scientists and other professional people, have to operate' (1988: 24f.). Thus, Strange combines aspects of the second and third faces of power in her concept. Her approach is similar to more recent analyses of the power of business in its emphasis on the role of production, knowledge, and finance in the new 'diffused' power in the international system. (She adds a fourth source of power: security, which she relates to state power, but which, with the present trends of a privatization of security, may soon gain prominence in analyses of business power as well.) According to Strange, having control over these sources of power and the ability to determine access to them, allows actors to exercise structural power and gain the capacity to define the terms on which needs in the global political economy are satisfied and whose needs are satisfied. In other words, Strange collapses the aspect of control over policy input and control over norms and ideas in her analysis, which, unfortunately, reduces the analytical value of the concept for the present analysis.

6   Some authors posit the independence of stable societal power structures from actors. Luhmann (1975), for example, argues that power is reflected in institutionalized

rules, which regulate contingency and determine the range of acceptable behaviour. According to him, these rules of institutionalized power rather than acts of self-interested use of power are the dominant influences on every day life in society. Likewise, Foucault (1980) perceives power as a universal societal phenomenon that exists prior to all arguments, discourses, and knowledge. It is not something an actor possesses, but exists in every social act and interaction and is practised on the basis of discursive everyday practices. One consequence of the degree of institutionalization of social power structures claimed by these authors, is the difficulty associated with the identification of the sources and beneficiaries of political decisions. The latter can easily hide behind intransparent networks of political and administrative decision making. The institutionalization of social power structures, in other words, implies the depersonalization and anonymization of power processes, which, according to these scholars, are among the defining characteristics of modern societies.

7   Such a perspective is similar to Gramsci's concept of hegemony (1971, 1995), which captures the existence of specific social and economic structures that systematically work to the advantage of certain actors. Due to the creation of legitimacy on the basis of moral and intellectual leadership and ideological reproduction, these structures foster 'the projection of a particular set of interests as the general interest' (Levy and Newell 2002: 87). Ideas, material capabilities, and institutions, and the mutually reinforcing relationships between them, define the boundaries of acceptable action (op. cit.: 97).

8   Other forms of political activity included by scholars in analyses of the first face of power include advocacy, monitoring of compliance of governments, or protest (Arts 2003).

9   In the 2000 US election, corporations contributed about 14 times as much as labour and 16 times as much as other interest groups (UNDP 2002). Similar trends emerge around the world. In India, for instance, corporations were the dominant source of funding for parties in 1996, providing approximately 80 per cent of contributions. In countries with more restrictions on corporate political contributions and the use of private media time in elections, however, these trends tend to be less pronounced and the extent of a personalization of elections is a little more controversial (Kaase 1994; Pappi and Shikano 2001; Weßels 2000).

10 In fact, scholars have frequently demonstrated that voluntary self-regulation is developed with the specific aim of avoiding more stringent public regulation (Clapp 2001; Ronit and Schneider 1999).

11 King and Lenox (2000), for instance, demonstrate the potential for failure of voluntary self-regulation in the case of the Responsible Care Programme of the Chemical Industry. Their statistical analysis reveals that dirtier companies make use of the potential for opportunism and free riding provided by the programme, that dirtier firms are more likely to participate in the programme, and the absence of evidence for a positive influence of the programme on the rate of environmental improvement among members.

12 Neoliberal ideas and values are not always promoted by business, of course. Companies asking for protection from foreign competition or regulated monopolies clearly do not follow neoliberal notions at that point. However, fundamentally, business tends to be sympathetic to neoliberal principles, especially TNCs, which generally prefer as little government intervention in and government regulation of their global activities.

13 Even in Germany, where observers had reported half-hearted attempts at reform and symbolic privatization earlier (Esser 1994; Grande 1989), more recent studies

document that significant changes took place in the 1990s (Grande and Eberlein 1999).

14 In fact, the redefinition of public goods and their best provision has gone so far that the even the water supply, traditionally seen as too sensitive a good to be left to the market, is being privatized (Finger and Allouche 2002).

References

Altvater, E. and Mahnkopf, B. (2002) *Globalisierung der Unsicherheit*, Münster: Westfälisches Dampfboot.

Ansolabehere, S., De Figueiredo, J. and Snyder, J. (2003) 'Why is there so little money in U.S. politics?', in *Journal of Economic Perspectives*, 17(1), 105–30.

Arendt, H. (1970) *On Violence*, London: Penguin Press.

Arts, B. (2003) *Non-State Actors in Global Governance. Three Faces of Power*, Preprint, Max-Planck-Projektgruppe, Recht der Gemeinschaftsgüter, 003(4), Bonn: Max-Planck-Gesellschaft.

Bachrach, P. and Baratz, M. (1970) *Power and Poverty. Theory and Practice*, New York: Oxford University Press.

Beck, U. (2002) *Macht und Gegenmacht im globalen Zeitalter. Neue weltpolitische Ökonomie*, Frankfurt am Main: Suhrkamp.

Berle, A. (1957) *Economic Power and the Free Society*, New York: Fund for the Republic.

Berry, J. (1997) *The Interest Group Society*, New York: Longman.

Bonefeld, W. and Holloway, J. (eds) (1995) *Global Capital, National State and the Politics of Money*, New York: St Martin's Press.

Brühl, T., Debiel, T., Hamm, B., Hummel, H. and Martens, J. (eds) (2001) *Die Privatisierung der Weltpolitik*, Bonn: Dietz.

Campbell, J., Hollingsworth, J.R. and Lindberg, L. (eds) (1991) *The Governance of the American Economy*, Cambridge: Cambridge University Press.

Caporaso, J. and Haggard, S. (1989) 'Power in the international political economy', in Stoll, R. and Ward, M. (eds), *Power in World Politics*, Boulder, CO: Lynne Rienner Publishers.

Cashore, B. (2002) 'Legitimacy and the privatization of environmental governance', in *Governance*, 8(4), 503–29.

Clapp, J. (2001) *Toxic Exports: The Transfer of Hazardous Wastes from Rich to Poor Countries*, Ithaca: Cornell University Press.

Clapp, J. (1998) 'The privatization of global environmental governance: ISO 14000 and the developing world', in *Global Governance*, 4, 295–316.

Clawson, D., Neustadt, A. and Scott, D. (1992) *Money Talks*, New York: Basic Books.

Cook, W. (1891) *The Corporation Problem*, New York: G.P. Putnam's Sons.

Cox, R. (1987) *Production, Power, and World Order*, New York: Columbia University Press.

Cutler, C., Haufler, V. and Porter, T. (eds) (1999) *Private Authority and International Affairs*, Albany: State University of New York Press.

Dahl, R. (1957) 'The concept of power', in *Behavioral Science*, 2, 201–15.

Dalton, R. and Wattenberg, M. (eds) (2000) *Parties without Partisans: Political Change in Advanced Industrial Democracies*, Oxford: Oxford University Press.

Drache, D. (ed.) (2001) *The Market or the Public Domain?* London: Routledge.

Dunning, J. (ed.) (1997) *Governments, Globalization, and International Business*, New York: Oxford University Press.

Eppler, E. (2002) *Vom Gewaltmonopol zum Gewaltmarkt*, Frankfurt am Main: Suhrkamp.

Esser, J. (1994) 'Germany: Symbolic privatizations in a social market economy', in Wright, V. (ed.), *Privatization in Western Europe*, London: Pinter.

Ferguson, Y. and Mousbach, R. (1999) 'Global politics at the turn of the millennium', in *International Studies Review*, 1(2), 77–107.

Finger, M. and Allouche, J. (2002) *Water Privatisation: Transnational Corporations and the Re-regulation of the Water Industry*, London: Spon.

Fischer, K. (1997) *Lobbying und Kommunikation in der Europäischen Union*, Berlin: Berlin Verlag.

Foucault, M. (1980) *Power/Knowledge: Selected Interviews and Other Writings 1972–1977*, (ed.), C. Gordon, Brighton: Harvester.

Fuchs, D. (2002) 'Globalization and global governance', in Fuchs, D. and Kratochwil, F. (eds), *Transformative Order and Global Change*, Münster: LIT Verlag.

Galbraith, J.K. (1983) *The Anatomy of Power*, Boston: Houghton Mifflin.

Galtung, J. (1969) 'Violence, peace and peace research', in *Journal of Peace Research*, 6, 167–91.

Garrett, G. (2000) 'Globalization and national autonomy', in Woods, Ngaire (ed.), *The Political Economy of Globalization*, New York: St Martin's Press.

Garrett, G. (1998), 'Global markets and national politics: Collision course or virtuous circle?' *International Organization*, 52(4), 787–824.

Getz, K. (1997) 'Research in corporate political action', in *Business and Society*, 36(1), 32–73.

Gill, S. (1995) 'Globalisation, market civilisation, and disciplinary neoliberalism', in *Millenium: Journal of International Studies*, 24(3), 399–423.

Gill, S. and Law, D. (1993) 'Global hegemony and the structural power of capital', in Gill, S. (ed.), *Gramsci, Historical Materialism and International Relations*, Cambridge: Cambridge University Press.

Gramsci, A. (1995) *Further Selections from the Prison Notebooks*, Minneapolis: University of Minnesota Press.

Gramsci, A. (1971) *Selections from the Prison Notebooks*, New York: International Publishers.

Grande, E. (2001) 'Institutions and interests: Interest groups in the European system of multi-level governance', Working paper no. 1/2001, Technische Universität München, Lehrstuhl für Politische Wissenschaft.

Grande, E. (1989) *Vom Monopol zum Wettbewerb?* Wiesbaden: Deutscher Universitätsverlag.

Grande, E. and Eberlein, B. (1999) 'Der Aufstieg des Regulierungsstaates im Infrastrukturbereich', Working Paper no. 2/1999, Technische Universität München, Lehrstuhl für Politische Wissenschaft.

Grayson, K. (2001) 'Human security in the global era', in Drache, D. (ed.), *The Market or the Public Domain?*, London: Routledge.

Greenwood, J. (1998) 'Regulating lobbying in the European Union', in *Parliamentary Affairs*, 51(4), 587–99.

Haufler, V. (2001) *A Public Role for the Private Sector*, Washington: Carnegie Endowment for International Peace.

Helpman, E. and Torsten P. (2001) 'Lobbying and legislative bargaining', in *Advances in Economic Analysis and Policy*, 1(1), 31–64.

Higgott, R., Underhill, G. and Bieler, A. (eds) (2000) *Non-State Actors and Authority in the Global System*, London: Routledge.

Himmelstein, J. (1997) *Looking Good and Doing Good. Corporate Philanthropy and Corporate Power*, Bloomington: Indiana University Press.

Hirsch, J. (1995) *Der nationale Wettbewerbsstaat*, Berlin: ed. ID-Archiv.
Hummel, H. (2001) 'Die Privatisierung der Weltpolitik', in Brühl, T., Debiel, T., Hamm, B., Hummel, H. and Martens, J. (eds), *Die Privatisierung der Weltpolitik*, Bonn: Dietz.
ILO (2002) *Codes of Conduct and Multinational Enterprises*, Geneva: International Labor Organization.
Kaase, M. (1994) 'Is there personalization in politics? Candidates and voting behavior in Germany', in *International Political Science Review*, 15, 211–30.
Kaul, I. (2001) 'Public goods', in Drache, D. (ed.), *The Market or the Public Domain?*, London: Routledge.
Kell, G. and Ruggie, J.G. (2001) 'Global markets and social legitimacy: The case of the "Global Compact"', in Drache, D. (ed), *The Market or the Public Domain?*, London: Routledge.
King, A. and Lenox, M. (2000) 'Industry self-regulation without sanctions', in *Academy of Management Journal*, 43(4), 698–716.
Kobrin, S. (1997) 'The architecture of globalization', in Dunning, J. (ed.), *Governments, Globalization, and International Business*, New York: Oxford University Press.
Kohler-Koch, B. (2000) 'Unternehmensverbände im Spannungsfeld von Europäisierung und Globalisierung', in Bührer, W. and Grande, E. (eds), *Unternehmerverbände und Staat in Deutschland*, Baden-Baden: Nomos.
Kolk, A. and van Tulder, R. (2002) 'The effectiveness of self-regulation: Corporate codes of conduct and child labour', in *European Management Journal*, 20(3), 260–71.
Koller, P. (1991) 'Facetten der Macht', in *Analyse und Kritik*, 13, 107–33.
Kurbjuweit, D. (2003) *Unser effizientes Leben. Die Diktatur der Ökonomie und ihre Folgen*, Reinbek: Rowohlt.
Lawton, T., Rosenau, J. and Verdun, A. (eds) (2000) *Strange Power*, Aldershot: Ashgate.
Leander, A. (2001) 'Global ungovernance: Mercenaries, states and the control over violence', Working Paper, Copenhagen Peace Research Institute.
Levy, D. and Egan, D. (2000) 'Corporate political action in the global polity', in Higgott, R., Underhill, G. and Bieler, A. (eds), *Non-State Actors and Authority in the Global System*, London: Routledge.
Levy, D. and Newell, P. (2002) 'Business strategy and international environmental governance: A neo-Gramscian synthesis', in *Global Environmental Politics*, 2(4), 84–101.
Lock, P. (2001) 'Sicherheit a la carte?', in Brühl, T., Debiel, T., Hamm, B., Hummel, H. and Martens, J. (eds), *Die Privatisierung der Weltpolitik*, Bonn: Dietz.
Lord, M. (2000) 'Constituency-based lobbying as corporate political strategy: Testing an agency theory perspective', in *Business and Politics*, 2(3), 289–308.
Luhmann, N. (1975) *Macht*, Stuttgart: Enke.
Lukes, S. (1974) *Power, a Radical View*, London: Macmillan.
Mazey, S. and Richardson, J. (1997) 'Policy framing: Interest groups and the lead up to the 1996 Inter-Governmental Conference', in *West European Politics*, 20(3), 111–33.
Messner, D. (2002) 'The Concept of the "World Economic Triangle"', IDS Working paper 173, Institute of Development Studies, Brighton.
Messner, D. and Nuscheler, F. (1996) 'Global governance', Policy Paper 2, Bonn: SEF.
Milner, H. (1991) 'The assumption of anarchy in international relations theory: A critique', in *Review of International Studies*, 17, 67–85.
Morgenthau, H. (1948) *Politics Among Nations: The Struggle for Power and Peace*, New York: Knopf.

Nadvi, K. and Wältring, F. (2002) 'Making Sense of Global Standards', INEF Report 58, Institute for Development and Peace, University of Duisburg.

Naßmacher, K.-H. (ed.) (2001) *Foundations for Democracy: Approaches to Comparative Political Finance*, Baden-Baden: Nomos.

Neyer, J. (2002) 'Politische Herrschaft in nicht-hierarchischen Mehrebenensystemen', in *Zeitschrift für Internationale Beziehungen*, 9(1), 9–38.

Nye, J. (2002) *The Paradox of American Power*, Oxford: Oxford University Press.

Nye, J. (1991) *Bound to Lead. The Changing Nature of American Power*, New York: Basic Books.

Pappi, F.U. and Shikano, S. (2001) 'Personalisierung der Politik in Mehrparteiensystemen am Beispiel deutscher Bundestagswahlen seit 1980', in *Politische Vierteljahresschrift*, 42(3), 355–87.

Parsons, T. (1967) *Sociological Theory and Modern Society*, New York: Free Press.

Robé, J.-P. (1997) 'Multinational enterprises: The constitution of a pluralistic legal order', in Teubner, G. (ed.), *Global Law without a State*, Aldershot: Dartmouth.

Römmele, A. (2002) 'Politische Parteien und professionalisierte Wahlkämpfe', in Fuchs, D., Roller, E. and Wessels, B. (eds), *Bürger und Demokratie in Ost und West*, Opladen: Westdeutscher Verlag.

Ronit, K. and Schneider, V. (1999) 'Global governance through private organizations', in *Governance*, 12(3), 243–66.

Schmidheiny, S. (1992) *Changing Course*, Cambridge: MIT Press.

Sell, S. (2000) 'Structures, agents and institutions', in Higgott, R., Underhill, G. and Bieler, A. (eds), *Non-State Actors and Authority in the Global System*, London: Routledge.

Shaiko, R. (1998) 'Lobbying in Washington: A contemporary perspective', in Herrnson, P., Shaiko, R. and Wilcox, C. (eds), *The Interest Group Connection*, Chatham: Chatham House Publishers.

Sinclair, T. (1999) 'Bond-rating agencies and coordination in the global political economy', in Cutler, C., Haufler, V. and Porter, T. (eds), *Private Authority and International Affairs*, New York: State University of New York Press.

Sklair, L. (1998) 'As political actors', in *New Political Economy*, 3(2), 284–7.

Smith, M. (2000) *American Business and Political Power*, Chicago: University of Chicago Press.

Solomon, M. (2003) *Conquering Consumerspace*, New York: Amacom.

Strange, S. (1996) 'A theory of structural power in the international political economy', in *Global Society*, 10(2), 167–218.

Strange, S. (1988) *States and Markets*, London: Blackwell.

Sturm, R., Dautermann, G. and Dieringer, J. (2000) *Regulierung und Deregulierung im wirtschaftlichen Transformationsprozess*, Opladen: Leske & Budrich.

Teubner, G. (ed.) (1997) *Global Law Without a State*, Dartmouth: Aldershot.

Thomas, C. (2000) *Global Governance, Development and Human Security*, London: Pluto Press.

Underhill, G. (2001) 'The public good versus private interests and the global financial and monetary system', in Drache, D. (ed.), *The Market or the Public Domain?*, London: Routledge.

UNDP (2002) *World Development Report*, New York: United Nations.

Verba, S. and Orren, G. (1985) *Equality in America*, Cambridge: Harvard University Press.

Walter, A. (2001) 'NGOs, business, and international investment', in *Global Governance*, 7, 51–73.

Waltz, K. (1979) *A Theory of International Politics*, Reading: Addison-Wesley.
Weber, M. (1980) *Wirtschaft und Gesellschaft*, J. Winckelmann (ed.), 5. rev. Aufl., Tübingen: Mohr.
Weßels, B. (2000) 'Kanzler – oder Politikwechsel', in Van Deth, J., Rattinger, H. and Roller, E. (eds), *Die Republik auf dem Weg zur Normalität*, Opladen: Leske & Budrich.
Wilson, G. (1990) *Interest Groups*, Oxford: Blackwell.

8
Transnational Private Authority and Corporate Governance[1]

Andreas Nölke

Locating transnational private authority in the study of global economic governance

Global economic governance does not only consist of traditional inter-governmental regulation in form of international organizations and regimes such as the World Bank, the International Monetary Fund (IMF) or the World Trade Organization (WTO). A radical departure from the conventional inter-governmental model lies in the evolution of 'private authority in international affairs' (Cutler *et al.* 1999a). Here, firms (and other non-state actors) cooperate transnationally to establish rules and standards of global commerce, without directly involving governments at all. International or, more appropriately, transnational private authority may be empirically identified based on three criteria: 'First, those subject to the rules and decisions being made by private sector actors must accept them as legitimate, as the representations of experts and those "in authority". Second, there should exist a high degree of compliance with the rules and decisions. Third, the private sector must be empowered either explicitly or *implicitly* [emphasis in original] by governments with the right to make decisions for others' (Cutler *et al.* 1999b: 19).

Thus, private authority should not be confused with private power. The core difference is that authority rests on the combination of power *and* legitimacy:[2] '*Legitimacy* ... refers to the normative belief by an actor that a rule or institution ought to be obeyed. It is a subjective quality, relational between actor and institution, and defined by the actor's *perception* [emphases in original] of the institution' (Hurd 1999: 381).

Power (or influence), in contrast, may also only be based on coercion (Hurd 1999: 400f.), resting on military, financial or analytical means.[3] Furthermore, private authority also has to be enforced. The mere proclamation of rules and principles will not be sufficient. Finally, although private actors make the rules and decisions, there is at least an implicit toleration of this authority by public actors. Thus, private authority does not necessarily undermine the role of governments – the latter are, at least in principle, able to reverse this form of authority allocation.[4]

Until most recently, the issue of private authority has largely been neglected in the discipline of International Relations (IR). The main reason for this negligence is the state-centric bias of the discipline, leading to a more or less exclusive focus on governmental actors and intergovernmental negotiations. As far as non-governmental actors have been taken into account, the focus was on the lobbying activities of actors such as NGOs, think tanks and business upon decisions finally taken by governments and intergovernmental entities, whereas self-regulation by non-governmental actors was not taken into consideration. Similarly, the relevant sub-discipline of international political economy/IPE has a strong macroeconomic bias. Thus, empirical studies mostly focus on issues such as the regulation of financial markets, currency questions, or the negotiation of international trade agreements. There are far fewer studies about the behaviour of business. The only notable exception relates to the research on multinational enterprises. Here, however, the research agenda has largely been narrowed down to the (effects of and negotiation over the) allocation of production between home and host countries, with a particular focus on developing countries.

Given this contrast between empirical developments and academic treatment, it has been concluded that the issue of private authority on issues such as bond rating is at the cutting edge within the discussion on globalization in general and on financial markets in particular (Cohen 2002: 442). This contribution concurs that the evolution of private authority is one of the most significant recent developments in global economic governance. Existing empirical research on transnational private authority has not yet realized the overall dimension of this development, but has mainly dealt with more peripheral aspects of economic governance (Chapter 2). More specifically, existing research on transnational private authority has largely excluded the important issue of corporate governance. Traditionally, this issue – which is central for the way capitalism is organized in modern societies – has been dealt with at the national level. Transnational private authority, however, appears to be at the core of current pressures for convergence of national models of capitalism (Chapter 3). Established theories of IR/IPE are unable to deal with the issue of private authority. Furthermore, the development of more appropriate theories is in a very early stage, still mostly being limited to broad typologies of transnational private authority (Chapter 4). In order to study transnational private authority on corporate governance in a more systematic manner, a theoretical framework is constructed based on a combination of a transnational policy network approach with a political economy perspective on capitalist diversity (Chapter 5). Three features of private authority over questions of corporate governance are singled out for a more detailed study, namely the work of rating agencies, private codes of 'good corporate governance' and the transnational harmonization of accounting standards (Chapter 6). The contribution concludes that the increasing role of transnational private authority for the convergence of different models of capitalism raises important normative concerns and, more particularly, asks for the identification of alternative agency (Chapter 7).

State of empirical research on transnational private authority

Although Susan Strange (1996) made wide-ranging claims regarding the increasing role of private authority on a global scale, these claims have not yet been matched with systematic research. Existing empirical studies very much concentrate on a selected number of issues that mostly carry a somewhat peripheral character for the organization of economic activity. Three main empirical fields may be differentiated:

- voluntary codes for 'good corporate conduct', mainly in terms of human rights and the environment (Braun 2001; Haufler 2001; Wolf 2002), are the result of NGO activism to press business to pay more attention to unwelcome side effects of some its activities
- technical standards in the widest sense are meant to lower transaction costs with regard to a number of issues which are not dealt with in much detail by governments, such as the governance of the internet (Spar 1999), technical standards in the narrow sense of that term (Salter 1999) or private international law/*lex mercatoria* (Cutler 1999)
- self-regulation of certain industries, such as insurance (Haufler 1997; Strange 1996: ch. 9), mineral markets (Webb 1999) or maritime transport (Cutler 1999).

These studies have been very important to bring the issue of transnational private authority on the academic agenda. Furthermore, they have already raised a number of the fundamental questions regarding this issue, such as the effectiveness and legitimacy of private self-regulation. All of these studies, however, deal with highly specific features of global economic governance. There is no systematic empirical evidence of which sectors and which organizational formats are suited at all to host transnational self-regulation (Ronit 2001: 564). Most existing studies of transnational private authority focus on cases where only a limited number of industries or a selective part of the economic process is being regulated, whereas the fundamental organization of economic life is not affected. Furthermore, and somewhat more irritating, private authority mostly carries a rather useful, positive character. Most of these studies demonstrate that business is able to govern itself and that it can deal with certain negative side effects of economic activity. Although there are some critical comments on the legitimacy and accountability of the private authority involved, most normative assessments more or less obviously focus on the efficiency of this type of regulation and frequently try to develop proposals to further improve this efficiency.

In contrast to this 'mainstream' literature, this contribution argues that private authority also affects more fundamental aspects of economic governance. Furthermore, conventional notions of efficiency may be too narrow to assess the impact of this form of regulation. Instead, this contribution proposes to look at the role of private authority for a fundamental convergence of capitalist models. Thus, a more embedded perspective on business activities is being taken, relating core elements of economic life to each other. Furthermore, it is also advisable to look at the long-term distributive consequences of transnational private authority and at its effects on less obvious stakeholders.

Corporate governance as a neglected issue of transnational private authority (research)

Currently, one of the most important issue areas of transnational private authority appears to be in the field of corporate governance.[5] Corporate governance may be broadly defined as the rules and practices governing the power relations between the various stakeholders in the modern corporation: shareholders, creditors, managers, workers and elements of the society (and the state) at large (cf. Hopt *et al.* 1999: 5; O'Sullivan 2000: 1). Within this configuration, three sets of relations are central: management–shareholder, management–employee and company–society relations. In order to delimit its empirical scope, the focus of this contribution is on shareholder relations: relations between shareholders and management are at the heart of the quintessential struggle over ownership and control (Becht *et al.* 2002; Berle and Means 1932/1991).

Management–shareholder relations in turn consist of three major components. Here, we follow the common distinction between exit and voice (Hirschman 1970) or between external (through the market for corporate control and evaluation) and internal (through the governing structure of the corporation itself) mechanisms of control (Jensen 1993). The third key issue is that of transparency and accountability, the regulation of which is highly relevant to both internal and external dimensions. We thus arrive at the following three key instances of corporate governance regulation:

- the internal governance structure of the firm
- the external control and evaluation of the firm
- regulation affecting transparency and accountability.

Corporate governance has, in the 1990s, become a buzzword of the global business community and is now receiving even wider attention given the worldwide economic, societal and political repercussions of the Enron collapse and other recent corporate breakdowns. Although it remains to be seen in which direction the regulatory reforms that are now called for would take us (Hopt 2002), it is clear that already long before Enron, the regulation of corporate governance has been in a process of major transformation worldwide. There are strong transnational pressures to change the structure of corporate governance within the Rhenish model of capitalism (particularly the German one). Given a wave of recent research on corporate governance in Germany, there already is abundant evidence for radical changes within this governance structure (cf. Deeg 2002). Changes in corporate governance, however, may have far-reaching consequences for the capitalist model as a whole (cf. Nölke 1998, 1999). Core comparative advantages of the Rhenish model traditionally are the fairly balanced and consensual relationship between labour and capital, and the availability of patient capital being provided by major banks ('Hausbanken') and internally generated funds. Management has to meet an arrangement with well-organized representatives of both labour and capital, which often participate directly in the decision making process. Thus, these decision making processes may take a long time, but the implementation of jointly made decisions is comparatively smooth. Moreover, the Rhenish model of corporate finance leads to a relatively long-term perspective with regard to the economic well-being of firms. 'Hausbanken' are less interested in short-term price movements on the stock markets than in the long-term solvency of their loans. The same long-term perspective applies to other sources of investment capital. At the same time, stable ownership structures provide firms with considerable protection against take-over. All of these factors also support the long-term investment in human resource development that is crucial for the Rhenish specialization in high skill and high quality products. These comparative advantages may now, however, be undermined by a shift of corporate governance structures in favour of shareholders. This may, in turn, lead to the familiar 'pressures of "short-terminism" that plague American and British companies – pressure from shareholders to maximize dividends by concentrating on quarterly results and short-range return on investment variables' (Sally 1995: 69), and to a more conflictive relationship with the representatives of labour. Radical changes in corporate governance structures, therefore, may threaten the very basis of the Rhenish capitalist model, because its elements are highly interdependent and may not be easily transferred and exchanged.

Some observers applaud these recent developments, since they assume that the Rhenish model is systematically underperforming, if compared with its Anglo-Saxon rival. Still, further erosion of the Rhenish model appears to be problematic. Even if the Anglo-Saxon model is assumed to be generally more efficient, a selective transfer of the US system of corporate governance into the German system of capitalism hardly appears to be promising, given the strong interdependencies between the different elements of national systems of capitalism. Thus, the selective 'disembedding' of single mechanisms of national models of capitalism for a transfer into another national model has rarely proved to be an attractive perspective, as several attempts to export the German system of apprenticeship have demonstrated.[6] The alternative of the Rhenish model completely shifting towards the Anglo-Saxon model of capitalism would, however, appear equally unattractive (at least in the short and medium term), given the inability of the Rhenish model to compete in simple low-cost products on the one hand and, on the other, products which demand high short-term investments in more risky business ventures on rapidly changing markets. Thus, the disembedding of Rhenish corporate governance may lead to a loss of its comparative advantages in high skill and high quality products, without providing an attractive reform perspective. This would not only be to the disadvantage of Germany (and other 'Rhenish' countries), but also to the overall welfare of capitalist societies:

> To the extent that national or other institutional specifities serve as niches allowing firms and economies to develop competitive new products and processes, their disappearance must diminish the aggregate entrepreneurial creativity and vitality of capitalism as a system. It is furthermore highly unlikely that any one approach to running a capitalist economy will monopolize all the virtues – which would seem to offer good Popperian, or even Hayekian, reasons for seeking to preserve the innovative potential inherent in a healthy level of 'socio-diversity' within global capitalism (Crouch and Streeck 1997b: 15).

Whereas ongoing changes within continental corporate governance systems (and their implications for the Rhenish model as a whole) are well documented by now, there is, however, far less evidence on the transnational forces that support these changes. Most research on corporate governance – and on its embeddedness in the more general 'varieties of capitalism' – is strictly comparative, thus excluding the transfer mechanisms between (national) models (cf., for example, Crouch and Streeck 1997a; Hall and Soskice 2001). Within remaining research, the conventional explanation of the evolution of transnational convergence of corporate governance focuses on the functional requirements of liberalized markets (cf. O'Sullivan 2000; Weil *et al.* 2002). Furthermore, competing substantial claims are mostly being discussed in a technical manner, assuming that standards are mainly a question of the most (market-) efficient solution. This explanation is at least incomplete, given the remaining diversity of corporate governance models and the fact that a number of potential movements towards convergence are highly controversial political issues. As far as there is a political explanation, authors focus on the role of national governments and, most prominently, the European Union as the dominant transfer mechanisms for corporate governance standards (for example, Bieling and Steinhilber 2002; van Apeldoorn 2002). Issues such as financial liberalization or European Company Law are at the forefront.

In contrast, this contribution argues that politically less visible, but potentially more important developments are happening within the private sector, especially in the wider context of the financial markets. First, there is a comparatively limited role of public regulation on issues of corporate governance. Market developments are very dynamic. Dominant actors prefer to keep governments out of this issue area, because a homogeneous regulation might not do justice to the complexity of situations involved. Furthermore, international public regulation of corporate governance is frequently being blocked because of the high national stakes involved, as in the cases of European Company Law or the Take-over Directive. As far as we can still find successful public regulation in this sector, it is largely based on private self-regulation. Thus, for example the European Union requires business to adopt international accounting standards (IAS) by 2005. Finally, there are private actors that are very actively promoting a convergence of corporate governance (towards the Anglo-Saxon model) on their own, such as institutional investors and rating agencies. In sum, effects of transnational private authority may be a crucial part of any explanation for current changes in corporate governance and, thus, for the basic organization of economic life.

State of theories on transnational private authority

As mentioned before, established (mainstream) theories of IR/IPE are unable to address the issue of transnational private authority, because of their state-centric bias. Existing theories on private self-regulation on the national level (for example, Streeck and Schmitter 1985) may only to a limited extent be transferred to the transnational level, because they are frequently linked to certain features of corporatism which are absent outside of the domestic context (especially the participation of labour). Correspondingly, the development of theories on transnational private authority is still in an early stage. Due to the absence of links with established theories, conceptual development very much follows an inductive approach. Thus, broad classifications and typologies of different forms and mechanisms of transnational private authority (such as informal industry norms, coordination service firms, production alliances, cartels or private regimes) dominate the field (cf. Cutler *et al.* 1999b).[7] Furthermore, there are some rather general explanations regarding the emergence and the operating principles of transnational private authority (cf. Cutler *et al.* 1999c). For some very specific cases of transnational private authority, such as rating agencies, more elaborate theoretical models are being developed (cf., for example, Kerwer 2001), without, however, being placed in a more comprehensive, comparative perspective. Although both the problem solving as well as the legitimacy dimensions of the evolution of transnational private authority have been highlighted, there is as yet no systematic theoretical reflection on how to assess these normative implications.

In an overall perspective, the current state of theory development on transnational private authority is not yet satisfactory. Broad typologies are a valuable option for early theory development, but have to be complemented by more advanced approaches focusing on the explanation of the working of transnational private authority as well as on the precise conditions under which this element of global governance is relevant. Furthermore, the normative focus of existing theories may be too narrow and too ahistorical. In order to assess the implications and desirability of transnational private authority within global economic governance, we have to embed this phenomenon into a more general and historical perspective of economic activity. Finally, it may be wise not to attempt to design a general theory of transnational private authority at once, but rather focus on a specific subcategory such as coordination service firms first. This could help to overcome not only the conceptual limitation of mere typologies (which frequently go hand in hand with a too broad approach), but also the risk of an idiosyncratic approach based on only one case of transnational private authority.

Elements of an alternative approach: transnational policy networks and varieties of capitalism

One promising point of departure for conceptual development is the resource dependency theory on transnational policy networks (cf. Nölke 2000). In marked contrast to conventional theories of international relations, this approach gives considerable space to the activities of private actors. Transnational policy networks, however, focus on public–private interaction and on policy advocacy or on policy participation of private actors at most, but not on private self-regulation (cf. Porter and Coleman 2002: 3). The degree of private influence on governmental or inter-governmental decisions, which is a good indicator for the relevance of transnational (global) policy networks, therefore misses the point as far as private self-regulation is concerned. Furthermore, policy network approaches are quite weak on political economy issues. Thus, they are unable to identify the larger picture and the significance of socio-economic changes that may be caused by transnational private authority, as well as the historical context that has given birth to this type of authority. Here, we can draw on theories of capitalist diversity (Crouch and Streeck 1997a; Hall and Soskice 2001), which are weak on the analysis of transnational governance, but strong on the overall relevance of current and historical developments for the organization of capitalist economies.

As a concrete analytical instrument an (inter-) organizational approach is chosen, since single firms and their inter-organizational networks appear to be at the centre of most forms of transnational private authority. Thus, the issue of transnational private authority is phrased in terms of a network of private organizations which are able transnationally to influence the conduct of other private organizations, *inter alia* based on legitimacy accepted by the latter and on a more or less implicit empowerment of (inter-) governmental actors. Sociological approaches on resource dependencies in inter-organizational networks (cf. Nölke 1995: 72–85) may serve as a starting point for the analysis of relationships between single companies, but have to be embedded in more general concepts of political economy. Thus, these organizations are representing the interests of different socio-economic groups, such as managers (various categories of), shareholders and employees. Policy networks assume that political decision making and implementation is mainly based on the exchange of material and immaterial resources between mutually – but frequently asymmetrically – dependent organizations. Typical resources to be exchanged in policy networks include finance, information and legitimacy (cf. Nölke 1995: 98f.). Within the framework of transnational private authority in global economic governance, legitimacy appears to be a core resource, but will always be combined with more conventional power resources such as finance and information.[8] The outcome of resource exchanges in a transnational political economy perspective, however, may very much transcend the corporate actors involved in these exchanges, given the potentially far-reaching relevance of private corporate governance standards for the organization of capitalist economies as a whole. In order to analyze these outcomes, the organizational logic of policy networks thus has to be combined with a comprehensive (transnational) political economy perspective. The same logic applies to the preconditions for the evolution of transnational private authority that also can only be properly understood in the context of the historical development of capitalist economies.

Coordination service firms and corporate governance

The activities of so-called 'coordination service firms' (Cutler *et al.* 1999b: 10f.) such as rating agencies, institutional investors, trade exchanges, investment banks, multinational law, accounting, insurance and management consultancy firms are at the core of transnational private authority on corporate governance. Recently, the Enron (and Worldcom and so on) debacle has demonstrated the importance of these institutions for corporate governance. The basic assumption is that these firms by setting and enforcing standards of company behaviour enjoy considerable authority over other firms – and, correspondingly, over more general issues of socio-economic governance. Thus, private actors take over (regulatory) roles, which traditionally are held by governments, with far-reaching consequences.

Based on the theoretical discussion outlined above, the remainder of the contribution will undertake a first cut of empirical developments in these fields, in order to give an assessment of the importance of this type of private transnational authority for global economic governance. Corresponding to the three key instances for corporate governance regulation mentioned above, the contribution will focus on three groups of coordination service firms:

- Institutional investors develop (and enforce) codes of conduct for the internal corporate governance structures of listed companies
- rating agencies assess the value of bonds issued by firms and other institutions, thereby inducing certain types of business behaviour
- major accounting firms favour certain standards of transparency and accountability over others, thus affecting the financial management of listed companies.

Institutional investors and internal corporate governance structures[9]

The evolution of codes of conduct for corporate governance has considerably intensified during the last years – out of the 35 codes currently existing in the EU Member States, 25 have been issued since 1997 (Weil *et al.* 2002: 2). Although there are a number of competing standards, there also has been a strong tendency towards substantial convergence. Remaining differences primarily reflect the strong historical association of corporate governance systems with different (national) models of capitalism. Furthermore, public authorities, on the national, European and global level have endorsed some private standards. Thus, codes of conduct on corporate governance have become enmeshed in a complex web of multi-level governance. Given the dominance of economic and legal literature on corporate governance, the political struggle behind this evolution of private authority is largely unaccounted for. The most important driving force for the development and enforcement of these codes, however, appears to be institutional investors. The term institutional investor generally refers to 'an investor with money under professional management in an organization that invests on behalf of a group of individuals, another organization, or a group of organizations' (Brancato 1997: 21). In the USA, the most important investors are mutual funds and pension funds. In the last few decades, the importance of these investors vis-à-vis individual investors has increased rapidly. The share of institutional investors in terms of all US financial assets rose from 8.4 per cent in 1950 to 12.3 per cent in 1970, and further to 20.5 per cent in 1990 (Harms 1997: 15). Whereas in 1965, 84 per cent of all US industry shares were owned by individual investors (and 16 per cent by institutional investors), in 1990 individual investors held only 54 per cent (as opposed to 46 per cent by institutional investors) (ibid.: 21). This accumulation of shares leads to a considerable concentration of power within the hands of institutional investors which is further intensified by a comparatively high degree accumulation of assets in the hand of a few, rather large investors.

Since the early 1980s, this concentration process has led to a very active role of institutional investors in terms of corporate governance. Accordingly, institutional investors no longer limit themselves to the option of exiting, selling their shares if they are not satisfied with the share development of a certain company, but use the voice option and directly influence corporate governance. To be sure, the classical system of operation on the basis of decisions to sell ('The Wall Street Walk') had also had an effect on corporate governance. Yet these effects were largely limited to a more indirect, structural influence, whereas the exercise of direct, active influence on management decisions remained rather rare, in comparison to the more recent, active behaviour. This behaviour has, *inter alia*, become necessary due to the increasing concentration of shares of a particular company with a particular institutional investor – if the exit option is chosen and shares are sold in large numbers, a downturn of prices now is unavoidable. In terms of internal corporate governance structures, institutional investors increasingly have put pressure on the companies they (partially) own, especially in comparison to the more passive approach of atomized individual investors. Typical issues include altering the structure and election practices of a company's board of directors, splitting the roles of chairman and chief executive, increasing current dividend payments and altering executives' and directors' compensation packages. The financial resources of institutional investors are complemented by the legitimacy that these organizations and their associations have accumulated as the leading experts on questions of internal corporate governance standards. Recommendations which were developed by organizations of the movement for 'institutional activism', such as the Council of Institutional Investors (CII) or the Investors' Rights Association of America (IRAA) are accepted as basis for the collective enforcement of corporate governance standards. These general guidelines are complemented by the accumulation of intelligence on companies with deviant behaviour (cf. Brancato 1997: ch. 3).

More recently, (US) institutional investors are slowly beginning to transnationalize their investments. While the principal US institutions making foreign equity investments (that is, pension funds and mutual funds) increased their foreign equity holdings from $97.5 billion in 1990 to $281.7 billion in 1994, this represents an aggregate increase in pension fund assets devoted to foreign equities from 3.1 per cent in 1990 to only 5.5 per cent in 1994, and an increase in mutual fund assets from 1.7 per cent to 3.9 per cent (Brancato 1997: 127). According to the long-term policy statements of many US institutional investors, an expansion of the international component of their shareholding portfolios towards a 20 per cent share is to be expected (Black *et al.* 1998: 201). The repercussions of this transnationalization process are already to be felt within other economies.[10] By 1997, international institutional investors already held shares of around 20 per cent and more in some of the most important German firms (Siemens 18 per cent, RWE 19 per cent, BASF 27 per cent, Hoechst 51 per cent; all figures taken from Balzer and Nölting 1997). Furthermore, the assets of German investment funds are also growing rapidly – in 1996 they amounted to DM 62.5 billion, more than five times the amount in 1991 (BVI 1997: 10).

The transnationalization of institutional investing is not limited to the acquisition of shares, but also comprises investor activism. Thus, German investment funds, while mostly being administered by German banks, increasingly differ from the traditionally more reluctant behaviour of their parent companies. They are not only beginning to issue general guidelines for changes in corporate governance of German companies, but also take a more critical stance at the general meetings of individual German firms where they hold shares (cf. Balzer and Nölting 1997: 80). Still, they have not yet reached the more aggressive behaviour of their US counterparts, such as the famous California Public Employees' Retirement System (CalPERS). CalPERS and other institutional investors have teamed up in institutions such as the International Corporate Governance Network (ICGN) in order aggressively to challenge traditional practices of corporate governance in Germany and other countries that deviate from the Anglo-Saxon model (cf. Balzer and Nölting 1997: 88f.). Typical issues of concern include voting rights of shareholders, executive remuneration or the composition of corporate boards. Given the absence of binding public regulations on internal corporate governance structures, these networks play a core role in developing and enforcing private or semi-private corporate governance codes. These codes increasingly define what the global business community considers adequate corporate governance. Correspondingly, a large part of recent changes in German (and other continental) corporate governance mechanisms has been attributed to the activities of Anglo-Saxon institutional investors and their networks (cf. Cioffi 2000: 585; Detomasi 2001: 20–8; Lannoo 1999: 287–90).

The basic mechanism of transnational private authority of institutional investors over internal corporate governance structures consists of the pooling of their analytical, financial and legitimacy resources. These assets are then used to exploit the dependency of other companies on these resources; for example, by issuing guidelines for correct corporate governance, selling shares and using voting rights or publishing lists of companies with deviating corporate governance practices. Given the existence of a multitude of corporate governance codes and of an even greater variety of institutional investors, their ability to exercise transnational private authority has, however, not yet been optimized.

Rating agencies and external evaluation

Debt rating agencies work towards the same direction of spreading Anglo-Saxon standards of corporate governance, although through a somewhat different mechanism. They exercise their authority in two manners (cf. King and Sinclair 2001: 4). On the one side, they shape the behaviour of market participants by limiting thinking to a range of legitimate possibilities. On the other, less frequent side, they may even occasionally exercise an explicit veto over certain options, by using a ratings downgrade. Rating agencies have received the most attention for their evaluation of public institutions, because this assessment forms one of the most obvious cases of political relevance of transnational private authority (cf. Hillebrand 2001). Although the proper task of rating agencies is to assess the 'quality' of other companies' (and public institutions') debts, they also have influence on issues of corporate governance, since the latter form an important element of their assessment criteria for business enterprises. Furthermore, the authority of both institutional investors and rating agencies is the product (and core element) of an ongoing (US-led) process of the disintermediation of finance, which is leading to a decreasing role of commercial banks for the provision of capital (cf. King and Sinclair 2001: 5–8). Insofar as the epistemic authority of rating agencies favours the US system of disintermediated finance, it is not politically neutral, but rather actively favours a specific socio-economic model which is very much in line of the short-term investment horizon of the Anglo-Saxon approach (Sinclair 1994: 149).

The resource base of rating agencies is somewhat different from the one used by institutional investors. Whereas the authority of the latter is mainly based on their financial resources (and on their legitimacy as standard-setters for internal corporate governance structures), rating agencies derive their authority from their analytical resources (and the legitimacy that is derived from the expert character of these analytical resources in the perception of market participants). The demand for the analytical output of rating agencies stems from the overwhelming quantity of information available to market actors. Rating agencies condense this information into some sort of recommendation, which is then used as a benchmark for other market actors. Although the latter may depart from these marks, they still are the standards for the work of other actors (King and Sinclair 2001: 4f.). Analytical resources (and the related legitimacy), however, are somewhat more unstable than financial resources, since they may be severely affected by perceived rating miscalls. Thus, the reputation as global experts for debt quality which has been accumulated by rating agencies over decades may be eroded quickly, as indicated by the Mexico crisis and the Asian financial crisis of the 1990s (King and Sinclair 2001: 10). Resource dependencies between rating agencies and other business companies exist not only in case of institutional investors, but also with the companies whose debts are rated by these agencies. It is here that rating agencies exercise their main authority over corporate governance, since most companies cannot afford a low ranking and will therefore consider adjusting their corporate governance structures, if these give concern to a rating agency. Although based on less tangible resources than those available to institutional investors, the authority of rating agencies over the basic organization of capitalist economies should not be underrated. Even if a company that is issuing a bond does not agree with a particular rating, it has to take account of other market actors that will be acting upon that particular rating (King and Sinclair 2001: 11).

Compared with institutional investors, rating agencies are considerably assisted in their exercise of transnational private authority by a far higher concentration within this business sector. Although there is intensified competition and an increasing number of agencies since the 1990s, the two major agencies of Moody's Investor Service (Moody's) and Standard & Poor's (S&P) still largely dominate the market. Other agencies rather occupy niche markets, such as Fitch Ratings for municipal and financial institutions. The dominating role of Moody's and S&P is not limited to the USA. It is their transnational authority over European and Asian market actors that has caused the most controversy (King and Sinclair 2001: 12). This controversy has been intensified by the Basle II capital adequacy proposals which mandate rating agency outputs for less sophisticated banks (cf. King and Sinclair 2001: 17–25). As in case of the semi-public corporate governance codes being elaborated by institutional investors, private authority here becomes enmeshed in a public–private system of multi-level governance. Third-party enforcement of debt rating has a long history in the USA (cf. Kerwer 2001; King and Sinclair 2001: 14–17), but now goes global. These most recent developments have not only been criticized because of a number of practical problems involved, but also because they may further undermine the Rhenish model, in this case especially the financial basis of some 'Mittelstand' companies.

Accounting companies and transparency standards

Both institutional investors and rating agencies rely upon accounting companies for accurate information about the performance of business. Without proper accounting figures, neither bond-rating nor institutional investing may be done in an acceptable manner. Regulations of transparency and accountability are a core element of corporate governance. In contrast to institutional investors and rating agencies, the role of accounting companies within the (transnational) political economy of modern capitalism has hardly been studied yet. Still, the potential of accounting companies for the development of powerful transnational private authority has already been indicated by Susan Strange's seminal study on the 'Retreat of the State' (1996, ch. 10). Strange focuses on the extreme concentration of the accountancy market, where the Big Six (after the dissolution of Arthur Andersen now the Big Five) have market shares of more than 95 per cent in the most important national markets, thereby giving them considerable structural power.

Even more important than the structural power of the big accountancy companies observed by Susan Strange may be the authority conferred by the elaboration of transnational private accounting standards. Traditionally, accounting standards have been developed on the national level, in most cases with a strong involvement of national governments. Economic transnationalization and the disintermediation of finance, however, have recently asked for a harmonization of national standards. Accounting companies are also in favour of pooling their resources in transnational standard setting bodies, since this will strengthen their position towards national regulators and single clients. Transnationally harmonized accounting standards are also important for the legitimacy resource base of the whole profession, because it increasingly becomes obvious that different (national) standards lead to dramatically different results for the same company (Sundgren 1997: 15). In the absence of inter-governmental cooperation for the regulation of the accountancy profession, the shift of standard setting to the transnational level leads to a further case of the evolution of powerful transnational private authority over issues of corporate governance. In contrast, the importance of national public regulations, such as the German Handelsgesetzbuch (HGB), is being tremendously eroded. Given the dominance of professional literature within accounting studies, the political struggle behind this evolution of private authority is yet largely unaccounted for, although transnational private accounting regulations are not only very much contested, but also the basis for international public regulation. The first substantial attempts for cross-border harmonization of accounting regulations have already been undertaken, in the early 1970s. During the 1990s, the controversy between the Generally Accepted Accounting Principles (GAAP) of the US, the transnational International Accounting Standards (IAS) set by the International Accounting Standards Board (IASB) and various national standards in Europe dominated the issue area. Numerous European companies have applied the GAAP to be listed on the New York Stock Exchange. Outside of the USA, the London-based IAS has increasingly been adopted. Recently, the EU has decided that European companies have to adapt the (private) IASB standard by 2005. In the aftermath of Enron, even US authorities consider the acceptance of (some of) these rules. Conventional explanations of the evolution of private authority on accounting focus on the functional requirements of liberalized markets for the harmonization of standards. Furthermore, competing substantial claims are mostly being discussed in a technical manner, assuming that standards are mainly a question of the most (market-) efficient solution. From the perspective of this contribution, however, these standard-setting procedures have to be understood within the context of the variety of capitalist models and the concrete interests of different socio-economic groups. Thus, the rather conservative, debtor-oriented accounting standards of the German (HGB) may be explained, for example, by the strong role of the

German banks during the evolution of this model of capitalism. The complex, case-oriented structures of the US GAAP are, *inter alia*, due to the lobbying efforts and the evasive behaviour of US companies in diverse economic sectors. Since accounting standards are not neutral towards different models of capitalism, transnational standard setting may severely threaten established practices on the national level. Increasing importance of transnational accounting standards, thus, recently led to the foundation of a German committee for accounting standards (Deutsches Rechnungslegungs Standards Committee/DRSC) by major German companies, with the prime intention of participating in international standard development. As of 27 March, 2003, this committee has already been severely reorganized, in order to improve its ability to influence the setting of private transnational accounting standards, which so far has been fairly limited. Again, private authority based on Anglo-Saxon preferences is increasingly undermining the Rhenish model – in this case the long-term perspective of German business based on considerable hidden reserves that will be made more difficult through the increased application of transnational accounting standards.

Conclusion and issues for further research

All three types of coordination service firms favour a convergence of corporate governance standards towards the Anglo-Saxon model, although the case of accounting also demonstrates that there may be considerable differences between British and US approaches. All three types of coordination service firms have considerably gained in importance through the process of disintermediation of finance during the last decades. One decisive factor for the success of transnational private authority in the field of accounting and even more so in the field of bond rating appears to be the high concentration within the market. This concentration very much assists the development and enforcement of common standards within a small group of organizations. The same principle is to be detected in case of institutional investors, but here concentration is still too limited to make a set of common standards easily available. In all cases, transnational private authority is based on the resource dependencies of other companies. These dependencies may be based on the financial resources of institutional investors, or the information which is provided by accounting and rating companies. All three types of coordination service firms furthermore enjoy considerable legitimacy resources as standard setters for different aspects of corporate governance.

The studies cited so far, however, have not yet been matched by investigations in other types of coordination service firms, such as law or management consultancy companies and stock exchanges: there is as yet little reflection of the interrelationships between these different mechanisms. Institutional investors, for example, rely on rating agencies and on accountancy companies for their investment decisions (Hillebrand 2001: 161). Furthermore, one may assume that these agencies coordinate their efforts for the implementation of Anglo-Saxon standards within alternative capitalist environments. In order to establish firmly the actorliness of these coordination service firms, it also has to be demonstrated that alternative courses of action – in terms of investment criteria, rating standards, accounting rules and so on – are possible. Otherwise, these firms are only the 'implementing agencies' of anonymous market pressures, and thus of very limited relevance. Correspondingly, further research may seek an alternative network of institutional investors, rating agencies and other coordinating firms, such as labour-dominated pension funds (Blackburn 1999), socially responsible investing (Guay and Jansons 2002) or alternative rating concepts focusing on social/political stability (Hillebrand 2001: 169f). The existence of an alternative to the dominating form of transnational private authority also becomes relevant from the perspective of the adaptability of the Rhenish model of capitalism, since it is fundamentally at odds with the prerogatives of the established transnational coordination service firms. There are obvious considerations – already made by others – that some aspects of this type of private authority are problematic; for example, the collusion between coordination service firms of different sectors/functions as in the case of cross selling between accountants and management consultants within one company. The utilization of private authority for public regulation as in the case of the Basle II capital adequacy proposals has also been severely criticized. These conclusions, however valid, remain within the narrow concern of short-term economic efficiency. Other observers have added that it is difficult to combine the existence of transnational private authority with conventional notions of democratic legitimacy and accountability. In a broader perspective, however, the influence of transnational private authority on a possible convergence of capitalist diversity towards an Anglo-Saxon model may be the most pressing policy issue.

Notes

1 This contribution has been written in the context of the research proposal 'The Transnational Political Economy of Corporate Governance Regulation' (NWO Programme 'Shifts in Governance'). I am heavily indebted to my colleagues Henk Overbeek and Bastiaan van Apeldoorn for numerous contributions. An earlier version was presented at the 'Global Economic Governance', conference of the section for International Relations of the German Political Science Association (DVPW) in Arnoldshain, 10–12 April, 2003. I am grateful to the participants for their helpful comments, especially to Stefan Schirm.
2 For a similar definition of transnational private authority as based on power combined with legitimacy, see Hall and Biersteker 2002: 4.
3 Private authority should also not be confused with Nye's concept of 'soft power' or Strange's 'structural power'. Besides the conceptual woolliness of the latter concepts (cf. Baldwin 2002: 184f., 186), both do not necessarily comprise a

combination of power *and* legitimacy. Thus, private authority may also be based on structural power (besides relational power) as well as on Nye's intangible resources (besides tangible resources such as information and finance) – but always has to include legitimacy.

4   In some cases, private actors may even have authority over public actors, as in case of rating agencies and their 'sovereign' ratings (Hillebrand 2001: 165–7). The focus of this article, however, is on self-regulation within the private sector.

5   The following conceptualization of corporate governance is largely taken from Nölke *et al.* 2003, ch. 11.

6   For a similar argument regarding the difficulties of importing selected mechanisms of the German model within the French context, cf. Boyer 1997: 92f.

7   There are some obvious parallels between the discussion on transnational private authority and the early discussion on transnational relations in general. In case of the latter, a too broad and general approach towards the subject inhibited the development of a coherent alternative to state-centric approaches, cf. Risse-Kappen 1995: 7f., 14f.

8   Compare this assumption with the observation made by Cutler *et al.* 1999c: 345, taking into account the close relationship between legitimacy and authority: 'Two distinct roles played by power in private authority can be discerned: The first, ex ante consideration, is the role of power in making it possible for firms to establish private authority in the first place … The second, an ex post consideration, is the importance of the power produced by private authority once it is established. Actors with power create private authority, and private authority creates power.'

9   This section partially draws on Nölke 1998.

10   The following examples focus on the case of Germany. A comprehensive European perspective is provided by Lannoo 1999: 287–91.

References

Apeldoorn, B. van (2002) *Transnational Capitalism and European Integration*, London: Routledge.

Baldwin, D.A. (2002) 'Power and international relations', in Carlsnaes, W., Risse, T. and Simmons, B.A. (eds), *Handbook of International Relations*, London: Sage, 177–91.

Balzer, A. and Nölting, A. (1997) 'Großanleger greifen an: Internationale Fonds gegen deutsche Manager', in *manager magazin*, 27(8), 72–89.

Becht, M., Bolton, P. and Rock, A. (2002) 'Corporate governance and control', ECGI Working Paper Series in Finance, European Corporate Governance Institute: Brussels.

Berle, A.A. and Means, G.C. (1991 [1932]) *The Modern Corporation and Private Property*, New Brunswick: Transaction Publishers.

Bieling, H.-J. and Steinhilber, J. (2002) 'Finanzmarktintegration und Corporate Governance in der Europäischen Union', in *Zeitschrift für Internationale Beziehungen*, 9(1), 39–74.

Black, A., Wright, P., Bachman, D.E. and Davis, I. (1998) *In Search of Shareholder Value: Managing the Drivers of Performance*, London: Financial Times, Pitman Publishing.

Blackburn, R. (1999) 'The new collectivism: Pension reform, grey capitalism and complex socialism', in *New Left Review*, 233, January/February, 3–65.

Boyer, R. (1997) 'French statism at the crossroads', in Crouch, C. and Streeck, W. (eds), *Political Economy of Modern Capitalism: Mapping Convergence and Diversity*, London, Thousand Oaks, New Delhi: Sage.

Brancato, C.K. (1997) *Institutional Investors and Corporate Governance: Best Practices for Increasing Corporate Value*, Chicago, London, Singapore: Irwin Professional Publishing.

Braun, R. (2001) 'Konzerne als Beschützer der Menschenrechte? Zur Bedeutung von Verhaltenskodizes', in Brühl, T., Debiel, T., Hamm, B., Hummel, H. and Martens, J. (eds), *Die Privatisierung der Weltpolitik: Entstaatlichung und Kommerzialisierung im Globalisierungsprozess*, Bonn: Dietz, 257–81.

Brühl, T., Debiel, T., Hamm, B., Hummel, H. and Martens, J. (eds) (2001) *Die Privatisierung der Weltpolitik: Entstaatlichung und Kommerzialisierung im Globalisierungsprozess*, Bonn: Dietz.

BVI (1997) *Investment 97: Daten, Fakten, Entwicklungen, Bundesverband Deutscher Investment Gesellschaften*, Frankfurt am Main: Bundesverband.

Cioffi, J.W. (2000) 'Governing globalisation? The state, law, and structural change in corporate governance', in *Journal of Law and Society*, 27(4), 572–600.

Cohen, B. (2002) 'International finance', in Carlsnaes, W., Risse, T. and Simmons, B.A. (eds), *Handbook of International Relations*, London, Thousand Oaks, New Delhi: Sage, 429–47.

Crouch, C. and Streeck, W. (eds) (1997a) *Political Economy of Modern Capitalism: Mapping Convergence and Diversity*, London, Thousand Oaks, New Delhi: Sage.

Crouch, C. and Streeck, W. (1997b) 'Introduction', in Crouch C. and Streeck, W. (eds), *Political Economy of Modern Capitalism: Mapping Convergence and Diversity*, London, Thousand Oaks, New Delhi: Sage, 1–32.

Cutler, A.C. (1999) 'Private authority in international trade relations: The case of maritime transport', in Cutler, A.C., Haufler, V. and Porter, T. (eds), *Private Authority and International Affairs*, Albany: State University of New York Press, 283–332.

Cutler, A.C., Haufler, V. and Porter, T. (eds) (1999a) *Private Authority and International Affairs*, Albany: State University of New York Press.

Cutler, A.C., Haufler, V. and Porter, T. (1999b) 'Private authority and international affairs', in Cutler, A.C., Haufler, V. and Porter, T. (eds), *Private Authority and International Affairs*, Albany: State University of New York Press, 3–30.

Cutler, A.C., Haufler, V. and Porter, T. (1999c) 'The contours and significance of private authority in international affairs', in Cutler, A.C., Haufler, V. and Porter, T. (eds), *Private Authority and International Affairs*, Albany: State University of New York Press, 333–76.

Deeg, R. (2002) 'New paths in German finance and corporate governance?', Paper presented at the Annual Meeting of the American Political Science Association, 28 August–1 September, Boston.

Detomasi, D. (2001) 'The political economy of corporate governance', Paper presented at the Annual Meeting of the American Political Science Association, 1 September, San Francisco.

Guay, T. and Jansons, M. (2002) 'The politics of socially responsible investing', Paper presented at the International Studies Association annual meeting, 24–27 March, New Orleans.

Hall, P. and Soskice, D. (eds) (2001) *Varieties of Capitalism: Institutional Foundations of Comparative Advantage*, Cambridge: Cambridge University Press.

Hall, R.B. and Biersteker, T.J. (2002) 'The emergence of private authority in the international system', in Hall, R.B. and Biersteker, T.J. (eds), *The Emergence of Private Authority in Global Governance*, Cambridge: Cambridge University Press, 3–22.

Harms, A. (1997) 'Privatizing hegemony: institutional investors and the reproduction of neoliberalism', Paper prepared for presentation at the 38th Annual Meeting of the International Studies Association, Toronto, 18–22 March.

Haufler, V. (2001) *A Public Role for the Private Sector: Industry Self-Regulation in a Global Economy*, Washington: Carnegie Endowment.

Haufler, V. (1997) *Dangerous Commerce*, Ithaca, NY: Cornell University Press.

Hillebrand, E. (2001) 'Schlüsselstellung im globalisierten Kapitalismus: Der Einfluss privater Rating-Agenturen auf Finanzmärkte und Politik', in Brühl, T., Debiel, T., Hamm, B., Hummel, H. and Martens, J., *Die Privatisierung der Weltpolitik: Einstaatlichung und Kommerzialisierung in Globalisierungprozess*, Bonn: Dietz, 150–73.

Hirschman, A.O. (1970) *Exit, Voice and Loyalty: Responses to Decline in Firms, Organizations and States*, Cambridge: Harvard University Press.

Hopt, K. (2002) 'Modern company and capital market problems: Improving European corporate governance after Enron', ECGI-Law Working Paper no. 05, European Corporate Governance Institute: Brussels.

Hopt, K., Hamada, H., Roe, M.I., Wymeersch, E. and Prigge, S. (1999) *Comparative Corporate Governance: The State of the Art and Emerging Research*, Oxford: Oxford University Press.

Hurd, I. (1999) 'Legitimacy and authority in international politics', in *International Organization*, 53(2), 379–408.

Jensen, M.C. (1993) 'The modern industrial revolution, exit, and the failure of internal control systems', in *Journal of Finance*, 48, 831–80.

Kerwer, D. (2001) *Standardising as Governance: The Case of Credit Rating Agencies*, Max Planck Project Group Common Goods – Law, Politics and Economics, Bonn: Max.

King, M.R. and Sinclair, T.J. (2001) 'Grasping at straws: A ratings downgrade for the emerging international financial architecture', Paper presented to the Annual Meeting of the American Political Science Association, 30 August–2 September, 2001, San Francisco.

Lannoo, K. (1999) 'A European perspective on corporate governance', in *Journal of Common Market Studies*, 37(2), 269–94.

Nölke, A. (2000) 'Regieren in transnationalen Politiknetzwerken? Kritik postnationaler Governance-Konzepte aus der Perspektive einer transnationalen (Inter-) Organisationssoziologie', in *Zeitschrift für Internationale Beziehungen*, 7(2), 331–58.

Nölke, A. (1999) 'Transnational economic relations and national models of capitalism', Paper presented to the workshop on 'National models and transnational structures – Globalisation and public policy', directed by Philip G. Czerny and Wolfgang Streeck, ECPR Joint Sessions of Workshops, 26–31 March 1999, Mannheim.

Nölke, A. (1998) 'Nichtkonventionelle Strukturen bei der Unternehmensfinanzierung: Kapitalismustypen und die Auswirkungen der Globalisierung am Beispiel der institutionellen Investoren', in *Comparativ*, 8(4), 45–62.

Nölke, A. (1995) *Geberkoordination für die Länder Afrikas südlich der Sahara: Analyse eines interorganisatorischen Netzwerkes zwischen bi- und multilateralen Entwicklungshilfeagenturen*, Baden-Baden: Nomos.

Nölke, A., Overbeek, H. and van Apeldoorn, B. (2003) 'The transnational political economy of corporate governance regulation', Research Proposal to the NWO, Vrije Universiteit, Amsterdam.

O'Sullivan, M. (2000) *Contests for Corporate Control: Corporate Governance and Economic Performance in the United States and Germany*, Oxford: Oxford University Press.

Porter, T. and Coleman, W.D. (2002) 'Transformations in the private governance of global finance', Paper prepared for presentation at the International Studies Association Annual Meeting, 25 March, New Orleans.

Risse-Kappen, T. (1995) 'Bringing transnational relations back in. Introduction', in Risse-Kappen, T. (ed.), *Bringing Transnational Relations Back In: Non-State Actors,*

Domestic Structures and International Institutions, Cambridge: Cambridge University Press, 3–36.

Ronit, K. (2001) 'Institutions of private authority in global governance: Linking territorial forms of self-regulation', in *Administration & Society*, 33(5), 555–78.

Sally, R. (1995) *States and Firms: Multinational Enterprises in Institutional Competition*, London, New York: Routledge.

Salter, L. (1999) 'The standards regime for communication and information technologies', in Cutler, A.C., Haufler, V. and Porter, T., *Private Authority and International Affairs*, Albany: State University of New York Press, 97–128.

Sinclair, T.L. (1999) 'Bond-rating agencies and coordination in the global political economy', in Cutler, A.C., Haufler, V. and Porter, T., *Private Authority and International Affairs*, Albany: State University of New York Press, 153–68.

Sinclair, T.L. (1994) 'Passing judgement: Credit rating processes as regulatory mechanisms of governance in the emerging world order', in *Review of International Political Economy*, 1(1), 133–59.

Spar, D.L. (1999) 'Lost in (cyber)space: The private rules of online commerce', in Cutler, A.C., Haufler, V. and Porter, T., *Private Authority and International Affairs*, Albany: State University of New York Press, 31–52.

Strange, S. (1996) *The Retreat of the State: The Diffusion of Power in the World Economy*, Cambridge: Cambridge University Press.

Streeck, W. and Schmitter, P. (eds) (1985) *Private Interest Government: Beyond Market and State*, London: Sage.

Sundgren, J. (1997) 'Self-regulatory initiatives in the global economy: Exploring the concept of private regimes', Paper prepared for the International Studies Association Annual Meeting, 18–22 March, Toronto.

Webb, M.C. (1999) 'Private and public management of international mineral markets', in Cutler, A.C., Haufler, V. and Porter, T., *Private Authority and International Affairs*, Albany: State University of New York Press, 53–96.

Weil, Gotshal & Manges (2002) 'Comparative study of corporate governance codes relevant to the European Union and its member states', on behalf of the European Commission, Internal Market Directorate General, *Final Report*, Brussels.

Wolf, K.D. (2002) 'Civil society and the legitimacy of governance beyond the state: Conceptional outlines and empirical explorations', Paper presented at the International Studies Association Annual Meeting, 24–27 March, New Orleans.

9

Corporate Social Responsibility in Global Economic Governance: A Comparison of the OECD Guidelines and the UN Global Compact

Lothar Rieth

Introduction

It has become almost common wisdom that processes of globalization have significant effects on the role of the state in international politics. Susan Strange has coined the term 'retreat of the state', others such as Raymond Vernon have alleged for a long time that state's sovereignty is at bay, being under attack by transnational corporations (TNCs) (Strange 1996; Vernon 1971). In their seminal book on 'Governance without Government', James Rosenau and Ernst-Otto Czempiel realized that power can be exercised without formal public authority (Rosenau and Czempiel 1992: 5). Some years later, Claire Cutler, Virginia Haufler and Tony Porter spoke explicitly about the importance of profit seeking entities wielding private authority in international politics (Cutler *et al.* 1999). And in the latest of important publications almost closing the circle of arguing, Hall and Biersteker speculate about the reversibility of private authority back to public authority (Hall and Biersteker 2002: 213).

So, one might ask, what is still left to be researched? But by saying this, one would go too far. The research programme is still in its infancy and results are currently at the preliminary stage. The afore-mentioned publications provide a succinct overview of the development of the research programme on global governance. The 'global governance debate' is still very much state-centred. It has focused, in particular, on the relocation and delegation of political authority between various layers of governance, but still taking the state as the point of departure, be it for heuristic or empirical analytical reasons (Gilpin and Gilpin 2001; Held and McGrew 2002).

Having in mind this slight 'state bias' of the current literature, these contributions add two aspects to the current debate. First, they seek to shed some light on the difference between the authority of actors and the authority of institutions. Second, they seek to change the perspective of assessing the authority of institutions by taking a TNC's perspective and not, as is common, a states' perspective.

It is argued that in issue domains that are affected by backlashes of globalization, TNCs feel the need to respond to social demands (Haufler 1999, 2000). This applies, for example, to business activities in developing countries, where TNCs are reproached for ignoring human and labour rights and the protection of the environment. Confronted with possible risks of being targeted for regulation or for attention from transnational activists, some TNCs have realized that for these and other reasons, it is in their own interest to abide by certain internationally agreed social principles stated in international conventions, declarations and guidelines (Haufler 2001).

It is assumed that TNCs are willing to commit actively to aspects of corporate social responsibility (CSR) although additional costs might be incurred, because at the same time their reputation with stakeholders will be lifted at each level by following recognized corporate responsibility instruments. But choosing a standard is not a simple thing, because there are more than a dozen standards available that TNCs can choose from (Kolk *et al.* 1999; OECD 2000). Many corporations start by developing their own code of conduct, but then try to become part of a larger initiative to extend the visibility of their engagement. These larger often independent initiatives are very often characterized by external rule setting or rule monitoring.

In the following, it will be explained why certain corporate responsibility instruments are more acceptable to TNCs than others. Corporate responsibility instruments are more specifically defined as governance mechanisms.

It is argued that the acceptance level of a governance mechanism is determined by TNCs' assessment of the authoritative dimensions of a governance mechanism. The higher the degree of authority attributed to a governance institution, the more likely a TNC is willing to participate in a governance mechanism. Participation in this sense is defined as the attempt to act in accordance with the provisions laid out in a governance mechanism, or at least to show aspects of engagement.

First, the concept of corporate social responsibility will be explained and, moreover, why there is no international regulation of TNCs concerning social aspects in place, neither on the national nor on the international level. In addition, it will be delineated why some companies still want to make use of corporate responsibility instruments. Second, authority dimensions of actors and institutions will be introduced. It will be discussed why there is an emergence of private authority in global politics even in non-economic areas, such as social global challenges. Third, the concept of governance mechanisms as a major category is presented and linked to the concept of authority. Three authority dimensions (coercion, self-interest and legitimacy) are presented that are considered crucial to the authority of a governance mechanism. Lastly, these three authority dimensions will be tested in an illustrative comparative case study by comparing two governance mechanisms in the field of corporate social responsibility. One more 'traditional' (state-oriented) governance mechanism, the *OECD Guidelines for Multinational Enterprises*, will be contrasted with a more 'new type' (non-state oriented) governance mechanism, the United Nations Global Compact.

Corporate social responsibility

Social and ecological activities of TNCs in the field of human rights, labour and environment are summarized in the concept of corporate citizenship or corporate social responsibility. It is about business taking greater account of its social and environmental footprint (Zadek 2001). The concept of corporate citizenship or corporate social responsibility (CSR) is a very amorphous one.[1] Different definitions are thrown into the debate with very different emphasis, depending on the interest of the author. Definitions of CSR by corporations or trade associations are usually very vague and stress the voluntary nature of CSR. NGOs focus more on the societal impacts and concentrate on the core business processes of the organization.

A useful way to differentiate between different models of CSR has been introduced by Richard Locke. He distinguishes between the supposed beneficiaries of corporate action (shareholders vs broader societal stakeholders) and the motivation behind these actions (instrumental vs moral/ethical).

One of the most sophisticated and extensive definitions of a strategy of CSR was put forward by Alyson Warhurst: 'CSR...defined as the internalization by the company of the social and environmental effects of its operations through proactive pollution prevention and social impact assessment so that harm is anticipated and avoided and benefits are optimized' (Warhurst 2001: 61). This definition highlights the possibility that a company would seize opportunities and make use of capabilities originally created to achieve traditional economic competitive advantages and employ these to sustainable development goals. This concept would be located in the lower-right of Locke's matrix and would constitute a far-reaching realization of CSR based on current knowledge.

Table 9.1 Alternative models of corporate citizenship

		Motivation	
		Instrumental	Moral/ethical
Beneficiaries	Shareholders	Minimalist	Philanthropic
	Stakeholders	Encompassing	Social activist

Source: Locke, R.M. (2002), 'Note on Corporate Citizenship in a Global Economy', prepared for the Sloan School of Management 50th Anniversary Celebration/ MIT, p. 3.

The overall goal of this contribution is to understand through which governance mechanisms TNCs are more willing, and make additional efforts, to move into the direction of 'social activists'. It is assumed that the noticeable rise of corporate action in the field of CSR, which can be seen in a stronger corporate emphasis on social and ecological matters instead of output and financial performance, is linked to new forms of governance mechanisms. Zadek summarizes this assumption very eloquently: 'Corporate Citizenship will only be effective if and where it evolves to a point *where business becomes active in promoting and institutionalizing new global governance frameworks* that effectively secure civil market behavior' (Zadek 2001: 13, emphasis added).

Thus, this study is in search of appropriate (global economic) governance mechanisms that trigger TNCs' behaviour in the field of CSR. Before looking into aspects of authority and governance mechanisms in more detail, the global context which has been touched upon in the introduction will be laid out in more detail.

Regulation of TNCs in global politics

There is a widespread belief that corporations are primary beneficiaries from the wave of 'globalization' outpacing many different actors, such as states as well as individuals in underdeveloped countries, but also in developed countries. It appears as if TNCs find themselves in an 'anarchic situation' where their scope of action is almost unlimited.[2] The buzz word 'globalization' is primarily connected to the internationalization of markets. Protesters from around the world complain that TNCs exercise too much power. The lines of argument and causal chains presented are not always easy to grasp and are far from simple. Sometimes, it seems as if the complexity of the issue is the biggest enemy of critics of globalization. Strong critics proclaim, for instance, that TNCs are free riding on the international system or rule the world (Korten 2001; Morgan 2003). It is claimed that TNCs take advantage only of absolute economics not paying attention to any negative side effects, such as on social aspects of workers or on the environmental living conditions in various communities around the world.

Corporations themselves take advantage of the fact that they can 'enter' and 'exit' national markets in order to maximize the well-being of their shareholders, without accepting any direct responsibility for the consequences of their actions in individual national jurisdictions. This approach is in diametrical opposition with the regime of nation states, which is built on the principle that the people in any national jurisdiction have a right to try to maximize their well-being (Vernon 1998: 28f.).[3] But is it really true that national policy makers cannot do anything against corporate power? To make a sound judgment on the relationship between the state and TNCs, the legal status of TNCs in the national arena and in the global arena needs to be clarified.

From a legal point of view, it is important to note that only states can confer international legal personality to companies (Malanczuk and Akehurst 2000: 104). So far, TNCs have not yet been upgraded by states to international subjects proper (Malanczuk and Michael 2000: 104). TNCs are neither considered legal persons nor subjects of international law and are therefore not directly bound by international law. Instead, sovereign states are obliged to implement and enforce conventions, declarations and guide-lines concerning TNCs that have been adopted on the international level (Kimminich and Stephan 2000: 154), such as the *Universal Declaration of Human Rights*, the International Labour Organization's (ILO) *Declaration on Fundamental Principles and the Rights to Work*, the ILO *Tripartite Declaration of Principles concerning Multinational Enterprises and Social Policy*, as well as the *Rio Declaration on Environment and Development* and the *Johannesburg Declaration on Sustainable Development*.

The impact of these various declarations is well-known. It is rather limited. While investing in the OECD world, TNCs observe the above-mentioned dec-larations in the majority of cases. However, in many other parts of the world, in particular in less-developed regions, TNCs can more or less act under lawless conditions, which are more characterized by anarchic traits than by aspects of rule of law. In this part of the world, neither the provision of national law nor international conventions, declaration or guidelines are enforced by national authorities. For these reasons, some globalization crit-ics argue that TNCs violate internationally recognized labour standards. This might be true, but that still does not mean that, at the same time, they violate national law. National standards are sometimes not in place or fall behind international standards (see ratification chart of ILO Fundamental Conventions).[4]

However, it can be also stated that, independent of the national situation, TNCs do comply selectively with internationally agreed norms, in particular, when it suits their needs. This leads to the first conclusion that, on a volun-tary basis, TNCs are hardly willing to implement high international social standards, such as labour standards or environmental standards in less devel-oped parts of the world.[5]

In addition, states in less developed parts of the world lack the power or the political will, sometimes both, to put international standards into national legislation that would impose constraints on TNCs. In some cases, states lack the administrative infrastructure, in others they do not want to upset potential investors.[6] This leads to the second conclusion, that national governments with given instruments are not willing to implement interna-tional standards effectively.

Summing up, TNCs are not always willing to comply with social standards and public authorities are not able to guarantee TNCs' adherence to social standards. For these reasons, the issue of 'authority' needs to be explored in more detail in order to see how instruments of corporate social responsibility can be become more effective and compensate for these shortcomings in the international economy.

Public and private authority in global politics

Owing to rising levels of interdependence, the nation state is no longer capable, unilaterally or multilaterally together with other nation states, of achieving its processual and material governance targets (Zürn 2002). At the same time, a growing number of actors, other than the state, have taken on authoritative roles and functions in the international system, such as private corporations in bond-rating agencies or in private international trade law (Cutler 1999; Sinclair 1999).

Based on these and other examples, it has become common knowledge that solutions to problems of global governance are related to the reconfiguration of authority between various layers of infrastructure. David Held and Anthony McGrew conclude that contemporary global governance involves a relocation of authority from public to quasi-public and to private agencies (Held and McGrew 2002: 10). James Rosenau speaks of a bifurcated system, including two worlds of world politics, one interstate system and another more multicentric system that has emerged as a rival source of authority with state and non-state actors that sometimes cooperate with, often compete with, and endlessly interact with the state-centric system (Rosenau 2002: 73). In this debate, it is not so much in question that authority is not reserved to public actors, but much rather 'what authority is made of'.

Two aspects of authority need to be highlighted. First, that authority cannot only be attributed to actors but also to institutions, being defined here as formal or informal rules, and second, that authority is based on the concepts of coercion, interest and legitimacy. It is argued that it is very important to differentiate whether the authority of an actor or an institution will be analyzed. In some cases the presence of an actor can enhance the authority of an institution, in other cases an actor vested with authority can make use of institutions to exercise its authority. Research on aspects of private authority and its properties usually has focused on actors *or* institutions. However, the difference between the two has not always been clearly stated, instead research results have been applied to actors *and* institutions, without any distinction (see Cutler *et al.* 1999; Hall and Biersteker 2002; Hurd 1999).

This research makes use of the analytical separation that was introduced by Thomas Franck. He, although focusing in particular on aspects of legitimacy, distinguishes between a property of a rule *or* rule-making institution which itself exerts a pull towards compliance on those addressed (Franck 1990: 16). This separation has the advantage that the authority of a rule or, in this case, of a governance mechanism, can be analyzed, leaving open the possibility that each of the actors involved in a governance mechanism might have an effect on the authority of a governance mechanism.

The concept of authority itself is a difficult one to define. It has been defined in many different ways, focusing on aspects of power, legitimacy and interests. In a strict legal sense, (state) authority has traditionally been associated with the necessary power to impose rules and regulations (Seidl-Hohenveldern 2001: 1368–70). Many authors in international relations ascertain that authority lies beyond the power of coercion by government. They locate authority between power and legitimacy (Cutler *et al.* 1999), between negotiation and coercion (Hurd 1999), and between legitimacy and utilitarian cost-benefit calculations (Young and Levy 1999).

Thus, these three conceptualizations of the term 'authority' pay tribute to the three main explanatory variables in institutional analysis in international relations. Hasenclever *et al.* have differentiated between interest-based, power-based and knowledge-based theories (Hasenclever *et al.* 1997). All of these factors might be of importance when discussing the authority of a rule. In general, a rule has authority if it receives the recognition and the consent of those governed by that authority (Biersteker and Hall 2002). This recognition and consent is granted if the three dimensions of authority are met satisfactorily. A rule does not have to be set up by a public actor.

Private authority of rule-making institutions and rules does work in the global system in some issue areas. However, it has not been shown, so far, that it works in the area of corporate social responsibility. Virginia Haufler has shown in her studies on the private sector in a global economy that factors such as risk, reputation and learning are driving factors for industry self-regulation (Haufler 2001). She also mentions a number of other factors that allegedly determine the success of industry self-regulation in global governance, such as engagement, transparency, accountability, role of governments and international organizations, monitoring, harmonization of different systems, voluntariness of initiatives, leadership of key executives, competitive pressure and so on. Thus far, no systematic research has been conducted in identifying the significance of each of these factors, in particular, not as properties of a governance mechanism.

Governance mechanisms in global politics

Summing up the two previous chapters, it can be stated that governments are unable to frame and enforce policy goals in the issue domain of corporate social responsibility owing to their inability to regulate TNCs and owing to the emergence of private authority. Public authority has eroded on the national and international level. New forms of governance are needed to resolve this problem. As a result, it can be inferred that non-governmental actors, in this case TNCs, come into play and need to be included in one way or another when devising new governance mechanisms in order to achieve substantive results.

James Rosenau has suggested that the core of governance involves rule systems in which steering mechanisms are employed to frame and implement goals that move communities in the directions they wish to go, or that enable them to maintain the institutions and policies they wish to maintain (Rosenau 1995). In a later work, he also refers to these rule systems as steering mechanisms, through which authority is exercised in order to eventually move towards desired goals (Rosenau 2002). This account of governance is based on the increasing role of non-state actors including corporate actors. It results in the introduction of governance mechanisms which are defined as a steering mechanism vested with authority that induces TNCs to comply with its prescribed provisions.

Thus, it is assumed that the authority dimension of a governance mechanism entails potential explanatory power to explain the variance in the acceptance level of governance mechanisms by TNCs. Broad acceptance leads to TNCs' compliance with a governance mechanism. These governance mechanisms are institutions (Simmons and Martin 2002: 194).[7] They are considered formal rule systems, which have not yet become hard law (Abbott and Snidal 2000: 421f.),[8] which means that these rules may lack explicit and agreed legally binding status (Raustiala and Slaughter 2002: 551).

In general, TNCs, because of the aforementioned limits of TNC regulation in national and international politics, prefer and choose informal and often only loosely institutionalized forms of governance, such as discretionary standards, that permit cheating when necessary (Cutler 2002). The content of governance mechanisms themselves will only explain the behaviour of TNCs to a limited extent. They have always been known, and some have been in place for almost three decades (cp. some ILO Declarations). It can therefore be concluded that TNCs are in the privileged position to pick and choose which governance mechanism they want to follow. Therefore, it is claimed that other specific aspects, such as the authority of a governance mechanism, do determine the behaviour of TNCs in the field of CSR. Authority, as defined above, is located around three dimensions: coercion, self-interest and legitimacy.

Coercion is connected to formal structures that guarantee surveillance and enforcement. Thus, a governance mechanism will be tested on whether and how it can support compliance with a rule system. In security politics, the motivation for following international rules is fear of physical coercion. The analogy in business is fear and risk of litigation. Consequently, it very much depends on which competencies are assigned to any monitoring body within a governance mechanism. The coercion variable therefore focuses on any sort of enforcement capability built into a governance mechanism.

The negotiations of (self-)interest can be associated with the design of governance mechanisms by looking at the way in which rational actors, such as TNCs, design institutions purposefully to advance their joint interests (Koremenos *et al.* 2001). Thus, one basic way is to test the concept of self-interest by analyzing to what extent TNCs participate in the process of a governance mechanism. The self-interest variable process participation will therefore analyze to what degree TNCs are full participants of a governance mechanism.

The perceived legitimacy of a governance mechanism may influence the degree to which TNCs accept and internalize those rules (Raustiala and Slaughter 2002). Ian Hurd defines legitimacy as a normative belief by an actor that a rule or institution ought to be obeyed. He stresses the fact that it is a subjective quality which is defined by the actor's perception of the institution (Hurd 1999). Claire Cutler adds that legitimacy involves the respect accorded 'an authority', whose authority derives from specialized knowledge and practice that render such knowledge acceptable and appropriate. This form of legitimacy applied to governance mechanisms points to actors being involved in a governance mechanism. For these reasons, the legitimacy variable will concentrate on the type of actors involved in a governance mechanism and the degree of respect accorded to them.

Governance mechanisms in practice: *OECD Guidelines* vs *UN Global Compact*

The developed framework including the three variables (enforcement capability, process participation, and actor type) representing the three different dimensions of authority will be tested in an illustrated comparative case study analyzing the *OECD Guidelines for Multinational Enterprises* and the *UN Global Compact*. The goal is to test whether the three variables provide insights into why TNCs prefer one governance to another, and attempt to act in accordance with the provisions laid out in it.

These two governance mechanisms have been selected because they represent two very different traditions of governance mechanism along a public–private continuum. The former is dominated by states with tripartite elements, including business associations and trade unions at least in some bodies. The latter is a typical example of a public–private partnership model that provides a broader platform for private actors to voice their concern and to lead the action.

This comparative case study is based on two surveys conducted in 2001 and 2002, focusing on German and international TNCs (Rieth 2003; Seitz 2002). Before comparing the two selected governance mechanisms concerning the acceptance rate by TNCs, both are briefly introduced and contrasted.

The *OECD Guidelines for Multinational Enterprises* are recommendations by governments, prepared with the assistance of staff of an international organization (Gordon 2001). The *OECD Guidelines* are closely linked to a broader framework for international investment, the *OECD Declaration on International*

Investment. The OECD *Guidelines* constitute the most comprehensive CSR instrument currently available, covering all eight major issue areas in business ethics. It deals with matters of competition, financing, taxation, employment and industry relations, environment and science and technology (OECD 2001, 2002).

The follow-up and implementation process was refined in 2000. The Committee on International Investment and Multinational Enterprises (CIME) at the OECD is overseeing the guidelines. In addition, the effectiveness of the guidelines depends mainly on the work of 'National Contact Points (NCP)', which implements the Guidelines within member states. These NCPs of most member states are located in the ministry of economics. If problems occur in relation to specific instances of business conduct (violation of the guidelines), an NCP has authority to investigate and, if a violation is found, it tries to resolve them and mediate a settlement between the parties.

NCPs have to meet annually and report to CIME. The main task of CIME is periodically, or at the request of an adhering country, to provide clarifications about how the guidelines would apply in a given situation and to report to the OECD Council on the guidelines. In addition, business and trade unions may request consultations with the NCPs. The Business Industry Advisory Council (BIAC), representing national and international business associations and the Trade Union Advisory Council (TUAC) may also raise issues related to the *OECD Guidelines* directly with CIME. Moreover, CIME holds meetings with BIAC and TUAC on a regular basis.

The *UN Global Compact* is an initiative launched by the Secretary General of the United Nations, prepared with the assistance of the International Chamber of Commerce and with the explicit support of some member states.[9] It is a strictly voluntary initiative that asks TNCs that want to take part in the initiative to send a letter from the Chief Executive Officer to the Secretary-General of the United Nations expressing support for the *Global Compact* and its nine principles, which cover topics in human rights, labour and environment. A TNC is supposed to set in motion changes to business operations so that the *Global Compact* and its principles become part of strategy, culture and day-to-day operations. At least once a year, specific examples of progress TNCs have made or lessons they have learned in putting principles into practice should be send to the *Global Compact* office that will post these reports to their website. Only recently, TNCs were asked to publish their experiences in their annual environment or sustainability report. The *Global Compact* offers three additional engagement mechanisms. Within 'policy dialogues' topics, that are chosen by TNCs together with the *Global Compact* office, that are related to the nine principles, will be discussed in multi-stakeholder workshops throughout the year with the objective of identifying problems, finding solutions, and, if possible, initiating partnership projects with UN bodies. The 'Learning Forum' has a two-fold concept. In a formal meeting once a year, TNCs share their experiences and highlight good practices to a wide audience. The *UN Global Compact* homepage also provides a virtual platform where all interested stakeholders can access experiences created by TNCs. A final engagement mechanism rests on local structures. TNCs have coalesced in national networks that are primarily used as communication platforms to showcase practical actions and solutions. All activities are strictly voluntary. However, if a TNC wants to be officially listed at the *Global Compact* homepage as an *UN Global Compact* participant, it has to submit an annual report detailing experiences implementing one of the principles.

Many observers are of the opinion that *OECD Guidelines* and the *Global Compact* are complementary instruments (Chahoud 2001: 6; National Policy Association 2003). The *Global Compact* focuses on general principles, while the *OECD Guidelines* make quite specific recommendations, depending on the issue area. The *Global Compact* covers only three issue areas, while the *OECD Guidelines* basically cover all relevant issue areas. The *Global Compact* solicits company endorsement and seeks to create working relationships with endorsing corporations, whereas the *OECD Guidelines* do not actively seek endorsements from individual corporations, instead BIAC can get in touch with the OECD follow-up institutions on the international level, whereas national business associations and TNCs can directly contact an NCP on the country level. The *Global Compact* invites corporations to make extra efforts, to implement the nine principles and to report on the experiences created. The only 'negative' reporting structure to the NCPs of the *OECD Guidelines* does not necessarily encourage more participation by corporations. Moreover, the *OECD Guidelines* are mainly supervised by government officials on the national level, while the *Global Compact* is guided primarily by UN civil servants, much of the initiative is left to corporations.

To sum up, both governance mechanisms are essentially self-regulatory mechanisms under the auspices of an international organization with differences in particular regarding the implementation procedures, the number of issues covered, company participation and last but not least, involvement of government officials.

When TNCs were asked, in 2001, which governance mechanism had guided their behaviour only a limited number (about 15 per cent) of companies mentioned the *UN Global Compact*. Only slightly more (about 20 per cent) referred to the *OECD Guidelines* (Seitz 2002: 126). In a different study conducted in 2002, however, none of the companies cited the *OECD Guidelines* when explaining their activities in the field of CSR, but about half of the interviewed representatives of TNCs referred to the *UN Global Compact* (Rieth 2003: 10). As a result, it can be summed up that the *Global Compact* enjoys a slightly higher degree of acceptance among TNCs.[10]

So far, owing to the fact that most of the CSR initiatives are very young, there have only been a limited number of surveys available concerning the behaviour of TNCs and CSR activities. The results give only some indications

Table 9.2 Governance mechanisms and level of acceptance

Governance mechanism	Level of acceptance
OECD Guidelines	$-/O$
UN Global Compact	$O/+$

Key: $-$ = low level; O = medium level; $+$ = high level.

of the position of the leading CSR initiatives. Both surveys, however, gave solid answers about each of the authority dimensions introduced before.

OECD Guidelines provide, with the NCP on the national level and with the CIME on the international level, only a limited enforcement capability. The NCP and CIME accept reports that have been presented to them, but only give advice on how to implement the *Guidelines* instead of starting any sort of legal investigation. The *UN Global Compact* itself denies that it has any enforcement capability in place, instead it offers incentive structures such as the possibility that TNCs' reports can be posted on their website and invitations to TNCs to various meetings.

OECD Guidelines provide almost no agenda setting power and only to a limited degree the opportunity for process supervision by TNCs. TNCs can only approach NCPs for advice on a country level and, through the BIAC, contact the CIME on the national level. It can be concluded that the *OECD Guidelines* offer limited to 'no' process participation opportunities for TNCs. The *UN Global Compact* does endow TNCs with moderate agenda setting power. TNCs can actively choose topics for 'policy dialogues' and can, for example, approach different UN bodies to explore partnership opportunities. It therefore offers a high degree of process participation.

The OECD is an international organization with only a small secretariat compared to the United Nations system, of which the *UN Global Compact* is a part. Both UN and OECD are almost purely public organizations, however, with a different mandate. Primarily, the UN much rather focuses, next to aspects of peace and security, on issues such as human rights, labour and environment. The OECD has as its foremost focus the planning, coordination and deepening of economic cooperation among OECD member countries and to a limited extent, although increasingly, development of other countries on its agenda. For these reasons, the UN is granted a higher level of legitimacy by TNCs than the OECD.[11]

It can be concluded that the results of the two analyzed governance mechanisms are very heterogeneous. The test of the three different authority dimensions leads to very different results. The *OECD Guidelines* have some sort of enforcement capability in place but grant only limited opportunities for process participation. Moreover, the OECD is only regarded as moderately legitimate regarding social issues. The *UN Global Compact* instead

Table 9.3 Governance mechanisms and authority dimensions

Governance mechanism	Enforcement capability	Process participation	Legitimacy of actor
OECD Guidelines	− / O	− / O	O
UN Global Compact	−	+	+

Key: − = low level; O = medium level; + = high level.

provides no enforcement capability. However, it offers lots of opportunities for companies to participate actively and is highly regarded as having special expertise regarding social issues.

Conclusion

In general, CSR activities by TNCs have currently lost ground, because of the economic downturn in the past two years. Nevertheless, it can be concluded that the *OECD Guidelines* have, since revised in 2000, only prompted some additional commitment by corporations. In addition, most of the NCPs have, on their part not actively promoted particular company engagement regarding CSR issues either.

The *UN Global Compact* has instead become more active. More TNCs have joined the initiative, more and more are willing to share their experiences, and have implemented one or more of the nine principles. But even this initiative has faced severe problems because a number of TNCs have publicly committed to the principles without engaging in any extra activities. Thus, it needs to be seen in the near future how the CSR issue evolves.

From a theoretical point of view the causal connection between the acceptance level of governance mechanisms and the three introduced authority dimensions can only be assumed. The revised *OECD Guidelines* and the *UN Global Compact* are still very new governance mechanisms and more empirical research is needed in the coming years to prove any correlation and causal connection between authority dimensions of a governance mechanism and the behaviour of TNCs. What can be said, however, is that different governance mechanisms have different values on each of the authority dimensions. The authority dimensions focusing on self-interest (process participation) and legitimacy (legitimacy of actor) look especially promising and should be further tested.

Thus, authority in the issue area of CSR needs a private and public component it would appear; a private component that gives the TNCs the feeling that they are sitting in the front row, if not behind the steering wheel, of the bus and a public one that provides them with the signs on the road.

Notes

1 In this chapter, these terms are used interchangeably. There is a debate between different connotations of the two terms based on their origin. Corporate citizenship is more linked to the debate in the USA and Great Britain, and corporate social responsibility is more associated with Europe. So far, no substantive progress has been achieved in this debate.

2 For the purpose of this study, TNCs are treated as rational actors with well-defined preferences. TNCs' practice will be explained by reference to goal-seeking behaviour. The goals of TNCs are based on a strong belief in the free market economy they operate in. Typically, TNCs are associated with the priority goal to maximize profits (or to maximize return on equity) and to provide the community with the optimal amount of goods and services. In times of globalization, the focus shifts to the first goal, because there is no longer any specified community a multinational corporation does serve.

3 It needs to be added that Vernon speaks of 'stakeholder' instead of 'shareholder'. For the purpose of this confrontation, it is useful to stress the fundamental difference between states and corporations by using the term shareholder, because too many corporations still do not take into account the interests of all stakeholders, such as workers, residents, and so on.

4 The ratification chart shows the differences between states in ratifying the core conventions on forced labour, freedom of association, discrimination, and child labour. See *http://webfusion.ilo.org/public/db/standards/normes/appl/appl-ratif8conv.cfm? Lang=EN*, accessed 28 December, 2002.

5 In the global governance debate, this problem has been called 'incentive gap' (Brühl and Rittberger 2001: 22; Kaul and Stern 1999: xxvi).

6 In the global governance debate, this mismatch between 'transsovereign problems' and predominantly national public policy-making approaches has been called 'jurisdictional gap' (Brühl and Rittberger 2001: 21; Kaul and Stern 1999: xxvi).

7 Governance mechanisms can therefore be regarded by international institutions as sets of rules meant to govern international behaviour. The concept of regimes is not directly applied because explicit no added value was expected, although some aspects are included in this research analysis.

8 Hard law is attenuated if legally binding obligations are no longer precise and no formal authority is available that interprets and implements the law. The realm of 'soft law' begins once legal arrangements are weakened along one or more dimensions of obligation, precision, and delegation.

9 For basic information on the *UN Global Compact*, 'How the Global Compact works: Mission, Actors and Engagement Mechanisms' (2003): *http://www.unglobal compact.org/irj/servlet/prt/portal/prtroot/com.sapportals.km.docs/documents/Public_Do cuments/mission_actors.pdf*. For more details on the *UN Global Compact*: *http://www. unglobalcompact.org/Portal/*

10 It needs to be taken into account that the *Global Compact* was only established a year before the survey by Seitz was conducted and only two years before that of Rieth.

11 This assessment is based on many interviews which have been conducted with representatives of TNCs in Germany as part of the survey conducted in 2002 (see Rieth 2003).

References

Abbott, K.W. and Snidal, D. (2000) 'Hard and soft law in international governance', in *International Organization*, 54(3), 421–56.

Biersteker, T.J. and Hall, R.B. (2002) 'Private authority as global governance', in Hall, R.B. and Biersteker, T.J. (eds), *The Emergence of Private Authority in Global Governance*, Cambridge: Cambridge University Press, 203–22.

Brühl, T. and Rittberger, V. (2001) 'From international to global governance: Actors, collective decision-making, and the United Nations in the world of the twenty-first century', in Rittberger, V. (ed.), *Global Governance and the United Nations System*, Tokyo, New York: United Nations University Press, 1–47.

Chahoud, T. (2001) Der 'Global Compact' und die 'OECD-Leitsätze für multinationale Unternehmen' als globale Instrumente zur Förderung der Unternehmensverantwortung, Bundeszentrale für politische Bildung, Bonn. *http://www.bpd.de/popup druckversion.html?guid=862YQM*

Cutler, A.C. (2002) 'Private regimes and interfirm cooperation', in Hall, R.B. and Biersteker, T.J. (eds), *The Emergence of Private Authority in Global Governance*, Cambridge, New York: Cambridge University Press, 23–40.

Cutler, A.C. (1999) 'Locating "authority" in the global political economy', in *International Studies Quarterly*, 43(1), 59–81.

Cutler, A.C., Haufler, V. and Porter, T. (1999) *Private Authority and International Affairs*, Albany: State University of New York Press.

Franck, T.M. (1990) *The Power of Legitimacy among Nations*, New York: Oxford University Press.

Gilpin, R. and Gilpin, J.M. (2001) *Global Political Economy: Understanding the International Economic Order*, Princeton, NJ: Princeton University Press.

Gordon, K. (2001) *The OECD Guidelines and other Corporate Responsibility Instruments: A Comparison*, Paris: OECD.

Hall, R.B. and Biersteker, T.J. (eds) (2002) *The Emergence of Private Authority in Global Governance*, Cambridge, New York: Cambridge University Press.

Hasenclever, A., Mayer, P. and Rittberger, V. (1997) *Theories of International Regimes*, Cambridge, UK, New York: Cambridge University Press.

Haufler, V. (2001) *A Public Role for the Private Sector: Industry Self-regulation in a Global Economy*, Washington, DC: Carnegie Endowment for International Peace.

Haufler, V. (2000) 'Private sector international regimes, in non-state actors and authority', in Higgott, R.A., Underhill, G.R.D. and Bieler, A. (eds), *The Global System*, London, New York: Routledge, 121–37.

Haufler, V. (1999) 'Private sector international regimes', in Higgott, R.A., Underhill, G.R.D. and Bieler, A. (eds), *Non-state Actors and Authority in the Global System*, London, New York: Routledge, 121–37.

Held, D. and McGrew, A.G. (2002) *Governing Globalization: Power, Authority and Global Governance*, Cambridge, UK; Oxford; Malden, MA: Polity.

Hurd, I. (1999) 'Legitimacy and authority in international politics', in *International Organization*, 53(2), 379–408.

Kaul, I., Grunberg, I. and Stern, M.A. (1999) *Global Public Goods: International Cooperation in the 21st Century*, New York: Oxford University Press.

Kimminich, O. and Stephan, H. (2000) 'Einführung', in *das Völkerrecht*, Tübingen: Francke.

Kolk, A., van Tulder, R. and Welters, C. (1999) 'International codes of conduct and corporate social responsibility: Can transnational corporations regulate themselves?', in *Transnational Corporations*, 8(1), 143–80.

Koremenos, B., Lipson, C. and Snidal, D. (2001) 'The rational design of international institutions', in *International Organization*, 55(4), 761–800.

Korten, D.C. (2001) *When Corporations Rule the World*, San Francisco, Bloomfield, CN: Berrett-Koehler; Kumarian Press.

Locke, R.M. (2002) *Note on Corporate Citizenship in a Global Economy*, Cambridge. Sloan School of Management and MIT.

Malanczuk, P. and Akehurst, M. (2000) *Akehurst's Modern Introduction to International Law*, London: Routledge.

Morgan, J. (2003) 'The free rider principle: How privilege subsidized', Global Public Policy Forum, New York, ATTAC Working Paper, *http://www.globalpolicy.org/socecon/ tncs/2003/0115 freerider.htm*

National Policy Association (2003) The UN Global Compact and the OECD Guidelines, Public Policies to Promote Corporate Social Responsibility, Washington, DC, *http://www.multinationalguidelines.org/csr/ungc vs oecd.htm*

OECD (2002) *OECD Guidelines for Multinational Enterprises Annual Report 2002*, Paris: OECD.

OECD (2001) *OECD Guidelines for Multinational Enterprises Annual Report 2001*, Paris: OECD.

OECD (2000) 'Codes of corporate conduct: Expanded review of their contents', Paris: OECD Working Papers on International Investment 2001/6.

Raustiala, K. and Slaughter, A.-M. (2002) 'International law, international relations and compliance', in Carlsnaes, W., Risse, T. and Simmons, B.A. (eds), *Handbook of International Relations*, London: Sage, 538–58.

Rieth, L. (2003) Deutsche Unternehmen, Soziale Verantwortung und der Global Compact, Universität Tübingen: Tübingen. *http://www.uni-tuebingen.de/gk.globale- herausforderungen/html/Kollegiaten/riethpapers.htm*

Rosenau, J.N. (2002) 'Governance in a new global order', in Held, D. and McGrew, A. (eds), *Governing Globalization*, Cambridge, UK, Oxford; Malden, MA: Polity, 70–86.

Rosenau, J.N. (1995) 'Governance in the 21st century', in *Global Governance*, 1(1), 13–43.

Rosenau, J.N. and Czempiel, E.O. (1992) *Governance without Government: Order and Change in World Politics*, Cambridge, New York: Cambridge University Press.

Seidl-Hohenveldern, I. (2001) *Völkerrecht*, Neuwied [u.a.]: Luchterhand.

Seitz, B. (2002) 'Corporate citizenship: Zwischen Idee und Geschäft', in Wieland, J. and Conradi, W. (eds), *Corporate Citizenship*, Marburg: Metropolis-Verlag, 23–195.

Simmons, B.A. and Martin, L.L. (2002) 'International organizations and institutions', in Carlsnaes, W., Risse-Kappen, T. and Simmons, B.A. (eds), *Handbook of International Relations*, London: Sage, 192–211.

Sinclair, T.J. (1999) 'Bond-rating agencies and coordination in the global political economy', in Cutler, A.C., Haufler, V. and Porter, T. (eds), *Private Authority and International Affairs*, Albany: State University of New York Press, 153–68.

Strange, S. (1996) *The Retreat of the State: The Diffusion of Power in the World Economy*, Cambridge, England; New York, NY: Cambridge University Press.

Vernon, R. (1998) *In the Hurricane's Eye: The Troubled Prospects of Multinational Enterprises*, Cambridge, MA: Harvard University Press.

Vernon, R. (1971) *Sovereignty at Bay: The Multinational Spread of U.S. Enterprises*, New York: Basic Books.

Warhurst, A. (2001) 'Corporate citizenship and corporate social investment: Drivers of tri-sector partnerships', in *Journal of Corporate Citizenship*, 1(1), 57–73.

Young, O.R. and Levy, M.A. (1999) 'The effectiveness of international environmental regimes', in Young, O.R. (ed.), *The Effectiveness of International Environmental Regimes: Causal Connections and Behavioral Mechanisms*, Cambridge, MA: MIT Press, 1–32.

Zadek, S. (2001) *The Civil Corporation*, London and Sterling, VA: Earthscan Publications Ltd.

Zürn, M. (2002) 'From interdependence to globalization', in Carlsnaes, W., Simmons, B.A. and Risse, T. (eds), *Handbook of International Relations*, London: Sage, 235–54.

Part IV

International Organizations and Regional Institutions

10
Mechanisms of Global Trade Governance: The 'Double Standard' on Standards in the WTO

Sieglinde Gstöhl and Robert Kaiser

Trade vs non-trade concerns in the WTO

The rapid growth of global trade has increased the need for more specified regulation of products and production processes. The World Trade Organization (WTO) has been coming under pressure to reconcile the requirements of free trade with requests for guarding certain health, environmental or labour standards as well as intellectual property rights, which carry both the promise of legitimate demands and the risk of non-tariff protectionism. In this chapter, we investigate the WTO's role at this intersection of trade and non-trade concerns. We understand global trade governance as the process by which different public and private actors from the local to the global level govern international trade in a cooperative mode.[1] Contrary to a common misunderstanding, the WTO itself does not set international standards and therefore has to find other ways to 'govern' trade-related regulation. The impact of standards on global trade is widespread – one estimate claims that up to 80 per cent of trade is affected by standards or associated technical regulations (OECD 1998: 4, 10). Nevertheless, 'the literature on standard setting generally lacks a sustained theoretical argument to explain or assess *institutional* standards arrangements past or present', and in contrast to some economic and legal studies, 'work on standards by political scientists practically does not exist' (Mattli 2001: 331f.).[2]

Standards are agreed criteria by which a product or a service's performance, its technical and physical characteristics, and/or the process and conditions under which it has been produced or delivered, can be assessed (Nadvi and Wältring 2002: 6). They address a wide range of issues, including technical, health and safety norms, and they provide for minimum quality, information and compatibility. From the point of view of their legally binding nature (and the actors involved), there are two kinds of standards: voluntary and regulatory. 'Voluntary standards' are defined by industry or non-governmental bodies. 'Regulatory standards' or regulations are publicly defined (in national or international public law) and mandatory.

Many voluntary standards have over time developed into regulatory standards. While the WTO agreements concern both voluntary and regulatory standards, its dispute settlement deals only with regulatory standards.[3]

Since the mid-1980s, an additional distinction has been drawn between 'product standards' and 'standards of process and production methods' (PPM), be they voluntary or regulatory. Product standards focus on the characteristics of a product, while process standards deal with the practices in the production process.[4] Regulations of working conditions, for example, are typical PPM standards, while environmental rules may concern the good or its manufacturing process. The distinction between product and process standards has first been confirmed by the GATT *tuna/dolphin I* panel report of 1991, which, however, was never adopted. The panel concluded that the USA could not embargo tuna imports from Mexico simply because Mexican regulations on *the way tuna was produced* did not satisfy US regulations; it could only apply its regulations on *the quality or content* of the tuna imported (cf. GATT 1991). A few other cases on this 'product–process doctrine' followed (cf. Hudec 2000).

The WTO has thus established a 'double standard': while member states may apply product standards equally to domestic and imported goods, they may enforce standards of process and production methods only at home; that is, the principle of non-discrimination remains restricted to how imported goods are and widely ignores how they have been made. Why is there such a 'double standard' on standards in the WTO, and is it likely to disappear in the near future? We argue that this distinction is due to the following three intertwined reasons:[5] institutions, interference, and interests. As a result, the 'double standard' is likely to be durable.

First, the institutional context of the World Trade Organization provides constraints and opportunities with regard to the introduction and application of standards. Since the WTO itself is not the appropriate institution to set standards but non-trade concerns increasingly affect free trade, it has developed two techniques – reference and ruling – to cope with the issue. On the one hand, the Agreement on Technical Barriers to Trade (TBT) and the Agreement on the Application of Sanitary and Phytosanitary Measures (SPS) refer to and encourage member states to adopt both voluntary and regulatory, product and PPM standards set by other bodies.[6] On the other hand, WTO case law has recently opened towards standards of process and production methods, and it may continue to do so within certain limits. On the whole, the WTO has used cross-references in agreements with regard to (voluntary and regulatory) product standards and rulings of the dispute settlement body (DSB) with regard to (regulatory) PPM standards.

Second, product standards aim at avoiding damage or other problems that might be caused at home by the use or consumption of (domestic or imported) goods, whereas the imposition of PPM standards on foreign goods concerns the pollution, inhumane working conditions or other problems in the exporting countries and might thus collide with foreign jurisdictions. An enforcement of PPM standards by the DSB or by inclusion of PPM standards in the treaties therefore entails sovereignty concerns in terms of interference by the WTO or by member states, because it would give the producing country a right to access the importing country's market without discrimination.[7]

Third, the future inclusion of regulatory PPM standards in the WTO agreements is fraught with conflicting interests among the member states. A 'codification' of environmental and social standards seems out of question. Such a treaty revision, which would not only introduce the possibility of references but allow for future rulings, meets with fierce resistance especially from developing countries. They fear not only an intrusion in domestic affairs, but severe economic disadvantages. Developing countries, however, constitute the majority of member countries in the WTO and treaty amendments need to be decided by consensus. Moreover, a codification of PPM standards would obstruct the work of other international institutions such as the International Labour Organization (ILO) and multilateral environmental agreements (MEAs).

As a result, the WTO is unlikely to codify PPM standards in its agreements due to institutional constraints as well as member states' sovereignty concerns and conflicting interests – even though the 'quasi-supranational' dispute settlement mechanism has led to a certain opening with regard to the enforcement of PPM standards, however only in connection with environmental and not labour standards. Institutions account for this – one-sided – case law opening, while interests matter most regarding the unlikely future codification of PPM standards.

For Abbott and Snidal (2001: 361f.), 'all standards issues are governance issues' in terms of blending private expertise with public representativeness. The development and application of standards typically involves networks of different actors ranging from private business, non-governmental organizations and trade unions to the public sector, operating at local, national and global levels (cf. Nadvi and Wältring 2002: 9ff.).[8] Many actors have thus an interest in standards affecting international trade in the different stages of the policy cycle: standard setting, standard monitoring, assistance in achieving standards, and sanctions for non-compliance (Nadvi and Wältring 2002: 5f.). While the WTO is not involved in the setting of standards, it helps to monitor and enforce them. WTO rules have raised the importance of both international standards (such as those referred to in the WTO agreements) and national or regional standards (in particular regarding WTO case law). An example for the WTO's assistance in achieving standards is the 'Standards and Trade Development Facility' recently established together with the World Bank in order to help developing countries develop and implement international standards on food safety, plant and animal health (WTO 2002a). The WTO does not require member states to have standards,

but its rules aim at ensuring that voluntary or regulatory standards or testing and certification of products do not constitute unnecessary barriers
to trade.

The following section sets out how and to what extent standards have
already been incorporated into WTO agreements. We then analyze how
standards have been applied in the WTO dispute settlement process, thereby
beginning to widen the scope of multilateral trading rules on process and
production methods. Next, we evaluate the prospects for an explicit integration of environmental and social standards into the WTO treaties, and
the chapter closes with some conclusions based on the findings.

Introducing standards in the WTO agreements

Even though the basic WTO principles (that is, national treatment and the
most-favoured nation clause) provide for non-discrimination in trade, they
do not prevent member states from setting all kinds of national standards.
Article xx GATT even authorizes measures, *inter alia*, to protect public
morals, human, animal or plant life or health, and to conserve exhaustible
natural resources, subject to the requirement that such measures are not
applied in a manner which would constitute a means of arbitrary or unjustifiable discrimination between countries where the same conditions prevail, or a disguised restriction on international trade.[9] Yet, Article xx GATT
had proved ineffective in thwarting standards as trade barriers, and as a
result of the Uruguay Round more specific rules on the treatment of foreign
goods and services – the TBT and SPS Agreements – were introduced into the
WTO scheme. They acknowledge the importance of harmonizing standards
internationally so as to minimize the risk of sanitary, phytosanitary and
other technical standards becoming barriers to trade.

Agreement on technical barriers to trade

The TBT Agreement was originally negotiated during the Tokyo Round and
took effect in 1980.[10] In 1995, it was superseded by the WTO Agreement on
Technical Barriers to Trade which, unlike its predecessor, is applicable to all
WTO members. The TBT Agreement covers all technical regulations, voluntary standards and the testing and certification procedures to ensure that
these are met (except for sanitary or phytosanitary measures). It embraces
both product and PPM standards[11] and aims at ensuring that they do not
create unnecessary obstacles to international trade. The TBT Agreement rec-
ognizes that countries may adopt the standards (for human, animal or plant
life or health, for the protection of the environment or consumers, and so
on) they themselves consider appropriate. In order to prevent too much
diversity, however, the TBT Agreement encourages WTO members to use
international standards. This pressure extends not only to new but also to

pre-existing standards, as a contracting party may ask another member state to justify any regulation it is 'preparing, adopting, or applying' (Article 2.5). Central government bodies are not permitted to discriminate or adopt technical regulations that are more trade-restrictive than necessary. In addition, a code of good practice applies regarding the preparation, adoption and application of voluntary standards, and WTO members are to take reasonable measures to ensure that local government, non-governmental and regional standardizing bodies comply with this code as well. Conformity assessment procedures are equally subject to non-discrimination, and if relevant guides or recommendations issued by international standardizing bodies exist, they are to be used. The elimination of technical barriers to trade has a significant bilateral dimension in the form of mutual recognition agreements (MRAs) in which countries agree to recognize each others' standards and conformity assessment procedures, and to accept them as equivalent. The European Union (EU), for example, has concluded several MRAs, *inter alia* with the United States, Australia, Japan and Switzerland. They usually cover industrial sectors in which the participants' trade volumes are especially high (for example, machinery, telecommunications terminal equipment and medicinal products).

Agreement on the application of sanitary and phytosanitary measures

Sanitary and phytosanitary measures (SPS) are requirements imposed by governments to ensure the safety of products for consumption or the environment. These national regulations usually apply equally to foreign and domestically produced goods, plants or animals. The SPS Agreement was negotiated as part of the Agreement on Agriculture and is *lex specialis* to the TBT Agreement. It encompasses product and PPM standards, but 'the definition is somewhat unclear as to whether voluntary "standards" are covered, although the focus is plainly on mandatory measures' (Sykes 1995: 82). The definition of SPS measures includes only measures that protect health within the territory of the regulating WTO member. It thus excludes regulations seeking to standardize processes and production methods in the exporting state with the goal of protecting health there (Marceau and Trachtman 2002: 862). However, the SPS Agreement includes measures of importing states regulating PPM standards abroad where the goal is to protect health within their territory (for example, regulation of foreign slaughterhouse practices). Most SPS PPM standards are product-related since they focus on the health risk of imported food products (including standards concerning transport of animals and plants).

According to the SPS Agreement, food safety and health standards shall not be more trade-restrictive than necessary to fulfil a legitimate objective such as national security requirements, protection of human health or safety, animal or plant life or health, or the environment. In addition, SPS measures must be based on scientific principles and must not be maintained without sufficient scientific evidence.[12] In case of a lack of such evidence, the precautionary principle (Article 5.7) allows a member state to take provisional measures restricting trade on the basis of pertinent information, including that from the relevant international organizations or from other members of the SPS Agreement. However, in doing so, member states are obliged to seek to obtain additional information in order to pursue a more objective risk assessment within the transition period.

The SPS Agreement goes a step further than the TBT Agreement and explicitly encourages member countries to use the standards set by the following three bodies: the FAO-WHO Codex Alimentarius Commission in Rome for food safety, the International Office for Epizootics based in Paris for animal health, and the FAO's Secretariat of the International Plant Protection Convention for plant health. These international standard setting organizations, which are often referred to as the 'three sisters', offer ready-made benchmarks for WTO members to use in developing their regulations. They are observers to SPS Committee meetings, and they can also be called in as experts to give advice to WTO dispute settlement panels. Most WTO members are actively involved in the three sisters, but they may also refer to any other international organization or agreement whose membership is open to all WTO members.

Hence, although the adoption of international standards remains voluntary, the SPS Agreement confers a new status on them as the only justification for not using them are scientific arguments resulting from a proper assessment of the potential health risks.[13] By contrast, under the TBT Agreement, governments may decide that international standards are not appropriate for other reasons than potential health risks, including fundamental technical problems or geographical factors. Moreover, WTO members must accept the SPS measures of other contracting parties as equivalent, if the exporting country can demonstrate that they achieve the desired level of protection.[14]

Conclusion: bringing standards in by references

Under the WTO regime, standards certainly gained more attention as non-tariff barriers to trade. While GATT has concentrated on negative integration, the SPS and TBT Agreements add greater support for positive integration, through strengthened incentives for adoption of international standards and promotion of recognition and harmonization.[15] Even though the World Trade Organization has not evolved into a standard-setting body itself, it makes increasingly use of regulatory activities pursued by specialized international bodies. The TBT and SPS Agreements make reference to such institutions with regard to both voluntary and regulatory standards as well as product and PPM standards. Within this context, member states are still entitled to apply standards with higher levels of protection than international standards, but such an endeavour meets considerable institutional restrictions. Under the TBT Agreement, national standard setting bodies have to consider scientific information, whereas the SPS Agreement requires scientific justification. Since 1995, those prerequisites have led to an increasing number of dispute settlement cases over standards which subsequently pushed forward the emergence of WTO case law on the application of standards.

Spreading standards through WTO case law

With the establishment of the World Trade Organization, the trade dispute resolution system has been significantly strengthened, in particular through shortening the procedures and abolishing the member states' veto against panel decisions. The new institutional setting has widened the scope of standards in recent rulings by recognizing the importance of non-trade concerns. In the following, we briefly present pertinent decisions of the DSB which underline how multilateral case law on standards has spread since 1995.

The 'sardines' case

The 'sardines' case was the first ruling under the Agreement on Technical Barriers to Trade. In September 2002, the Appellate Body decided in favour of Peru that the EC Council Regulation 2136/89 violated Article 2.4 of the TBT Agreement, as it allowed for the import and marketing of preserved sardines only if they were prepared exclusively from fish of the species *Sardina pilchardus Walbaum* (cf. WTO 2002b). Other types of fish of this family were allowed to be freely marketed within the EU as long as they did not use the trade description 'sardines' even if accompanied by a geographical indication. By referring to a standard on preserved sardines and sardine-type products adopted by the Codex Alimentarius in 1978 ('Codex STAN 94'), which among others also covers *Sardinos sagax sagax*, a species found mainly in the Eastern Pacific Ocean, Peru was able to show that the EC regulation was inconsistent with international standards, and the European Union agreed to bring its regulation in line with the TBT Agreement.

The 'beef hormones' case

The 'beef hormones' case illustrates the difficulty of providing the sufficient scientific evidence which the SPS Agreement requires. In 1986, when the USA had asked the Codex Alimentarius Commission to decide on the safety of beef hormones, a majority of member states had rejected the advice of its scientific committee that the growth-promoting hormones were safe. When it was asked again in 1995, a new majority of Commission members narrowly approved their use (Skogstad 2001: 496).[16] This stamp of approval led the USA and Canada to petition the WTO to rule the European Union's ban on imported beef produced from cattle treated with growth hormones illegal. In 1998, the Appellate Body affirmed the panel decision sustaining the US–Canadian complaint that the EU's ban on imported beef produced from cattle treated with growth hormones – albeit the ban also applied to domestic beef in the EU – violated the SPS Agreement because the EU had not conducted the necessary risk assessment (WTO 1998a).

This case reveals the growing importance of specialized international standard organizations. Five of the six growth hormones in question were in line with recommendations issued by the Codex. Since the EU was not able to justify the import ban with a scientific risk assessment, the non-application of international standards violated the SPS Agreement. The EU also failed to invoke Article 5.7 of the SPS Agreement which would have provided for the opportunity to justify the import ban as a provisional measure. Consequently, the Appellate Body authorized Canada and the USA to impose suspensions of tariff concessions in reaction to the EU's violation of the SPS Agreement (cf. Skogstad 2001).

The 'shrimp/turtle' case

The 'shrimp/turtle' case originated from a US embargo on shrimp products harvested with methods resulting in incidental killing of sea turtles. In May 1998, Malaysia, Thailand, India and Pakistan initiated a dispute against the USA reacting to a 1996 US court decision which required that Section 609 of the Endangered Species Act was to be enforced without geographical limitation in order to make sure that no shrimp commercially harvested without using turtle exclusion devices (TEDs) could be imported into the USA (cf. Kelemen 2001: 637ff.; Shaw and Schwartz 2002: 146 ff.).

Even though the Appellate Body referred to several multilateral environmental agreements, in particular the Convention on International Trade in Endangered Species of Wild Fauna and Flora (CITES), to argue that sea turtles were indeed endangered, the US import ban was considered inconsistent with Article xx GATT.[17] For the first time, however, a WTO ruling recognized that governments have a right to take measures to conserve exhaustible resources even abroad. The USA lost the case because it discriminated between Caribbean and Southeast Asian countries in providing the former with technical and financial assistance and transition periods for fishermen to start using TEDs (WTO 1998b; Shaw and Schwartz 2002: 146–9). This decision gave rise to a more comprehensive consideration of environmental concerns. First, it recognized that trade restrictions based on PPMs could be used for the purpose of environmental protection. Second, it allowed in principal for the application of such trade sanctions outside member states' borders. Third, the Appellate Body did not dismiss comments (*'amicus curiae* briefs') made by US-based environmental NGOs, thus admitting that WTO panels could consider unsolicited information submitted by interested private groups (Kelemen 2001: 638). Nevertheless, the scope of the Article xx(g) exception validated by the decision is still uncertain, in particular as to the kind of environmental measures protected.[18]

Conclusion: bringing standards in by rulings

The new WTO dispute settlement mechanism has certainly promoted both (regulatory) product and PPM standards. Within this new institutional context, member states have been both constrained and empowered to apply their own standards. National standards based on scientific risk assessment or the existence of relevant scientific information may be applied to protect the environment or public health. In the absence of scientific proof, however, other WTO members may challenge them as non-tariff barriers to trade. The cases discussed in this section have exemplified the conflicts of interests in trade disputes – whose 'quasi-supranational' resolution may well raise fears of interference.

In contrast to Howse and Regan (2000: 252), for whom 'it is likely that the processes/product distinction will not long remain untouched by WTO jurisprudence', we maintain that this distinction is here to stay for quite some time, even though it might be challenged in some cases such as genetically modified foods. The WTO dispute settlement procedure is not well-suited to 'cases where taste may vary, deep issues of sovereignty are at stake or the offence lies in production process rather than in an observable characteristic of the good concerned' (Rollo and Winters 2000: 574). Even though economic costs might be high, a country may still prefer trade sanctions authorized by the WTO to a change of its national standards.

Finally, even though the 'shrimp/turtle' case might have worked to push environmental concerns into the exceptions of Article xx GATT, a negotiated settlement, as Jackson (2000: 306f.) argues, would be preferable to judicial activism. In other words, besides references in the WTO agreements recommending existing standards and DSB rulings referring to such standards, the WTO contracting parties could directly incorporate PPM standards.

Inscribing environmental and labour standards in WTO agreements?

The codification of environmental or labour standards in the global trade regime is a highly controversial issue. For example, Wolffgang and Feuerhake (2002) argue that due to their human rights character, core labour standards must necessarily be included in the WTO. By contrast, Maskus (2002) argues that on economic grounds, the case for environmental regulatory standards having cross-border effects is weak and core labour standards are even less desirable. Rollo and Winters (2000) altogether reject the idea of bringing environmental and labour standards under the WTO since the organization has neither the technical ability nor the political legitimacy to act effectively in these areas.

In fact, labour standards differ from environmental regulations in important ways that make them less eligible for inclusion in import restrictions. For example, applying the importing country's minimum wage requirement to foreign goods may simply be inappropriate to the economic conditions in the producing country. The discussion thus focuses on the so-called 'core' or 'internationally recognized' labour standards, yet there is no agreement on all the relevant rights, in particular with regard to acceptable conditions of work and the minimum age for the employment of children (cf. Leary 1996: 215f.). In its Declaration on Fundamental Principles and Rights at Work, the International Labour Organization identified four basic workers' rights on the basis of its most fundamental and widely recognized conventions: the freedom of association and collective bargaining, the elimination of all forms of forced labour and of discrimination in the workplace, and the abolition of child labour (ILO 1998). The ILO also declared that all member states have an obligation to implement the related core conventions even if they have not ratified them. According to the WTO, the ILO is the competent body to set and deal with these standards. It has not only the required staff expertise, but a unique tripartite structure including representatives of the main stakeholders (trade unions, business, and governments).

Activists for labour and environmental standards have looked to WTO trade agreements for help because of the organization's dispute settlement procedure – an enforcement mechanism which other institutions and agreements lack. However, we argue that the institutional context and conflicting interests among member states are likely to prevent the WTO from defining its own environmental or social regulations.

Institutional context

In the WTO, all member states enjoy equal voting power, and decision making is clearly driven by member states. In the past, GATT decision making worked well because there were fewer countries actively engaged and no compulsion for all members to adhere to the results. WTO decision making has been complicated by more participants with more diverse interests and more complex issues on the agenda. Even though decisions are taken by consensus,[19] negotiations within the WTO are either 'law-based' or 'power-based'. Steinberg (2002: 341) defines law-based bargaining as a situation in which member states take procedural rules seriously 'attempting to build a consensus … yielding market-opening contracts that are roughly symmetrical'. In power-based bargaining, however, member states refer to their market size and trade volume in order to 'generate outcomes that are asymmetrical' (Steinberg 2002: 341). He shows that the launching of trade rounds occurs through law-based bargaining but that the conclusion of such rounds and the (informal) agenda setting process in between are often power-based. Hence, in negotiations on the further reduction of trade barriers and on the accession of new member states, 'powerful' nations can rely on their market size and economic weight. Treaty revisions involving new issues requiring institutional changes to national systems are more likely to imply law-based bargaining since each member state, independent of its market size, can use the veto option. Another limit to 'invisible weighting' is disagreement between the US and the EU and the empowerment of new actors such as China or coalitions of developing countries (Steinberg 2002: 367ff.).[20] The incorporation of environmental and labour standards would require an amendment of the WTO agreements (for example, a modification of Article xx GATT), thus demanding consensus in law-based bargaining. Given the conflicting interests that exist among WTO member states, such a treaty revision seems to be unlikely in the foreseeable future, even if broad package deals are aimed at.

Conflicting interests

With regard to non-trade concerns, the WTO is subject to conflicting pressures: some governments and non-state actors are lobbying for its powers to be expanded (for example, to use trade sanctions to enforce agreements on labour, environmental or other standards), others are pushing in the opposite direction. While most 'advocacy' NGOs (human rights activists, environmental and development groups) as well as some labour unions demand higher social and environmental standards, most industries (and governments) in developing countries oppose them. Before the Singapore Ministerial Conference in 1996, the proponents of non-product related PPM standards advocated without success a reform of Article xx GATT to accommodate environmental concerns. In fact, whereas the EU suggested changing WTO rules, the USA – which is a non-party to many MEAs – claimed that WTO rules provide sufficient scope to protect the environment.[21] 'After 1996, the United States began to rely more on the WTO dispute settlement process, whereas the EU shifted its emphasis to civil society and political declarations on trade and environment' (Jha 2002: 476).

There are approximately 200 MEAs in place today, but only twenty of them contain trade provisions. States are reluctant to refer to them, and so far no MEA measure affecting trade has been challenged in the WTO dispute settlement system. At the Ministerial Conference in Doha (WTO 2001), it was agreed to clarify the relationship between existing WTO rules and specific trade obligations set out in MEAs (for example, the Montreal Protocol on Substances that Deplete the Ozone Layer, the Convention on Biological Diversity with the Cartagena Protocol on Biosafety, the Framework Convention on Climate Change with the Kyoto Protocol, or the Convention on International Trade in Endangered Species). Those MEAs involve bans on the production or trade of particular pollutants (such as chlorofluorocarbons in the Montreal Protocol), set out reductions in emissions (for example, for

carbon dioxide in the Kyoto Protocol), or call for the promotion of internationally agreed goals such as the preservation of biological diversity.

Another important issue arises from the fact that not all WTO members
have ratified the MEAs, so that the application of MEA sanctions could
induce economic damages in third parties and counter-reactions in the
WTO.[22] From this perspective, pressure could rise to globalize the MEAs
through adoption of their rules into the WTO.[23] In addition to clarifying the
issue of trade and MEAs, the Doha trade round is to negotiate a reduction
of trade barriers for environmental goods and services (for example, catalytic
converters, air filters) and to examine whether existing WTO rules stand
in the way of eco-labelling policies. The deadline for the negotiations on
the linkage between trade and environment and on environmental goods
and services, which are taking place in special sessions of the Trade and
Environment Committee, is 1 January, 2005. The eco-labelling policies were
on the agenda of the unsuccessful Fifth WTO Ministerial Conference in
Cancun in September 2003, but the controversial positions of many
member states remained unchanged.

In general, industrialized countries place high priority on the inclusion of
environmental considerations in trade negotiations, whereas developing
countries worry about protectionism (for example, interests of Western
labour unions hiding behind standards in textiles or steel industries) and
intrusion into domestic politics, for example by spill-overs into other areas
such as labour standards (Jha 2002: 475). At the same time, little headway
has been made on supportive measures for developing countries, such as
finance, access to environmentally sound technologies and capacity building. While eco-labelling was initially strongly championed by the USA and
Canada, these countries now question it with regard to GMOs, arguing that
the products were safe and testing would be prohibitively expensive.
Ironically, similar concerns raised by developing countries regarding
eco-labelling of textiles and footwear were dismissed on the grounds that
consumer preferences should be catered to (Jha 2002: 474f.). Nevertheless,
developing countries are not simply resisting changes in the WTO (for
example, modification of Article xx GATT, eco-labelling, environmental
reviews of trade policies), but actively seeking reforms of the TRIPs
Agreement regarding transfer of technology and biodiversity, of provisions
on market access and on trade in domestically prohibited goods.

The issue of trade and social standards continues to be an even more
controversial topic than the discussions on trade and environment (cf. Addo
2002). Labour standards are not subject to any WTO rules or disciplines yet,
except that Article xx(e) GATT permits member states to take measures
restricting market access for products of prison labour.[24] Therefore, the
agreements do not offer exceptions inviting broader interpretation in fayour
of labour standards by the DSB. A WTO agreement on core labour standards
might require member states to ban exploitative use of child workers,

eliminate forced labour, prevent discrimination and allow free association of workers and collective bargaining, and it might permit them to ban imports of offending goods.

In the final stage of the Uruguay Round in 1994, the USA and France suggested that a 'social clause' be incorporated into the WTO's framework (Hoekman and Kostecki 2001: 449). Their attempt to establish a working party on basic worker rights (excluding minimum wages) – presumably as a precondition for market access – failed. The issue was again put forward by the USA, Canada and France (supported by the EU) at the 1996 Singapore Ministerial Conference and three years later by the US government in the run-up to the Seattle Ministerial Conference. Once more, the idea was rejected by the developing countries as hidden protectionism and an interference in their domestic affairs. The Doha Ministerial Conference 2001 simply reaffirmed the declaration made at the 1996 Singapore meeting in which the International Labour Organization had been identified as the competent body. The ILO advocates the instrument of moral suasion rather than that of coercive trade sanctions to implement the labour standards which it sets and monitors. In any event, the Doha Ministerial Declaration allows for a first cooperation of the WTO with other international organizations in this area; for instance, regarding the ILO's 'Working Party on the Social Dimension of Globalization' (WTO 2001).

Conclusion: bringing standards in by treaty revision?

Given the consensus requirement for treaty amendments and the member states' conflicting interests, there is little reason to expect an inclusion of environmental or social standards in the near future. In fact, 'there is widespread recognition that trade policy has little if any role to play in the pursuit of environmental objectives, that the WTO does not restrict the use of green policies by members, that MEAs are the appropriate instrument to address global environmental problems, and that carrots, not sticks are called for if a country seeks to induce another to adopt stricter environmental norms' (Hoekman and Kostecki 2001: 448).

As an alternative to the cumbersome treaty revisions, one might attempt to raise national levels worldwide or to promote the adoption of voluntary standards, in particular by multinational enterprises. Among the voluntary social and environmental standards are company, sector-specific or generic codes and labels, for example the US–Canadian chemical industry's Responsible Care programme, Fairtrade, or the ISO 14000 environmental management standard (cf. Nadvi and Wältring 2002: 23). In addition, NGOs might push for voluntary eco- and social labelling or consumer boycotts ('naming and shaming') to create incentives for producers to adopt new technologies. In addition, uni- or multilateral aid could be used to motivate developing countries to increase their standards. Even though the WTO is not an agency for the protection of the environment or workers' rights, it needs to find a *modus operandi* regarding environmental and labour standards. Ignoring these issues might lead to more aggressive unilateral use of trade measures against countries with lower standards, to a lesser willingness of industrialized countries to maintain liberal trade policies, or to more regional integration agreements with side agreements on these issues (Anderson 2001: 245f.).

Conclusion: durable 'double standard' on standards

There are many ways by which the World Trade Organization is governing global trade. With regard to non-trade concerns, the WTO is importing externally produced standards instead of competing with – more competent – standard-setting institutions. Harmonization would indeed be a very cumbersome task for a consensus-driven intergovernmental trade organization with 148 members. The WTO does not lead regulatory practices, but it follows them; and it envisages the use of voluntary standards instead of compulsory regulation wherever possible. The principles of non-discrimination work on the presumption that if a state is applying an internationally agreed standard, its action cannot constitute a barrier to trade. The WTO's objective is not to regulate trade by standards, but to facilitate trade; and its dispute settlement system does not aim at regulatory control, but at resolving conflicts between states.

The mechanisms of global trade governance which introduce standards into the WTO regime rely on two techniques: references in the agreements and rulings. Both create linkages between the World Trade Organization and standard-setting bodies or agreements. In this governance effort, however, the WTO has established a 'double standard': while member states may apply product standards equally to domestic and imported goods, they may enforce standards of process and production methods only at home. Table 10.1 summarizes the sources of the different kinds of standards.

We have argued that this 'double standard' is due to the member states' fears of interference, their conflicting interests and the WTO's institutional

Table 10.1   Typology of standards

	Voluntary standards	*Regulatory standards*
Product standards	Business and NGOs National and international standardization bodies TBT and SPS Agreements	National laws, MEAs TBT and SPS Agreements GATT dispute settlement
PPM standards	Business and NGOs National and international standardization bodies TBT and SPS Agreements	National laws, MEAs, ILO TBT and SPS Agreements WTO dispute settlement

context, and we conclude that this dichotomy might well be durable. The option of directly codifying environmental and labour standards by a revision of the WTO treaties (or, respectively, even to refer to such existing international standards) faces very low chances. The WTO does not impose any constraints on a member state regarding the pursuit of environmental or social policies on its territory, but it does prevent the extraterritorial enforcement of national standards. PPM standards may only be applied to imports if it can be shown that the processes targeted have repercussions for the physical qualities of a product or if an exception under Article xx GATT is justified. In the 'shrimp/turtle' case of 1998, the WTO Appellate Body signalled that extraterritorial application of national standards can be legal under Article xx GATT. Developing countries' fears that this decision might open the door for import bans due to working conditions are, however, unfounded as Article xx makes no mention of labour standards.

An advantage of the 'double standard' is that the product–process distinction serves as a clear and simple rule regarding foreign products: production processes occur in the exporting state and are not under the jurisdiction of the importing state, while products coming into the territory of the importing state are. Bringing in external standards provides the WTO (1) a degree of insulation from criticism; (2) a device that may evade the need for unanimity, or at least consensus, within the WTO; (3) an opportunity for subject-matter specialists, as opposed to trade specialists, to take a leading role in formulating the standards; and (4) the possibility – subject to the difficulty of changing WTO law – still later to override outside sources of standards (cf. Marceau and Trachtman 2002: 840). In addition, Gehring (2002: 135) argues that the introduction of environmental and safety standards into the world trade order strengthens their binding force and at the same time creates incentives for raising the levels of protection.

Yet, the importation of standards by reference or ruling is not without problems. It runs the risk of taking over the problems that might come with those standards such as a lack of transparency and legitimacy of certain standard-setting procedures or a tendency to produce only minimum standards (Gehring 2002: 132f.). Moreover, the TBT and SPS Agreements strongly encourage countries to adopt product standards that are at least as rigorous as those developed by international standard-setting bodies. It can be assumed that over time, all WTO members implement such regulations. Developing economies thus have no choice but to meet those standards, at least for exports, even though they often lack the necessary capacities and resources (Wilson 2002: 437).

In sum, the World Trade Organization remains one important link in the network of private and public actors who are involved in the process of setting, monitoring and enforcing standards. The current mechanisms of global trade governance show that the coordination between trade and non-trade concerns can be improved without turning the WTO into a 'catch-all' organization.

Notes

1 We thus follow the analytical strand in the global governance debate, which attempts to investigate empirically how global governance actually works, instead of the normative strand searching for prescriptive solutions in view of normative goals.

2 There are a few studies on institutional change in standard setting in specific economic sectors such as information technologies (cf. Genschel 1995).

3 Voluntary standards may, all the same, constitute a source of technical barriers to trade, for instance when consumers prefer certain seals of approval or require compatibility with complementary products, or when government procurement or insurers require compliance (Sykes 1995: 13–15).

4 In some cases, the distinction is blurred as process concerns are incorporated into product features (for example, organic food).

5 In practice, institutions, interference, and interests are often hard to separate: the WTO institutional features such as the decision making and dispute settlement processes may involve fears of interference and conflicting interests, actors articulate their worries and interests within specific institutions, and sovereignty concerns themselves may be considered a specific interest.

6 In addition, the Agreement on Trade-related Aspects of Intellectual Property Rights (TRIPs), which deals with both product and PPM standards, directly requires the application of external minimum standards for the global protection of intellectual assets (for example, copyrights, patents, geographical origins, trademarks, industrial designs) and introduces a few new regulations.

7 The counter-argument claims that the sovereignty of the importing country is invaded by denying it the right to exclude products produced by processes it abhors.

8 As an example, quality management standards (for example, ISO 9000) are to a great extent business-driven and voluntary, except for health and food safety standards. Environmental and social standards range from company codes of conduct (for example, Reebok) and sector labels (for example, Eco-tex) to NGO-business defined standards (for example, Rugmark) and tripartite social minimum standards (for example, SA 8000) which try to give the conventions of the International Labour Organization more policy impact.

9 In addition, Article xxi GATT exempts measures in case of essential security interests. Similar provisions can be found in Article xiv and xivbis GATS (General Agreement on Trade in Services) and in Article 27 TRIPs.

10 The so-called Standards Code encouraged GATT members to resort to international (voluntary and regulatory) product standards and to justify decisions to depart from them on request (Sykes 1995: 70–7).

11 Some developing countries have argued that the TBT Agreement does not cover PPM regulations – in which case they would be examined under Articles iii/xi and xx GATT (Marceau and Trachtman 2002: 861f.).

12 The EU failed in its attempt to have other criteria such as 'genuine consumer concerns' and animal welfare included (Skogstad 2001: 493). These are legitimate criteria for technical regulations under the TBT Agreement but not under the SPS Agreement.

13 Marceau and Trachtman (2002: 838) argue that the SPS Agreement appoints the three sisters as 'quasi-legislators' of international standards in the sense that they have certain force in creating a presumption of WTO/SPS compatibility.

14 This equivalence provision mitigates somewhat the pressure to adopt the standards of the three sisters instead of higher levels of protection.

15 For a detailed legal description of the disciplines on domestic regulation provided by the GATT, SPS and TBT Agreements, see Marceau and Trachtman (2002).

16 By contrast, the EU Scientific Committee on Veterinary Measures concluded on the basis of scientific evidence that hormones could produce tumours.

17 The Appellate Body found that the measure at stake qualified for provisional justification under Article xx(g) ('conservation of exhaustible natural resources'), but failed to meet the requirements of the chapeau of Article xx (no 'arbitrary or unjustifiable discrimination between countries' or 'disguised restriction on international trade'), and, therefore, was not justified under Article xx GATT.

18 For example, the Appellate Body's observation that sea turtles belonged to no one and that some swam in US waters leaves doubts as to whether the decision might not be limited to protection of migratory species within the global commons (Hudec 2000: 188).

19 Consensus is achieved if no member state present disagrees with a decision. Votes rarely occur, but can be held if there is no consensus. According to Steinberg (2002: 365), the practice of consensus persists because it helps powerful states to generate legitimacy as well as the necessary information about the other members' preferences.

20 Developing countries increasingly demand procedural reforms to ensure inclusive and transparent negotiations. The traditional 'green room' process, in which a small number of self-selected, important countries resolves divisive issues before submitting them to the larger membership for final decision, excluded most developing countries.

21 On the different positions on how to settle the WTO–MEA debate, see Motaal (2001: 1218–26).

22 For example, in August 2003, the USA, Canada and Argentina requested the establishment of a WTO panel on the EU's authorization system for genetically modified organisms (GMOs). The USA is not a party to the Biosafety Protocol which regulates trade in GMOs and seeks to protect human health and biodiversity. While the WTO DSB would have to take this MEA into consideration, the result of a ruling is open to speculation.

23 Other suggestions include waivers, a specification of WTO rules, joint WTO–MEA interpretations, consultative mechanisms, or dispute settlement systems within the MEA themselves (cf. Sampson 2001; Shaw and Schwartz 2002: 134ff.).

24 The draft 1948 Havanna Charter of the ill-fated International Trade Organization included an article on fair labour standards.

References

Abbott, K.W. and Snidal, D. (2001) 'International "standards" and international governance', in *Journal of European Public Policy*, 8(3), 345–70.

Addo, K. (2002) 'The correlation between labour standards and international trade: Which way forward?', in *Journal of World Trade*, 36(2), 285–303.

Anderson, K. (2001) 'Environmental and labor standards: What role for the WTO?', in Krueger, A.O. (ed.), *The WTO as an International Organization*, Chicago: University of Chicago Press, 231–55.

GATT (1991) 'United States – Restrictions on Import of Tuna', Report of the Panel (DS21/R-39S/155).

Gehring, T. (2002) 'Schutzstandards in der WTO? Die schleichende Verknüpfung der Welthandelsorganisation mit standardsetzenden internationalen Institutionen', in Jachtenfuchs, M. and Knodt, M. (eds), *Regieren in internationalen Institutionen*, Opladen: Leske & Budrich, 111–39.

Genschel, P. (1995) *Standards in der Informationstechnik: Institutioneller Wandel in der internationalen Standardisierung*, Frankfurt am Main: Campus.

Hoekman, B.M. and Kostecki, M.M. (2001) *The Political Economy of the World Trading System: The WTO and Beyond*, 2nd edn, Oxford: Oxford University Press.

Howse, R. and Regan, D. (2000) 'The product/process distinction: An illusionary basis for disciplining "unilateralism" in international law', in *European Journal of International Law*, 11(2), 249–89.

Hudec, R.E. (2000) 'The product–process doctrine in GATT/WTO jurisprudence', in Bronckers, M. and Quick, R. (eds), *New Directions in International Economic Law: Essays in Honour of John H. Jackson*, The Hague: Kluwer Law International, 187–217.

ILO (International Labour Organization) (1998) 'Declaration on fundamental principles and rights at work', Geneva, 18 June, 1998, taken from *www.ilo.org/public/english/standards/decl/declaration/text/index.htm*

Jackson, J.H. (2000) 'Comments on shrimp/turtle and the product/process distinction', in *European Journal of International Law*, 11(2), 303–7.

Jha, V. (2002) 'Environmental regulation and the WTO', in Hoekman, B.M., Mattoo, A. and English, P. (eds), *Development, Trade, and the WTO: A Handbook*, Washington, DC: The World Bank, 472–81.

Kelemen, R.D. (2001) 'The limits of judicial power: Trade-environment disputes in the GATT/WTO and the EU', in *Comparative Political Studies*, 34(6), 622–50.

Leary, V.A. (1996) 'Workers' rights and international trade: The social clause (GATT, ILO, NAFTA, US laws)', in Baghwati, J. and Hudec, R.E. (eds), *Fair Trade and Harmonization: Prerequisites for Free Trade?*, vol. 2, Cambridge, MA: MIT Press, 177–230.

Marceau, G. and Trachtman, J.P. (2002) 'The Technical Barriers to Trade Agreement, the Sanitary and Phytosanitary Measures Agreement, and the General Agreement on Tariffs and Trade: A map of the World Trade Organization law of domestic regulation of goods', in *Journal of World Trade*, 36(5), 811–81.

Maskus, K.E. (2002) 'Regulatory standards in the WTO: Comparing intellectual property rights with competition policy, environmental protection, and core labor standards', in *World Trade Review*, 1(2), 135–52.

Mattli, W. (2001) 'The politics and economics of international institutional standards setting: An introduction', in *Journal of European Public Policy*, 8(3), 328–44.

Motaal, D.A. (2001) 'Multilateral Environmental Agreements (MEAs) and WTO rules', in *Journal of World Trade*, 35(6), 1215–33.

Nadvi, K. and Wältring, F. (2002) 'Making sense of global standards', INEF Report, 58, Duisburg: Institut für Entwicklung und Frieden der Gerhard-Mercator-Universität Duisburg.

OECD (1998) 'Regulatory reform and international standardisation', Paris: Working Party of the Trade Committee (TD/TC/WP(98)36/FINAL).

Robertson, D. (2000) 'Civil society and the WTO', in *The World Economy*, 23(9), 1119–34.

Rollo, J. and Winters, L.A. (2000) 'Subsidiarity and governance challenges for the WTO: Environmental and labour standards', in *The World Economy*, 23(4), 561–76.

Sampson, G.P. (2001) 'Effective Multilateral Environment Agreements and why the WTO needs them', in *The World Economy*, 24(9), 1109–34.

Shaw, S. and Schwartz, R. (2002) 'Trade and environment in the WTO: State of play', in *Journal of World Trade*, 36(1), 129–54.

Skogstad, G. (2001) 'The WTO and food safety regulatory policy innovation in the European Union', in *Journal of Common Market Studies*, 39(3), 485–505.

Steinberg, R.H. (2002) 'In the shadow of law or power? Consensus-based bargaining and outcomes in the GATT/WTO', in *International Organization*, 56(2), 339–74.

Sykes, A.O. (1995) *Product Standards for Internationally Integrated Goods Markets*, Washington, DC: The Brookings Institution.

Wilson, J.S. (2002) 'Standards, regulation, and trade: WTO rules and developing country concerns', in Hoekman, B.M., Mattoo, A. and English, P. (eds), *Development, Trade, and the WTO: A Handbook*, Washington, DC: The World Bank, 428–38.

Wolffgang, H.-M. and Feuerhake, W. (2002) 'Core labour standards in World Trade law: The necessity for incorporation of core labour standards in the World Trade Organization', in *Journal of World Trade*, 36(5), 883–901.

WTO (2002a) 'World Bank grant kicks off bank-WTO assistance on standards', Press Release, 314, 27 September, 2002. *www.wto.org/english/news_e/pres02_e/ pr314_e.htm*

WTO (2002b) 'European communities – trade description of sardines', Appellate Body Report (WT/DS231/AB/R).

WTO (2001) Ministerial Declaration, Doha, 14 November, 2001 (WT/MIN(01)/DEC/1).

WTO (1998a) 'EC measures concerning meat and meat products (hormones)', Appellate Body Report (WT/DS26/AB/R and WT/DS48/AB/R).

WTO (1998b) 'United States – import prohibition of certain shrimp and shrimp products', Appellate Body Report (WT/DS58/AB/R).

11
ASEAN+3: The Failure of Global Governance and the Construction of Regional Institutions

Dirk Nabers

Introduction

The debate that has taken place in IR between rationalists and social constructivists in the last fifteen years has been rather confusing, especially when it came to empirical testing of the various hypotheses put forward by one or the other side. The confusion stems from the simple fact that both theories are rooted in different metatheoretical orientations. As various German scholars suggested in the so-called 'ZIB-Debate' in the 1990s,[1] the IR community should not overstress the variation in metatheoretical orientations, such as rational choice capturing the 'logic of consequentialism' and constructivism covering either the 'logic of appropriateness' or the 'logic of arguing' (for example, Müller 1994; Risse 2000). Since both modes of action are ideal types that hardly ever happen in real life, one should rather stick to a combination of the two or ask which logic might dominate in a given situation.

Within the broad frame of rationalism, especially (neoliberal) institutionalism has convincingly shown that cooperation between states is likely when maximizing one's own interests is only possible through cooperative behaviour. However, constructivists maintain that states' interests and preferences are not fixed during the process of interaction, an important matter that is often neglected by rationalism. It might though be possible to combine institutionalist arguments for cooperation with the constructivist claim that agents do not exist independent from their social environment and intersubjective meanings (see Checkel 1997, 2001; Keohane 2000).

In the following analysis, I will try to show that rational utilitarianism can, in part, be compatible with ideational accounts that stress identity building, intersubjectivity and communicative action in international politics. My approach employs both institutionalist and constructivist insights, however stressing the 'value added' that constructivism brings in. Drawing on the development of a new regional institution in East Asia as a test case, I will try to specify how instrumental interests of state actors and ideas, cultural understandings and identities can be connected theoretically.

In the next section I will briefly explain my empirical case, before proceeding with an explanation of the rationalist–constructivist divide. After that I will lay down specifically my methodological approach. Finally, I illustrate my arguments through the analysis of the ASEAN plus three process. I will use discourse analysis as a tool to elucidate the rearticulation of identities over time and as a method that helps us comprehend the interpretative schemes that serve as the basis of state interests.

Puzzle: cooperation in East Asia

International cooperation in East Asia has been a hot topic since the beginning of the 1990s. The origin of a genuine regional cooperation process combining both Northeast and Southeast Asia can be seen in Malaysian Prime Minister Mahathir's proposal for an East Asian Economic Grouping (EAEG) in the early 1990s. This initiative was immediately rejected by non-East Asian countries. Japan, as the vital participant from Northeast Asia, also held back support because of concerns that its membership would antagonize the USA, its closest ally. However, ASEAN tried to save the idea by proposing an East Asian Economic Caucus (EAEC) within the framework of APEC (Hund and Ofken 2001; Layador 2000; Nabers 2002a,b).

In the years that followed, the political landscape in Asia changed to a great extent (Dosch and Mols 2000; Eilenberger *et al.* 1996; Mack and Ravenhill 1994; Maull and Nabers 2001; McGrew and Brook 1998; Ravenhill 2001; Rüland 2002), including the formation of new regional institutions like the ASEAN Regional Forum (ARF) or the ASEAN Free Trade Area (AFTA) as well as a new interregional institution, the Asia Europe Meeting (ASEM). The same countries that were the target of the EAEC/EAEG idea came together as one united group for the first time in ASEM, representing the East Asia component of that interregional process at the ministerial and senior official level (cf. Harris 2000: 511). The impetus for cooperation seemed to intensify amid widespread critique of the failure of the International Monetary Fund (IMF) during the Asian financial troubles. Public support for the IMF reform programmes was undermined by the fact that modern social safety nets in the ASEAN countries did not exist at the time. This intensified the perceived pain of restructuring (Lewis 1999). While already existing within the borders of ASEM, the first East Asian Summit (EAS) was held in Kuala Lumpur in December 1997. It was sponsored by ASEAN and paved the way for what has subsequently become known as the ASEAN plus three cooperation. Before long, a process of steady institutionalization developed within the institution, including ministerial rounds, senior official meetings (SOM) and proposals to establish an East Asia Vision Group.[2] It was in Hanoi in December 1998 where the heads of state or government of the ASEAN members plus China, Japan and South Korea decided that regular meetings be held among them. The next summit meetings took place in Manila in November 1999 and in Singapore in November of the following year. Other meetings of the forum included those of the finance and foreign ministers of the thirteen countries (Webber 2001).

The finance ministerial meeting of May 2000 in Chiang Mai, Thailand, can be seen as the basis for a beginning of region-wide financial and economic cooperation. The adoption of the so-called Chiang Mai initiative set a framework for cooperation in the areas of capital flow monitoring, self-help and support mechanisms, and international financial reforms. It seeks not only to switch information on capital flows and smooth the progress of mutual surveillance, but also to set up regional financing arrangements to complement the existing international facilities. The extension of the currency swap accord exemplifies the sincerity of East Asians to strengthen regional cooperation. This makes temporary foreign currency support available for crisis affected countries in East Asia (Henning 2002: 12–47; Layador 2000: 439).

In detail, the thirteen countries involved in the process agreed to execute a series of currency swap arrangements between their central banks, consenting to lend each other part of their hard currency reserves if any of their currencies came under speculative pressure. As a result of the Chiang Mai initiative, in May 2001, Japan announced bilateral deals with South Korea, Thailand and Malaysia. Together with the US$1 billion announced by the ASEAN countries in November 2000, the mutual central bank support comprised more than US$700 billion in reserves. In July, Japan and the Philippines reached a basic agreement to set up a US$3 billion-peso swap facility as part of the envisaged Asia-wide currency safety net (*South China Morning Post*, 14 July, 2001). Until the end of 2002, Japan signed swap arrangements with South Korea, Thailand, the Philippines, Malaysia, China and Indonesia (*Financial Times*, 28 March, 2002; Nabers 2003). In addition to the pact with Japan, China has another swap agreement with Thailand, while South Korea has also been holding negotiations with Malaysia, the Philippines and Thailand (*Financial Times*, 13 May, 2001; *Japan Times*, 8 May, 2002). China and South Korea have also worked out an deal for a bilateral swap agreement (*Financial Times*, 13 May, 2001). Fourteen agreements have been announced as of the end of 2002. Complementing this process are growing currency reserves in the respective ASEAN plus three countries. While South Korea's reserves have risen from US$74 billion to US$94 billion over a period of just one year, China exhibits an even higher growth rate, from US$260 billion to over US$300 billion (*Far Eastern Economic Review*, 12 July 2001).

For the time being, there is neither a central body or authority that is in charge of overseeing or administering the agreements, nor is there a pooling of foreign exchange reserves in a central account (Henning 2002: 18). ASEAN plus three, as an institution, cannot make a decision about the activation of a swap on its specific terms. What is happening under the initiative could rather be called 'organized bilateralism'. Nevertheless, the network of swap arrangements could be described as a rather significant development because potential borrowers have concluded multiple swaps, which are large in comparison to these countries' quotas with the IMF.

It is this process that requires further explanation. Why do countries such as Japan or China participate in the process? And in what direction have the interests and identities of the members developed since 1997? To answer these questions, it might be helpful to explore the theoretical literature about cooperation more closely. It will be illustrated that different approaches exist in IR theory for the explanation of the initiation and development of international institutions. The problem of explaining international institutionalized cooperation will prove a fruitful site for developing a broader conception of political science that is able to combine rationalist with constructivist approaches.

Method: identity-building in international politics

The main question to be addressed in the article is: What kind of pressures lead to communicative processes in international politics and how do initially self-interested actors eventually 'learn' to consider the interests of others as if they were their own? This question is closely connected with the concept of 'collective identity'. It means that state actors are still rational, but they start to calculate their interests on the basis of the group of which they are a member.

To make the process leading to collective identity a little clearer, let us first look at what makes international interaction or communication possible in the first place. Using institutionalist insights, one can assume that states initially engage in pro-communicative activities for egoistic reasons; for example, because state goals cannot be pursued unilaterally. The argument depends on a mechanism of functional institutional efficiency in order to account for social change. Yet, institutionalist theories can only explain initial short-term, behavioral cooperation; that is, the impetus for engaging in communicative action, but fail to account for the development of long-term communal collaboration (for a critique, cf. Sterling-Folker 2000). On the other hand, the social constructivist model maintains that agents themselves are in process when they interact, which means that their very properties rather than just behaviours are at issue. Interdependence, common fate and a homogenous culture can, in this sense, be seen as 'independent variables', good for instigating states' engagement in communicative processes (Wendt 1999: ch. 7).

In the classical definition of Keohane's and Nye's Power and Interdependence, the concept of interdependence refers to a state of mutual dependence; that is, a situation in which one actor is being determined or significantly affected by the forces of another actor. Interdependent relationships always involve costs, since autonomy of choice is restricted. Such a situation can either imply mutual losses or gains. It is the asymmetries of interdependence that provide sources of influence for states in their relations with other states (Keohane and Nye 2001: ch. 1). Interdependence can occur in the economic field (for example, through growing international trade) but also in the political, as Buzan puts it in his definition of a regional security complex: 'It is possible to identify regional *security complexes* as sets of states whose national securities are sufficiently interdependent that it is impossible to consider them separately' (Buzan *et al.* 1998: 71).

Buzan's definition of a security complex shows how closely the concept of interdependence is connected to a second possible reason for a country to engage in communicative action; that is, common fate. States face a common fate when the existence or interests depend on what happens to a group as a whole. The difference is that interdependence implies an interactive moment while common fate has no such insinuation, it 'is constituted by a third party which defines the first two as a group' (Wendt 1999: 349). Finally, another possible cause for engagement in communicative action is homogeneity. In the case of states, the variation could be in their domestic regime type – democracy or authoritarianism, capitalism or socialism – but it also entails a subjective dimension in that states categorize themselves as being alike with regard to the features that define a group (Wendt 1999: 353–4).

As has been said before these variables serve the purpose of setting off a state's engagement in communicative processes. Yet they seem to be inadequate for explaining the erosion of egoistic identities over time and the creation of collective ones. Few institutions will be steady if their members are occupied by an ongoing reckoning over whether norm-conformity serves their individual interests. Consequently, we assume that identities and interests are a continuing outcome of interaction, not just an input into the institutional process.

However, the question as to why identities and their corresponding interests are transformed in the institutional communicative process has not been answered. One question remains: What makes states change their respective standpoints in the institutional communicative context? We have seen that interdependence, common fate and homogeneity can be 'efficient' causes of pro-communicative engagement, which will eventually lead to a transformation of state identities. But this process can only ensue if states can surmount their apprehension of being engulfed by those with whom they would identify. The principle of 'reflected appraisals' introduced into IR theory by Wendt helps solve this problem. If one state treats the other as if it were a friend, then by this principle it is likely that the state internalizes that belief (Wendt 1999: 327). Creating a basic confidence is therefore the fundamental problem of international institution building. Wendt's process is described in Figure 11.1 (Wendt 1999: 330–1).

The political acts of the states that communicate with each other constitute signals about the role that one wants to play and about the corresponding role into which it wants to cast its opponent. If State B modifies its ideas because of State A's political action, then learning has taken place. If this is the case, the actors 'will get to know each other, changing a distribution of knowledge that was initially only privately held (a mere social structure) into one that is at least partly shared (a culture)' (Wendt 1999: 331). From a constructivist standpoint, the mark of a completely internalized culture is that actors identify with it, and include the wishes, ideas, and intentions of others into their own ideas. If identity is nothing other than to have certain ideas about who one is in a given situation, then the sense of being part of a group 'is a social or collective identity that gives actors an interest in the preservation of their culture' (ibid.: 337). Certainly, State A can also take the role of an egoist or cast State B in a position to be manipulated for the satisfaction of its own needs. This might then threaten the needs of State B, who will probably adopt an egoistic identity himself and act accordingly.

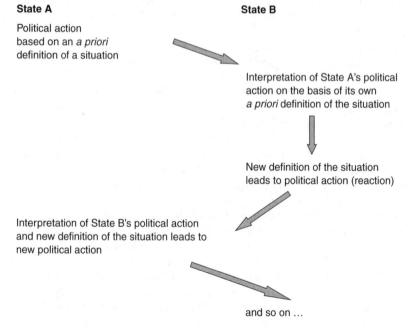

Figure 11.1   Learning processes in international politics
Source: Wendt 1999: 330–1.

In short, the nature of international relations is determined by the ideas and beliefs that states have about each other. This does not suggest that material power and interests are irrelevant, but rather that their implications and effects are constituted by the social structure of the system. In taking the state system as the central level of analysis, we do not have to scrutinize in detail what the state is made of: 'Even if we lacked detailed knowledge about actors and their intentions, we should be able to explain, and even predict, patterns of their behavior if we know the structure of rules in which they are embedded' (Wendt 1999: 184).

It is, in other words, the social structure of the system, the communication processes that occur in the institutional context, that have to be emphasized in the analysis; it is the 'material world' of institutional actors, the institutional-identitive linkages that have to be explored in the empirical scrutiny; it is discourse analysis that helps us come to terms with the rearticulation of identities over time and that helps us comprehend the interpretative schemes that insert meaning into state interests (Waever 1995). In this sense, discourses are treated as possible sources of foreign policy (Larsen 1997: 21) in that they construct social identities of actors, which eventually constitute state interests.

Before explaining the way that discourses can be studied, let us just briefly clarify how they are defined in the following empirical investigation. The most pragmatic definition is provided by van Dijk, who sees discourse quite generally as 'text in context' (van Dijk 1977). Van Dijk also points out that discourse should be understood as an act of communication. Because of intertextuality, there can, in principle, be no objective starting point and no conclusion of a discourse, since every speech act is connected with many others and can only be understood on the basis of others. As an act of communication, 'discourse is socially constituted as well as socially conditioned – it constitutes situations, objects of knowledge, and the social identities of and relationships between people and groups of people. It is constitutive both in the sense that it helps sustain and reproduce the social status quo, and in the sense that it contributes to transforming it' (Wodak 1996: 15).

In that sense, discourses also have transformative effects on culture. This point has to be emphasized because we expect current discourses in East Asia to have ongoing effects on the regional culture of cooperation. Altering values and norms are in a changing relationship with the social production of discourse and must therefore be included in the analysis (Titscher *et al.* 2000: 27). To put it briefly, the context of discourse is constantly being recreated through the discourse, which in turn influences the context of the latter.

An important question then is how we study discourses as a means of explaining the transformation of state identities in international institutions. The first aspect that is of relevance here is the exploration of repetitive statements in major speeches of government representatives because those speech acts 'convey the logic of the government as they wish to express it' (Hoffmann and Knowles 1999: 17). Whether or not political actors really mean what they say is of minor importance, because they will always put forward their arguments strategically; both opportunistic and honest arguments have real consequences for their advocates and the outcome of the debate (see also Schimmelfennig 2001: 66). Neither can we expect with absolute certainty that a dominant discourse will evolve. There is no warranty that one particular discourse will overpower all its contenders and become a predominant interpretative framework. The battle between discourses to become the leading interpretative structure actually tends to reveal the configuration of power relations in a given historical moment, but they are so multifaceted that we cannot foresee their exact outcomes (Smith 1998: 57). However, once a discourse reaches the stage of establishing a dominant perception of reality for all those participating in the communicative process, it reveals a lot about the course of action in collective identity formation (Hoffmann and Knowles 1999: 15). If it is reflected in the speech acts of all interacting agents, we can speak of collective identity. Our focus will thus be on intra-institutional discourses; that is, the deliberations leading to the emergence of a dominant institutional discourse.

Particularly in so-called 'organic crises' (Laclau 1977: 103, referring to Gramsci), existing identities are apt to collapse and new dominant discourses can evolve. In such a crisis, more and more actors open themselves up for innovative discourses, and hegemonic strategies can be successful. The network of existing social structures is increasingly considered an obstacle on the path to one's 'true self'; the evolving hegemonic discourse, on the other hand, reinforces a specific actor's identity crisis by offering alternative identity concepts.

As (in our case) it is multilateral in nature, this transition is a highly complex venture, encompassing a fundamental reconstruction of existing values and identities. It is a process that can be summed up as follows:

(1) At the beginning there is the 'organic crisis', a catastrophe like the Asian crisis starting in 1997, that might weaken dominant discourses; that is, dominant perceptions of reality.
(2) Alternative discourses start to compete in their interpretation of the crisis. Sooner or later, one predominant interpretation will evolve, which institutes the framework that determines what action is appropriate and what action is inappropriate to end the predicament (Laclau 1990: 64).
(3) Old identities tend to dissolve with the construction of newly established dominant interpretative frameworks.
(4) New identities will then generate new kinds of political action along the lines of the dominant interpretative framework (cf. also Laclau 1977). In short, the process, which will inform the following empirical analysis, evolves as shown in Figure 11.2.

While an analysis of a domestic discourse on a particular topic faces the problem of a boundless amount of available actors and sources, the fund is

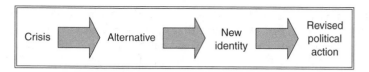

Figure 11.2 Collective identity formation in international politics

much easier to survey if limited to the international system. The study concentrates on speech-acts of decision makers that directly refer to the international institution, official statements – issued by state governments – concerning the institution, representative declarations and communiqués. In detail, it will bring together official statements by heads of states and governments, their respective foreign, finance and trade ministers as well as state secretaries of foreign affairs on issues of regional cooperation, press releases and summaries of press conferences by the member governments, background information issued by the various governments concerning ASEAN plus three, joint statements by the heads of states or foreign ministers of the ASEAN plus three countries and official speeches held by delegates during the ASEAN plus three forum.

I will now analyze the ASEAN plus three process along the lines of this methodical framework. As a result of the analysis, I expect to detect a profound change in existing identities as the basis of international cooperation in East Asia.

Analysis: interests and identities in East Asia

Crisis

Let us first look at the material interests behind the ASEAN plus three-initiative. It has been argued above that growing interdependence, common fate and a homogeneous culture can be seen as variables that are able to bring about states' engagement in communicative processes. Looking at the discourse concerning the Asian Crisis, those factors are of major importance. The progressive integration of markets in East Asia has obviously bestowed the countries of the region with shared economic interests.[3] The first aspect that is of importance here is interdependence. It was the Asian financial that eventually invigorated Mahathir's quiescent EAEC project.[4] Two factors apparently contributed to the establishment of ASEAN plus three: interdependence and an external shock. This is expressed clearly by Japan: 'If we are lax in these efforts towards integration, we may invite more region-wide upheavals similar to the currency crisis. It is therefore important to understand how and in what sense this region, including Japan, is a community with common fate' (MOFA 1999).

A third factor might be called the East Asia factor: it becomes obvious in the discourse over the establishment of the institution that Northeast and

Southeast Asia are integral members of a broader concept,[5] while it is debated whether Australia and New Zealand are part of the region. As Malaysian Minister of Industry and Foreign Trade Rafidah Aziz put it: 'They are not [part of] East Asia. They will have to fit into the APEC process' (*Asia Times Online*, 8 March, 2001). Malaysia's view is backed by Beijing: the last thing the Chinese government wants is Australia, a close US ally, to join the group. Contrary, in January 2002, Japanese Prime Minister Koizumi presented his vision of a vast trading zone covering ASEAN, Japan, China, South Korea plus Australia and New Zealand (for a discussion, see *FEER*, 13 June, 2002).

Categorically, all three factors are related to each other. The financial crisis compelled many Asian countries to re-evaluate their place in the world. 'The crisis has stimulated a new sense of East Asian regionalism and brought the countries closer together', says Tommy Koh, Director of the Institute of Policy Studies in Singapore (quoted in *Financial Times*, 13 May, 2001).

During the communicative process, in particular the region's dependence on the dollar has come to be viewed as problematic. As the Japanese Finance Minister put it on the height of the Asian financial chaos: 'It is now widely acknowledged that maintaining a virtual peg to the U.S. dollar was one of the main reasons for the crises in the emerging economies in Asia' (MOF 1998: 2). By many countries, the yen is seen as the most important currency in the region. Referring to the yen's ups and downs, Malaysian Prime Minister Mahathir Mohammad said in January 2002 that he was really 'interested in the course of the yen, which would affect the Chinese yuan and ASEAN currencies' (*The Nikkei Weekly*, 25 February, 2002).

All in all, the Asian financial crisis demonstrated that the countries of the region are vulnerable to contagion from one another. This effect buttresses the shared interest in crisis prevention and stabilization among countries in the region, which in turn sets them apart from countries outside East Asia (Henning 2002: 6). Malaysia brought its EAEC idea back to the table,[6] and, with no detailed programme at hand to bring the crisis to an end, the ASEAN governments reached out to the leaders of the three Northeast Asian nations – Japan, China and South Korea – in an effort to enliven their economies. In November 1997, the ASEAN heads of state and government invited their three counterparts from Northeast Asia to their summit meeting at Kuala Lumpur. This first meeting and the subsequent summits at Hanoi in 1998 and in Manila in 1999 set the stage for what has henceforth been dubbed the ASEAN plus three process.

Alternative discourses

During the financial crisis, it was widely conceded that the IMF is generally unable to contribute to the strengthening of the supply side of the countries it supports, while its major task is stabilizing the macroeconomic environment. It can help by providing liquidity; yet, it fails when asked for support for real economic activities, such as export financing or buttressing banks' lending capability. Moreover, the financial resources of the IMF are rather limited, since it is an institution with global responsibilities. A research report of the Japanese government concludes that: 'In a word, there is a need for a new institution that plays a role complementary to the IMF's. Such a framework cannot be established on a worldwide scale, though, because forming a consensus among a large number of countries will be difficult and require considerable time. In addition, crises are often a matter of regional concern, and it is perhaps only natural that deeply interdependent countries should help each other out' (*Japan Times*, 14 July 2001).

Many analysts agree that the IMF reform measures were too abrupt and too harsh (for example, Lewis 1999). Furthermore, deeper analysis of documents released by East Asian governments show widespread and open criticism. While the Japanese government points out that the 'crises in Russia and Brazil demonstrated the need to look at the risks inherent in the global financial system itself' (MOFA 2001b: 2), the South Korean government directly addresses the need of 'reforming the international financial architecture, and enhancing self-help and support mechanisms in East Asia through the ASEAN+3 framework' (MOFAT 1999: 1). Agreeing with this view, politicians such as the Japanese Finance Minister Kiichi Miyazawa and South Korean Prime Minister Kim Jong-pil have, from the beginning, encouraged an alternative approach to bringing the crisis to an end, advocating that the IMF is incapable of treating poorly performing Asian economies. Instead of IMF-lead reforms, Miyazawa in particular promotes an Asian Monetary Fund (AMF) as an alternative solution to the financial upheaval.

The first proposal to set up an AMF was advanced by then Japanese Vice Minister of Finance Eisuke Sakakibara in 1997, but was withdrawn later that year in the face of western, in particular American, opposition. Regional leaders, among them Kim Jong-pil, have henceforth incorporated the plan into several policy proposals, before Miyazawa again recommended supplementing IMF loans through 'some kind of regional currency support mechanism ... funded by countries in the region that are strongly dependent upon each other in the fields of trade and investment and that are conducting continuous dialogue with each other on their policy directions' (cited in Lewis 1999).

Above this, by pointing out the EU enlargement process of including former East and Central European states, the ASEAN plus three countries underline a compelling imperative for stronger regional institutions.[7] Member countries argue that this would be built on the principle of subsidiarity where certain functions not effectively served by other mechanisms – the IMF, the Worldbank or APEC – would be performed by this new grouping. Major topics in this context are capital flows, investment and the creation of a self-help support mechanism reducing dependence on funds of the traditional international financial institutions. Continuing in this manner, the institutionalization of the ASEAN plus three process will likely result in the reduction of dependence on institutions such as the IMF and the World Bank for monetary and fiscal assistance and development needs.

In the first couple of years of the ASEAN plus three process, the strategies for reaching economic unity in a common market nonetheless still varied from country to country. Whereas Japan and Singapore bolster the creation of Free Trade Areas (FTAs) in the region (Yun 2002), Malaysia's concept of integration does not necessarily mean the conclusion of such treaties. Instead, together with South Korea, it favours a broader approach to economic integration that would create a wider range of mutual support and benefits (Bae 2001). Yet, China, in November 2000, individually proposed an integration scheme with – according to the Chinese government – more potential than the bilateral trade agreements: an ASEAN–China free trade area. ASEAN hailed the proposal, but seems to be worried about the growing competitiveness of China, especially in light of its newly established membership of the WTO (*The Japan Times*, 29 April 2001).

This, in turn, lead to the Japanese government's decision to set up a study group on the conclusion of a free trade pact with ASEAN. Observers see this as a bid to compete with China (ibid.). Japan coins this strategy a 'multilevel trading policy'. As in the past, however, different identities seem to constitute Japan's, at times, contradictory behaviour in the process. On the one hand, Japan tries to emerge as a leader in the region, while on the other hand trying to maintain its close political and economic relations with the USA. This is the reason why Tokyo has for so long been reluctant to sign FTAs. It feared that this could lead to regional protectionism and criticism by Washington. Hence, it has only recently accepted the idea as a way to complement multilateral trade liberalization under the WTO and as a strategy to balance worldwide moves in the same direction.

Political action

In the first phase of the institutionalization process, political leaders in the region considered regionalism as a form of self-help mechanism in times of crises. The idea is echoed in a statement by Thai Deputy Prime Minister Supachai: 'We cannot rely on the World Bank, Asian Development Bank, or the International Monetary Fund but we must rely on regional cooperation' (quoted in *The Nation*, 10 June 2000).

The Chiang Mai accord of May 2000 was undeniably a good start in furthering talks on the establishment of an Asian Monetary Fund. Since that date, the region's countries for the first time take an active concern in their neighbour's economies in a multilateral framework; on the one hand contravening ASEAN's tradition of non-interference in other state's internal affairs, on the other hand, binding the three Northeast Asian countries far more closely to the Southeast Asian neighbours by substantial financial collaboration. There is, though, still a lot of work to be done. Important bilateral agreements under this initiative have been linked to the consent of the IMF for drawing down major parts of credit lines. If, for example, a member needs to draw more than 10 per cent of its agreed credit facility with the Japanese central bank, it needs IMF approval (*FEER*, 12 July 2001). This allows South Korea to draw only US$200 million from the fund, a sum that would hardly suffice in a liquidity crisis.

However, the Chiang Mai initiative is not the only achievement of the forum. During the institutionalization process, new topics either emerged or initially formulated policy goals, such as in the security field, were filled with substance.

The institutionalization within ASEAN plus three is in consequence also about community building that is facilitated by dialogues on issues of common concern that subsist outside the security and economic realms but concern social problems. What is particularly important in this respect is the backing of this development by Japan, which endorses 'cooperation for Asian countries to build up social safety nets in order to minimize unexpected negative impacts of globalization on their economy and society' (*Japan Times*, 14 July, 2000). The Japanese government already dubs itself 'a "sworn friend" of Asia [that] must actively provide Asian countries with resources in the areas of people, goods, money, and information' (MOFA 2001b). On the other hand, ASEAN members seem uniformly to appreciate assistance by the biggest economy, especially assistance in the wake of the financial crisis, as can be seen from remarks by Ali Alatas, Foreign Minister of Indonesia: 'I look forward to its [Japan's] playing an important role in our common endeavours to soften the social impact of the financial and economic crisis upon our peoples, and eventually to overcome that crisis altogether' (Department of Foreign Affairs, Indonesia 1999).

This view seems to be representative for ASEAN, as one finds similar or comparable statements in speeches by representatives from other ASEAN countries. To quote further examples, former Foreign Secretary Domingo L. Siazon of the Philippines goes so far as to aspire that ASEAN plus three 'can be the embryo for a free trade area in East Asia', calling Japan a 'major partner' in the process of economic and monetary integration (DFA, Philippines 2001); Surakiart Sathirathai, Minister of Foreign Affairs of Thailand sees ASEAN plus three's *raison d'être* in 'narrowing the development gap within ASEAN and between ASEAN and East Asia'. According to Sathirathai, '[through] the strengthening of financial and capital market linkages, the financial field will be another area of potential growth in this region' (*Ministry of Foreign Affairs*, Thailand 2001: 4). Finally, President Arroyo of the Philippines expects that the initial financial cooperation is the first step toward much deeper financial and monetary cooperation in East Asia: 'In the future, we can further explore the feasibility of having a common basket of currencies' (*The Nikkei Weekly*, 15 July 2002).

Consequently, the long-term goal of a cooperative monetary regime in East Asia has also repeatedly been outlined by Japan, the leading economy and major trading country in the region. In an interview in January 2000, Eisuke Sakakibara, former state secretary of the Japanese finance ministry, strongly advocates that kind of collaboration (World Bank, 12 January 2000). In line with the Japanese position, other Asian countries also encourage expanded cooperation in social and cultural fields. As Malaysian Minister of Industry and Foreign Trade Rafidah Aziz sees it, integration in areas like youth, academic and media exchanges should begin right away. Building on further exchange in these fields, the minister says officials of the thirteen participating countries can begin work on a customs compendium for the region (*Asia Times Online*, 8 March 2001; MOFA 2001a). Accordingly, politicians from China, Japan and South Korea reached agreement at the Singapore summit in March 2001 to begin a study to examine the feasibility of creating an East Asian economic community of the ASEAN plus three members (ibid.).

At the moment, it is astonishing that even China announced its participation in the ASEAN plus three process, thereby tentatively supporting the Japanese idea of a permanent monetary fund in East Asia. In times of increasing interdependence and exchange between the countries in the region, China for the first time actively engages in a multilateral regional institution. As Premier Zhu Rongji, attending an ASEAN plus three summit, put it:

> While pushing for financial cooperation, we should explore measures facilitating trade and investment so as to strengthen exchanges among the business community and promote free passage of information, goods and investment within the region. East Asian countries can exchange views on regional and international issues of common concern so as to strengthen coordination and enhance mutual understanding and trust (Foreign Ministry, People's Republic of China 2000).

For the time being, China's participation is mostly symbolic and therefore cannot be explained in a functionalist manner, except when long-term calculations are taken into consideration. Neither Japan nor China are expected to see short-term liquidity or balance of payment crises. Japanese participation is even more surprising since Tokyo is unlikely to need yuan in the near future. From a rationalist perspective, one can thus only conclude that future gains in a more integrated East Asian economy is what lies behind the two countries participation in the institution.

Likewise, the most seriously affected countries have steadily regained strength during the years after the financial system meltdown in 1997. On the basis of this finding, it is difficult to explain the continuing institutional dynamic of ASEAN plus three. Hence, we have to look at other factors; that is, the ideas that foster the process of regional cooperation. It is quite obvious that actors involved in the ASEAN plus three process do not always behave either strategically or on the basis of a common identity. We rather have to ask which mode of action captures more of the development of the institution in a specific situation.

New identity

As predicted by the theoretical arguments stated above, learning processes take place in international politics when the political acts of the states that communicate with each other constitute positive or affable signals about the role that each wants to play and about the corresponding role into which it wants to cast its opponent. If State A takes the role of an altruist or treats State B as an associate, then State B's trust in its opponent is likely to increase, as seems to be the case between ASEAN and Japan after the Asian Crisis: 'I would also like to take this opportunity to express our appreciation for the continuous support shown by Japan through out the years especially during the crisis in 1997–98. We are grateful for all the assistance, which Japan has so generously extended to us over the years. I believe Japan will continue to do so, particularly with respect to ASEAN programmes aimed at bridging the development gap within ASEAN' (MOFA, Malaysia 2002).

This shows that the concepts of interests and identity cannot be separated in international politics. In international politics, identity can be treated as a property of states that generates behavioural and motivational disposi- tions. Interests can thus change during the process of interaction. The mean- ings of identities often depend on whether other states' representations are the same or different. The formation of a collective identity makes cooper- ation possible in the first place. The members of the ASEAN plus three process are still rational, but the basis on which each member calculates its interests is the interest of the group. And it becomes obvious that new com- municative processes are emerging within the institutional context. As the Japanese Diplomatic Bluebook concludes:

> On the occasion of the ASEAN + 3 (Japan, China, the ROK) Summit Meeting in Manila, based upon a proposal from Prime Minister Obuchi, a trilateral leaders'-level dialogue among Japan, China and the ROK was realized for the first time in the form of a breakfast meeting ... the meeting marked an important first step toward trilateral Japan–China–ROK leaders'-level dialogue and the promotion of regional cooperation in East Asia' (MOFA 2000c: ch. I, C, 4a).

New proposals and new channels of communication are emerging in the process, as is explained in a statement by the South Korean government: '[The ASEAN+3 governments] noted the bright prospects for enhanced interaction and closer linkages in East Asia and recognized the fact that this growing interaction has helped increase opportunities for cooperation and

collaboration with each other, thereby strengthening the elements essential
for the promotion of peace, stability and prosperity in East Asia' (MOFAT
1999: 1).

The evolving cooperation will require even more communication in the
future, and that, in turn, will open new opportunities for association.
Interests and identities will change in the context of the institutional process,
they are not eternally fixed by some asocial authority that exists prior to
international interaction. The bilateral swap agreements, for example, provide a focus for concrete negotiations, periodic reviews among government
officials, and the basis for serious policy dialogue, which, in the words of
Randall Henning, is 'in fact path-breaking: Officials within the region have
never before had such intensive, continuous negotiations and policy dialogue on a regional basis on monetary and financial matters' (Henning
2002: 29).

Conclusion

It became evident in the empirical analysis that the ASEAN plus three
process can be explained through a combination of institutionalist and constructivist IR theories in which institutionalization is understood as a result
of social communication, reciprocal speech-acts and changing attitudes,
identities and interests of the states cooperating with each other. Those who
share the same values, norms, and, thereby, the same identity are integrating in one institution. It was undoubtedly egoism that helped to lift the
states into the same boat; though, at some points, rational considerations
were finally turned into normative ones. In effect, the institution is closely
related to a pan-Asian culture and history of which China, Japan and South
Korea are obviously an unquestionable part. Whereas in Europe, it was the
end of the Cold War that lead to the realization of the pan-European idea,
(that is, the Eastern Enlargement of the Union), it was the Asian crisis that
led to the institutionalization of the Asian idea. It is the deeper institutionalization of ASEAN plus three in the political field that is of particular interest, since this process obviously has nothing to do with the original *raison
d'être* of the forum. The original interest of the member countries obviously
was to stabilize East Asia after the Asian crisis. This goal was not abandoned,
but it was complemented by a wide range of political and social goals. It
seems as if the ASEAN Regional Forum (ARF) was responsible for traditional
security affairs, including confidence-building, while ASEAN plus three has
a much more complex mission, indicating a much wider security concept.[8]

To conclude, one can say that interests are by no means more important
for the establishment and functioning of an international institution, as
suggested by rationalists. Interests, when defined as ideas about how to meet
needs, are actually constituted by ideas. Otherwise, it would be impossible
to answer the question why there is a turn to Asia after the 1997 financial

turmoil; many other (for example, global) solutions may have been possible. In a further analytical step, it would also be difficult to explain the changing attitudes of the member countries towards the institution. Ideas are able to constitute certain collective identities in that they provide the causal power to induce actors to define the welfare of others as part of their own. Acting on the basis of a collective identity does not at all imply irrationality, but the basis on which states calculate their interests is a group of states. On the other hand, identity is neither stable nor undisputed. The international system contains a wide variety of different states with diverging interests and identities.

As predicted by the theoretical hypotheses that were introduced at the beginning of this chapter, existing identities tend to collapse during 'organic crises' such as the Asian crisis and new dominant discourses can be established. While both Malaysia – since the beginning of the 1990s – and later Japan and South Korea – have repeatedly put forward proposals for a strengthened region-wide collaboration, a new dynamic could be gained after 1997. The Chiang Mai initiative and the subsequent establishment of the swap facilities is similar in essence to the AMF plan of 1997, proposed by Japan but retracted amid a chorus of opposition led by the USA.

More and more actors opened themselves up for innovative discourses, and the network of existing (global) structures was increasingly considered an obstacle to a genuine Asian solution for the crisis. The evolving hegemonic discourse – considering ASEAN plus three the natural solution to the problems raised by the financial turmoil in the last years of the 1990s – offered alternative identity concepts for South- and Northeast Asia as one political group. Eventually, a fundamental reconstruction of existing values and identities became visible. New identities generated new kinds of political action along the lines of the established institution – ASEAN plus three.

It is true, as predicted by institutionalism, that large numbers of actors make cooperation more difficult, because they raise questions about how to share both the costs and the benefits of cooperation; in particular, when some states are richer, bigger, or more powerful than others (for this argument, see Koremenos *et al.* 2001). That is why the relationship between Japan and China is so crucial for ASEAN plus three. Moreover, uncertainty can be an obstacle to cooperation since it complicates the surveillance of other actors' actions. Thus, reducing uncertainty among actors is a key function of institutions. This will be a major task for the institution in the future. I am sure that the process will proceed and be even more complex in the years to come. We will only be able to grasp this complexity if we take account of the fundamental constructivist insight that human agents – hence, also states as an aggregation of many human agents – do not exist independently from their social environment and its collectively shared systems of meanings; that is, culture. The concepts of interests and identity can not be separated when analyzing international politics.

Notes

1   A debate that has taken place in the German IR journal *Zeitschrift für Internationale Beziehungen (ZIB)*.
2   The East Asia Vision Group (EAVG) was initiated by Korea's President Kim Dae-jung at the ASEAN+3 Summit in Hanoi in 1998 to discuss long-term cooperation in the region.
3   For a discussion of the depth of integration, see also Henning 2002: ch. 2.
4   Other authors reach the same conclusion. See, for example, Layador 2000.
5   Cf. *Japan Times*, 9 October, 2000, for this idea.
6   As suggested by the Malaysia government: 'With the support of ASEAN, Japan, China and the Republic of Korea, EAEC would not only serve as a catalyst for further economic development but would also ensure economic stability in the region' (MOFA, Malaysia, undated).
7   (*The Nation*, 6 October, 2002)
8   Interviews of the author in the Ministry of Foreign Affairs, Japan, and the Ministry of Economy, Trade and Industry, Japan, in November 2001.

References

Bae, G.C. (2001) 'ASEAN+3 Regional cooperation: Challenges and prospects', in *Korean Observations on Foreign Relations*, 3(1), 106–21.

Buzan, B., Waever, O. and de Wilde, J. (1998) *Security. A New Framework for Analysis*, Boulder and London: Lynne Rienner.

Checkel, J.T. (2001) 'Social construction and European integration', in Christiansen, T., Jørgensen, K.E. and Wiener, A. (eds), *The Social Construction of Europe*, London: Sage Publications, 50–65.

Checkel, J.T. (1997) 'International norms and domestic politics. Bridging the rationalist-constructivist divide', in *European Journal of International Relations*, 3, 473–95.

Dosch, J. and Mols, M. (eds) (2000) *International Relations in the Asia-Pacific. New Patterns of Power, Interest and Cooperation*, Hamburg and New York: Lit-Verlag.

Dijk, T.A. van (1977) *Text and Context: Explorations in the Semantics and Pragmatics of Discourse*, London: Longman.

Eilenberger, G., Mols, M. and Rüland, J. (eds) (1996) *Kooperation, Regionalismus und Integration im asiatisch-pazifischen Raum*, Hamburg: Mitteilungen des Instituts für Asienkunde nr. 226.

Harris, S. (2000) 'Asian multilateral institutions and their response to the Asian economic crisis', in *Pacific Review*, 13(3), 495–516.

Henning, R.C. (2002) *East Asian Financial Cooperation*, Washington DC: Institute for International Economics.

Hoffmann, A. and Knowles, V. (1999) 'Germany and the reshaping of Europe. Identifying interests – the role of discourse analysis', ESRC-IGS Discussion Paper 99/9.

Hund, M. and Okfen, N. (2001) 'Der East Asian Caucus (EAEC)/ASEAN-Plus-Drei', in Maull, H.W. and Nabers, D. *Multilaterale Kooperation in Ostasien-Pazifik. Probleme und Perspektiven im neuen Jahrhundert*, Hamburg: Institut für Asienkunde, 68–86.

Keohane, R.O. (2000) 'Ideas part-way down', in *Review of International Studies*, 26, 125–30.

Keohane, R.O. and Nye, J.S. (2001) *Power and Interdependence*, Glenview, IL: Longman.

Koremenos, B., Lipson, C. and Snidal, D. (2001) 'The rational design of international institutions', in *International Organization*, 55(4), 761–99.

Kwan, C.H. (2001) *Yen Bloc. Toward Economic Integration in Asia*, Washington, DC: Brookings Institution Press.

Laclau, E. (1977) *Politics and Ideology in Marxist Theory: Capitalism, Fascism, Populism*, London: Verso.

Laclau, E. (1990) *New Reflections of the Revolution of Our Time*, London: Verso.

Larsen, H. (1997) *Foreign Policy and Discourse Analysis. France, Britain and Europe*, London and New York: Routledge.

Layador, M.A.R.L.G. (2000) 'The emerging ASEAN plus three process: Another building block for community building in the Asia Pacific?', in *Indonesian Quarterly*, 28(4), 434–43.

Lewis, J. (1999) 'Asian vs. international: Structuring an Asian monetary fund', in *Harvard Asia Quarterly*, 3(4), *http://www.fas.harvard.edu/~asiactr/haq/199904/9904a005.htm* [22 September 2003].

Mack, A. and Ravenhill, J. (eds) (1994) *Building Economic and Security Regimes in the Asia-Pacific*, Canberra: Allen and Unwin.

Maull, H.W. and Nabers, D. (2001) *Multilaterale Kooperation in Ostasien-Pazifik. Probleme und Perspektiven im neuen Jahrhundert*, Hamburg: Institut für Asienkunde.

McGrew, A. and Brook, C. (eds) (1998) *Asia-Pacific in the New World Order*, London and New York: Routledge.

MOFA (Ministry of Foreign Affairs), Malaysia (undated): East Asian Economic Caucus (EAEC), *http://www.kln.gov.my/english/Fr-foreignaffairs.htm* [15 July 1998].

MOFA (Ministry of Foreign Affairs), Malaysia (2002) Remarks by H.E. Datuk Seri Syed Hamid Albar, Minister of Foreign Affairs of Malaysia, as the incoming Coordinator of the ASEAN-Japan Dialogue at the PMC 10 + 1 Session with Japan, 1 August, 2002, *http://www.kln.gov.my* [10 November 2002].

MOFA (The Ministry of Foreign Affairs) Japan (2001a) Japan–ASEAN Exchange Program for High School Students, 23 May, *http://www.mofa.go.jp* [25 July 2000].

MOFA (The Ministry of Foreign Affairs) Japan (2001b) Report of the Mission for Revitalization of Asian Economy; Living in Harmony with Asia in the Twenty-first century, *http://www.mofa.go.jp* [25 July 2001].

MOFA (The Ministry of Foreign Affairs) Japan (2000) Summary of ASEAN+3 Foreign Ministers Meeting, 26 July, *http://www.mofa.go.jp* [25 July 2000].

MOFAT (The Ministry of Foreign Affairs and Trade) Republic of Korea 1999, joint statement on East Asia Cooperation, 28 November, *http://www.mofat.go.kr* [10 September 2001].

Müller, H. (1994) 'Internationale Beziehungen als kommunikatives Handeln. Zur Kritik der utilitaristischen Handlungstheorien', in *Zeitschrift für Internationale Beziehungen*, 1(1), 15–44.

Nabers, D. (2003) 'The social construction of international institutions: ASEAN+3', in *International Relations of the Asia-Pacific*, 1/2003, 113–36.

Nabers, D. (2002a) 'Japans neuer Regionalismus – Die prozessuale Dynamik der ASEAN+3', in *Japan aktuell*, 1(2), 51–60.

Nabers, D. (2002b) 'Neuer Regionalismus in Ostasien – das Forum der ASEAN+3', in *Nord-Süd-aktuell*, 2/2002, 267–75.

Ravenhill, J. (2001) *APEC and the Construction of Pacific Rim Regionalism*, Cambridge: Cambridge University Press.

Risse, T. (2000) 'Let's argue! Persuasion and deliberation in International Relations', in *International Organization*, 54(1), 1–39.

Rüland, J. (2002) ' "Dichte" oder "schlanke" Institutionalisierung? Der Neue Regionalismus im Zeichen von Globalisierung und Asienkrise', in *Zeitschrift für Internationale Beziehungen*, 9(2), 175–207.

Sakakibara, E. (2001) 'The Asian Monetary Fund. Where do we go from here?' Institute of Strategic and International Studies (ISIS), Malaysia, 26 February.

Schimmelfennig, F. (2001) 'The community trap: Liberal norms, rhetorical action, and the Eastern enlargement of the European Union', in *International Organization*, 55(1), 47–80.

Smith, A.M. (1998) *Laclau and Mouffe. The Radical Democratic Imaginary*, London and New York: Routledge.

Sterling-Folker, J. (2000) 'Competing paradigms or birds of a feather? Constructivism and neoliberal institutionalism compared', in *International Studies Quarterly*, 44, 97–119.

Titscher, S., Meyer, M., Wodak, R. and Vetter, E. (2000) *Methods of Text and Discourse Analysis*, London: Sage.

Waever, O. (1995) 'Resisting the temptation of post foreign policy analysis', in Carlsnaes, W. and Smith, S. (eds), *European Foreign Policy: The EC and Changing Perspectives in Europe*, London, Thousand Oaks and New Delhi: Sage.

Webber, D. (2001) 'Two funerals and a wedding? The ups and downs of regionalism in East Asia and Asia-Pacific after the Asian crisis', in *Pacific Review*, 14(3), 339–72.

Wendt, A. (1999) *Social Theory of International Politics*, Cambridge: Cambridge University Press.

Wendt, A. (1992) 'Collective identity formation and the international state', in *American Political Science Review*, 88(2), 384–96.

Wodak, R. (1996) *Disorders of Discourse*, London: Longman.

Yun, C. (2002) *Japan's FTA strategy and the East Asian economic bloc*, translated from *Sekai* 699 (March 2002), *http://www.iwanami.co.jp* [18 March 2002].

12
New Regionalism and Global Economic Governance

Manuela Spindler

Introduction

With the European Union, the North American Free Trade Area (NAFTA), Asia Pacific Economic Cooperation (APEC), ASEAN or the Southern Common Market (Mercosur) – just to mention a few – the globalizing political economy is characterized by the persistence and even new building of regions. Since the 1990s, a 'second wave' of regionalism has been discovered by a broad academic community,[1] reminding us of the 'first wave' of building free trade areas, customs unions and common markets in the 1950s and 1960s. However, there is an ongoing controversy as to the nature of what is new about regionalism compared to the 'old'. Old regionalism has usually been associated with the protectionist provisions of European integration on one hand and Southern integration schemes based on import substitution policies on the other. Still, the phenomenon of new regionalism is seen as a protectionist measure while, at the same time, being associated with openness (open regionalism). This indicates a rather contradictory or even paradoxical nature of new regionalism and is linked to the question often asked about the relation between new regionalism and globalization. It is answered in many ways: from regionalism being a 'stepping stone' to regionalism being a 'stumbling block' with regard to globalization. Studies come to the (rather inconclusive) conclusion that new regionalism may 'represent globalization' or attempt to ride on it, to regulate it or to resist it (Hveem 2000: 71).[2] This is against the background of the emergence of a global, and thus borderless, economic space and prevailing (bounded) forms of political authority to 'govern' the global economy found at the state and regional level.

This chapter relates research on new regionalism to discussions on global governance and inquires about the (new) role of regions as part of attempts to govern an increasingly global economy. The chapter introduces a framework for understanding new regionalism by relating it to processes of structural change in the global political economy led by agency. It is particularly interested in the role of global market actors as globalizing forces at the level of regions. The argument is put forward that global business actors not only are the 'masters of the market', meaning that they create regionalized and globalized patterns of economic transactions due to economic firm strategies. As powerful actors, they have the strength to shape the political frameworks of governance found at the global (multilateral institutions), the regional (regionalism) and state level, making prevailing forms of political-economic governance at these levels more compatible with the requirements of a globalizing economy. It will be argued that with new regionalism, the predominant politics of the old regionalism found in the 'embedded liberalism' of the postwar world is in the process of undergoing a fundamental change which could be grasped as 'marketization' or opening. It is bound to the activities of global market actors as globalizing forces who have the strength to 'infuse' the logic of the market into traditional, old style regionalism. To expound the argument, the chapter proceeds as follows.

The next section starts off with a discussion of the concept of global governance in its relation to the question of global order and of the particular strand of 'global governance theory' that focuses on the role of non-state actors in bringing about order. This is based on the conviction that devoting greater attention to the role of non-state actors is of particular importance to increase our understanding of governance in a globalizing political economy. We follow this by going into more detail on the question of order, and provide a critical IPE understanding of order as being related to the specific (and changing) balances between political authority and the market in political economic governance at the national, regional, and global level. We then discuss the specific relationship between the market and political authority for regionalism in the political-economic order of the postwar world. The argument will be brought forward that regionalism then was based on the idea of the protectionist region. Next, we investigate the role of global market actors in the transition from old to new regionalism. This will be done by drawing on two cases of new regionalism. The first is discussing the role of the European Round Table of Industrialists (ERT) with regard to the European internal market programme, the second the role of business in similar forums to be found in Asia-Pacific regionalism (through APEC), such as the APEC Business Advisory Council (ABAC). This is to support the core argument of a changing balance between political authority and the market: a 'marketization' of the former protectionist regionalism found in the postwar world. The chapter concludes by discussing the implications of a 'marketized' regionalism for the prospects of global order.

Business actors and global governance: do corporations rule the world?[3]

At the heart of the concept of global governance is an increasing sensibility for questions of order in the global system, and therefore the chances of 'governing without government'. The general problem of theorizing global governance derives from the absence of government at the global level; that is, the lack of a sovereign and centralized system of sanctions. However, the concept of 'global governance' can be an important tool for understanding change in the global political economy (Cutler *et al.* 1999: 19; Hewson and Sinclair 1999a: 3). For Rosenau, governance is understood as the 'recurrent patterns that are developed purposively, that reflect the interventions of human will, the virtues of planning, the drawing up of constitutional charters, the organization of public affairs in such a way that goals are framed, ends realized, cooperation achieved, stable equilibria established, and order maintained' (Rosenau 1987: 10).[4]

His definition draws on a difference between governance and other forms of collective action at the global level such as the building of international regimes in specific issue areas. The term 'governance' in international politics should be reserved to the broader building of political frameworks through purposeful political action and the subsequent adaptation of actor behaviour according to the norms and principles 'written' into these frameworks (Kohler-Koch 1993: 116–17). As a politics of order (*Ordnungspolitik*) governance sets up the framework for actor behaviour and thus shapes the structures of international relations, that is it defines who gets what, and formulates norms and principles that guide actor behaviour within the established framework. As such, order becomes a 'product' of governance, that is of purposeful political action (Kohler-Koch 1993: 121).[5]

Due to different ontological perspectives on international relations there are different views of governance, above all with regard to the question 'who governs' – that is, who are the actors and what ability do they have to shape the contours of the global political economy?

State-centred views either point to the distribution of power among states, and thus to the most powerful actors in the system (neorealism), or focus on inter-state policy coordination and the building of international intergovernmental institutions and their role in solving global problems (liberal institutionalism).[6] Out of such a view, research on global governance is primarily focused on governance provided by states and international governmental institutions.

With a society-centred view, studies on transnational relations on the one hand and domestic approaches on the other emphasize the impact of non-state actors on global politics (Risse 2002; Risse-Kappen 1995). The former point to transnational actors such as INGOs and an emerging global civil society (Boli and Thomas 1999; Florini 2000; O'Brien *et al.* 2000; Princen and Finger 1994; Weiss and Gordenker 1996), cross-border social movements, transnational epistemic communities (Haas 1992) or transnational advocacy coalitions (Keck and Sikkink 1998). Domestic approaches theorize the role of non-state actors within the boundaries of the state such as interest groups and their lobbying of the state in order to get their particular interests on to the political agenda (Milner 1988, 1995; Keohane and Milner 1996).

The increasing importance of non-state actors in world politics is often related to a perceived 'retreat of the state' (Strange 1996), or a 'withering away of the state' (Ohmae 1990).[7] They increasingly possess capabilities to structure the global political economy and thus become important actors of governance, both in the domestic, regional, and global realm (see Higgott *et al.* 2000b). However, it is quite a wide range of actors subsumed under the term 'non-state actors'. There are basically two types: profit-oriented private sector corporate actors (such as MNCs and TNCs) and non-profit actors and organizations (such as INGOs, global social movements and so on) (Higgott *et al.* 2000a: 1).

Profit-oriented private sector actors, such as transnational corporations and economic elites, are often separately dealt with in the literature with most studies coming from International Political Economy (Bieler and Morton 2001; Cox with Sinclair 1996; Gill 1993; Stopford and Strange 1991). The rise of transnational corporations as global market actors is one of the central features of the global political economy.[8] Their number has increased dramatically since the 1970s. So has their importance in the global economy: manifest in the increase in their foreign direct investment activities, and their control of a growing share of international trade flows (partly through intra-firm trade), both of which are more and more beyond control by governments (Ruigrok 2000). It reflects the underlying change in the basic structure of the production process from the Fordist model of production to the post-Fordist model of flexible production – a fundamental reconfiguration of production space (Dicken 1998). The literature on TNCs has been expanding dramatically and there is a wide academic controversy on how to come to terms with the role of non-state actors of a market-oriented type.[9]

Recent studies acknowledge the important political role those global business actors play in the global economy (Cutler *et al.* 1999b; Hewson and Sinclair 1999b). Indeed, it is political frameworks of governance for international economic transactions that are increasingly created by private sector actors (and *not* by states or international institutions): the setting up of private sector regimes that create areas of rule making, standards setting and organization of industrial sectors.[10] Here, it is individual firms that are establishing international frameworks for their economic activities, now captured with the concept of international private authority over transnational affairs as a market-oriented source of authority (as opposed to the traditional understanding of authority as public or governmental by nature) (Cutler *et al.* 1999a: 4–5).[11]

Cutler *et al.* (1999a: 9–15) distinguish among six categories of cooperative arrangements among firms: (1) informal industry norms and practices; (2) coordination services firms; (3) production alliances and subcontractor relationships; and (4) cartels. Further, there is an increase in business lobbying activities at the international level, mainly done by business associations (category 5) representing their members to decision makers on issues of importance to industry.[12] There are more and more 'official positions' of firms and business associations within domestic political structures (such as industry advisory panels) or within international institutions. Internationally such associations have just begun to emerge and gain attention as formerly closed international negotiations are opening towards non-governmental organizations. Private regimes (category 6), as integrated complexes of formal and informal institutions that are sources of governance for an economic issue area as a whole, constitute the most institutionalized form of private authority. They are created by negotiation and interaction among firms within a particular industry sector or issue area.[13]

Studies on private authority show that the traditional focus on state authority and sovereignty that dominates theories of IR and IPE can only in part explain the evolving contours of the global political-economic order. A significant degree of global order is provided by individual firms cooperating formally or informally in establishing international frameworks for their economic activities. 'Private authority' thus points to the significant role of non-state actors as important ordering elements in the global economy.

However, a shortcoming of such analysis for theorizing governance is their narrow focus on specific industry sectors or issue areas.[14] As a consequence, broader aspects of order, going beyond sector- or issue-specific private regimes, are lost out of sight. The definition of governance by Rosenau, demanding to differentiate between governance and issue-specific regimes and the plea of Kohler-Koch to reserve the term governance for broader aspects of order, is not matched. This is particularly true for questions of world order. However, out of their holistic perspectives, critical approaches in IPE can provide important insights which will be shown in the next section.

Order and the global political economy

How the (global) economy is organized politically (that is how the economy is being embedded in broader, politically constituted, social and legal institutional frameworks within which political and economic activities take place), is one of the core questions in International Political Economy (Cox 1995: 32; Ruggie 1998: 23). It is based on the assumption that in order to function, a market (and particularly a global market) presupposes some kind of social order. '[T]he logic of the economy presupposes a solution to a problem that it can neither pose nor solve: the problem of the production of an *orderly system*, a social order, within whose context one can *legitimately* speak in singular, politically neutral terms of a definite set of system boundaries and a definite set of systemic structures' (Ashley 1983: 476; emphasis added).

For critical perspectives in IPE, this is a question of (world) order. According to Hettne (1999: 19–20), in IPE theory, world order is usually defined as an 'arrangement which provides the necessary framework for sustained transactions in the world economy'. There are specific solutions to the problem of order at a particular point in time: orders are historical. Polanyi's work (1944) is inspiring for thinking how those solutions might appear. His analysis of capitalism in the nineteenth and twentieth centuries provides a view of the modern society basically being the result of two forces or logics: the logic of market expansion and of attempts for self-protection by society against the disruptive and destabilizing effects of the market, in effect creating a specific balance between economics and politics, or *laissez-faire* and protectionism. This has to be understood as a 'dialectical process' of capitalism, called 'double movement'. The 'first movement' is attempts to impose a self-regulating market (that is, to dis-embed the economy from society so as to allow the market to function without social or political constraints). The 'second movement' is the reaction of society to bring the market under social and political control (such as by introducing factory legislation, social insurance and so on, culminating in the welfare state) (Polanyi 1944). Thus, there is a mutual relationship between politics and economics, the state and the market, protectionism and *laissez-faire*, or political authority and the market.[15] In line with this understanding for the purpose of the chapter, the term 'political economy' is used to describe the (changing) relationship between the market economy and forms of political authority. It implies a conception of the market and political authority as parts of the same 'integrated ensemble of governance' (Underhill 2000: 4), not as separate entities or principles of social organization. Order is reflecting a particular balance of both as a persistent pattern over time. The next section will investigate into that balance for the political economy of the postwar world and provide an understanding of the role regionalism plays therein.

The postwar order and old regionalism

Basically, it is the global regimes for money, finance, and trade that constitute the framework of the international political economy.[16] They build the institutional skeleton of the particular 'type' of international order developed after World War II that tried to reconcile an open world economy with an active role of the state in the domestic realm. Ruggie (1982) called it 'embedded liberalism'. As a domestic and international order, 'embedded liberalism' purposefully has been created with the intention to constrain 'orthodox liberalism', whose 'authority relations are constructed in such a way as to give maximum scope to market forces rather than to constrain them' (Ruggie 1998: 63f., 78). Thus, the model of the embedded economy is characterized by setting limits to the freedom of market forces through political intervention. This special balance between economics and politics has been institutionalized in the international system of economic multilateralism. It is predicated on domestic intervention: 'Keynes at home and Smith abroad', as Gilpin puts it (1987: 363). The 'generative grammar' of politics inherent in this 'compromise' represents a 'fusion of power with legitimate social purpose', with the shared purpose prescribing the domestic social and economic role of the state as the Keynesian or social democratic welfare state of the postwar era (Ikenberry 1992; Lacher 1999: 356; Ruggie 1998: 64, 84).

With regard to the world trading system, for a number of decades trade was shaped by a particular combination of liberalization and protection. The GATT made obligatory the most-favoured-nation (MFN) rule, but an exception from the cardinal principle of MFN was allowed for areas such as the regulation of commodity markets, restrictive business practices and international investments to protect a variety of domestic social policies; that is to serve Ruggie's 'legitimate social purpose'. Furthermore, it explicitly allows for regional trade arrangements (customs unions and free trade areas) under Article XXIV of the GATT (and its updated version in the WTO), under Part IV of the GATT, relating to economic development adopted in 1965 and under the enabling clause of the Tokyo Round in 1979 (WTO 1995: 7). The exemption provisions for regional agreements under Article XXIV of the GATT and the practice of regionalism in the postwar world are manifestations of the 'embedded liberalism compromise'. Basically, regionalism was associated with protectionism; that is, the closing up of regions to their international surrounding, the keeping of tariff and the new creation of non-tariff barriers to non-members for purposes such as the protection of vulnerable industries. The purpose of protectionism was to contend with the social externalities of the global market.

In sum, the regionalized order of 'embedded liberalism' was based on a protectionist form of regulating the market economy at the domestic, regional, and international level. The region of 'embedded liberalism' was the protectionist region. It was a manifestation of the victory of the interventionist, or welfare logic of politics over the pure market economy.

Global business actors, new regionalism and the construction of global order

Basically, in most studies, regionalism is associated with state-led projects leading to formal regional institutional arrangements (Hveem 2000: 72). Those perspectives are representative of regional integration theories' long-standing intellectual habits and the use of concepts and categories derived from earlier historical moments. For them, '[T]he question of what states are trying to do through regionalism, and why they are doing it ... is the critical issue' (Richards and Kirkpatrick 1999: 687). However, theorizing the process of regional integration by Haas, Deutsch and others did not take a global economy as its referent. At this time, the concept of an economic space transcending nation states did not really exist. Thus, as political-economic actors, global business has been absent from analyses of regionalism, which is largely due to the fact that global business (as firms with large scale transnational production and globalizing strategies) basically rose to prominence in the 1970s when the 'first wave' of regionalism had already come to an end (Ruigrok and van Tulder 1995: 128–30).[17] Since then, globally competitive firms are emerging in almost every region of the world. They cannot be left out when theorizing new regionalism; that is regionalism in the global political economy.[18]

Since the late 1980s, global business actors have shown a growing interest in regionalism. This is against the background of a growing 'misfit' between an increasingly borderless economic world and the prevailing forms of political-economic governance. 'In attempting to adapt to a range of complex changes in cultural, institutional and market structures, both political and market actors are increasingly seeking, directly or indirectly, wittingly or unwittingly, *to reinvent political structures* and institutions in a wider global context' (Cerny 2000: 117; emphasis added).[19] A consequence of the evolution of transnational corporations is the gradual emergence of an internationalized managerial élite and their meetings in informal clubs, mainly at the level of CEOs of the most globalized and strongest transnational corporate players. These meetings could be seen as sites for the discussion and creation of new concepts and ideas, concerned with the kind of global political-economic order preferred for the conduct of their economic transactions.[20] At the regional level, this happens in groups such as the European Round Table of Industrialists (ERT), directed at the European internal market, the Pacific Basin Economic Council (PBEC) or the APEC CEO Summits with regard to the APEC forum, or the Business Network for Hemispheric Integration (BNHI) promoting a Free Trade Area of the Americas (FTAA) – just to mention a few new regional activities of business. The actors involved are leading industrialists of global operating firms such as Unilever, TotalFinaElf, ThyssenKrupp, Nestlé, Philips, ICI, Royal Dutch/ Shell, Bayer, or Siemens in the European case (ERT webpage). Citigroup, TotalFinaElf, General Motors, Shell, HSBC, Mitsubishi Corp., AIG, Hyundai, Samsung, Fujitsu, Goldman Sachs, Allianz, or McDonalds are active in the Asia Pacific (APEC CEO Summit 2000a, 2000b).

With the free market logic at the core, the political frameworks advocated by those market forces both at the global and regional level are intended to support and promote further moves towards globalization. In the following, two cases will support the argument.

New regionalism in Europe (the internal market programme)

This is clearly to be seen in the role the European Round Table of Industrialists plays with regard to the European internal market.[21] The ERT has been identified as the major policy actor behind the single market initiative (Cowles 1995; Holman 1992; van Apeldoorn 2002) and a crucial force setting a trend towards openness that European regionalism within the single market follows since then. The initial purpose of the group was to develop projects which should promote an internal market, and to provide an 'alternative form of job and wealth creation' compared to the one offered by member states so far, and which were seen as too costly for their corporate operations in the face of international competition (Cowles 1995: 505). The creation of a unified European market was advocated because it would allow European firms to become more powerful competitors in world markets.[22] While, in the first years, the ERT has been dominated by import-competing firms for the European market, demanding a strong European home base protected by import quota or other forms of political interventionism (that is, the old protectionist model of regionalism of embedded liberalism), there has been a change since the late 1980s towards a 'globalist' orientation, leaving the old 'Europrotectionist' trend behind (van Apeldoorn 2002).[23] Since then, competition, free market integration and neoliberal deregulation are at the core of ERT's view of internal market regionalism: 'Industry wants a strong Europe in a growing world economy, which cannot be achieved by building a fortress closed against our neighbors. The largest companies of the European Round Table operate on a global scale and can clearly identify the causes of declining competitiveness… Industry… expects more open access to world markets, in return for giving our competitors better access to the Single Market in Europe' (ERT 1993: 10, 14).

Competitiveness has been the key word from the start of ERT. Stressing that most ERT members operate on a global scale, ERT constantly passes on proposals for reform of EU competition policy to EU institutions and governments, such as more recently in their message to the Stockholm European Council in March 2001 (ERT 2001) or in their proposals presented to Commissioner Monti in December 2000 (ERT 2000). It urges the Commission to define the world market as the 'relevant geographical market' and to examine barriers from a worldwide perspective rather than sticking to the old, narrow definition of EU markets as this constrains the ability of business to invest and compete in global markets (ERT 2000, 2001). Furthermore, they stress the need of an 'economics-based' interpretation of competition law (ERT 2000).

The Competitiveness Advisory Group (CAG) that was set up in February 1995 is often seen as an example of the 'institutionalization' of ERT access to EU decision-making structures with the reports published by the CAG closely reflecting ERT's views on competitiveness (Balanyá *et al.* 2000: 33).[24]

The ERT can be seen as a driving force of what, in principle, is a neoliberal restructuring of the European political economy, formerly adopting an approach of Keynesian regulation. With the previous paradigm being based on the old consensus on the role of protectionism and intervention, the new paradigm started to undercut the old consensus on the welfare state, questioning former economic redistributive and social economic policies in the EU economic regime. Hence, a fundamental restructuring of the relationship between political authority and the market trying to insulate markets from political interference (Hooghe and Marks 1999; Wallace 1997).

ERT members present and promote their views actively not only at the regional level but in a range of more global, or what could be called 'inter-regional', groups such as the Evian Group, the Transatlantic Business Dialogue (TABD) and the Trans-Atlantic Policy Network (TPN), the EU–Japan Industrialists Round Table, and the ASEAN–EU Industrialists Round Table. These groups basically promote a liberalizing world economy. However, as expressed by ERT Chairman Morris Tabaksblat at a meeting of the Evian Group, the call by business for liberalizing trade is not a plea for uncontrolled free world markets. What is needed is the creation of an 'appropriate regulatory framework'. Therefore, he calls for a 'better alternative to the current tendency towards regionalism, which if not managed well may sow the seeds of protectionism' (Tabaksblat 2001: 3, 6).

New regionalism in Asia Pacific: APEC

The 'European case' of ERT closely resembles the role business takes in the context of APEC.[25] However, the path towards regionalism pursued within the APEC Forum as an association of member economies was one of open regionalism and market-led integration from the very beginning. The idea of open regionalism taken with APEC implies the view of a process of regional economic cooperation whose outcome is not only the actual reduction of internal (intra-regional) barriers, but also the actual reduction of external barriers to economies that are not part of the agreement. To pursue open regionalism, four key policies have been proposed as a guide to regional cooperation. First, APEC members should unilaterally reduce trade and investment barriers to the maximum extent possible. Second, while they liberalize internal trade and investment barriers on a most favoured nation basis, they should also continue to reduce barriers to non-member countries. Third, APEC members should extend the benefits of regional liberalization to non-members on a mutually reciprocal basis. Fourth, individual members should be allowed to extend the benefits of their own APEC liberalization to non-members either on a conditional or unconditional MFN basis (APEC 1994).[26]

This road is further taken with the two-track procedure of Individual and Collective Action Plans as agreed in 1996. Individual Action Plans are unilateral measures that are taken domestically by each member according to its individual timetable. They include traditional market access issues such as the reduction and removal of tariffs and the elimination of WTO inconsistent non-tariff measures (Adlan 1998; Drysdale *et al.* 1998). APEC's Collective Action Plans are dealing with trade facilitation covering a wide range of issues from customs and standards to government procurement and intellectual property rights. They are jointly pursued by all members according to the same timetable (Adlan 1998). The idea of open regionalism is rooted in the view that Asia's economic boom has come about without the formation of a trading bloc or any other arrangements which grant special economic benefits to members and discriminate against non-members. The Asia Pacific – unlike the EU – has no tradition of 'old style', that is protectionist regionalism.

Similar to the case of the internal market, the initiative for APEC came from outside governments. The APEC Forum as such can be seen as the result of the networking and agenda setting activities through 'economic élites' active in groups such as the Pacific Basin Economic Council (PBEC) and the Pacific Economic Cooperation Council (PECC) (Harris 1994).[27] It was here that the idea of open regionalism and market-led integration was generated. In the late 1980s, it came to an acceptance in those circles that opening up an economy to import competition, even unilaterally, makes the economy more competitive internationally and supports exports. The consensus on open regionalism is part of a general strong commitment of business in Asia Pacific to GATT/WTO (Harris 1994: 389). It became the very principle on which APEC rests due to the close and mutual recognized relationships between business and APEC (Woods 1995: 815).

At the Osaka Summit in 1995, APEC's relationship with business was institutionalized through the creation of the APEC Business Advisory Council (ABAC) whose task it is to provide advice on the implementation of the APEC agenda. ABAC is now considered to be the private sector arm of APEC and the official voice of the private sector in the region. It has direct access to the highest political levels. In its reports to APEC Leaders, ABAC constantly calls on APEC for maintaining the momentum on market opening in the Asia Pacific. '[O]penness to trade and investment are critical for growth and development in the region' (ABAC 2000).[28] ABAC constantly is pointing to the top priority of getting a new WTO round started (APEC CEO Summit 2000a, 2000b).

In a similar way, PBEC provides comprehensive private sector views of what business views as crucial for a market-driven regulatory framework through APEC (PBEC 1998). Furthermore, of increasing importance is the interchange of ideas and views at the APEC CEO Summits taking place before APEC Leaders meet annually. Here, CEOs and Chairmen of global players such as Citigroup, TotalFinaElf, General Motors, Shell, HSBC, Mitsubishi Corp., AIG, Hyundai, Samsung, Fujitsu, Goldman Sachs, Allianz, or McDonalds meet and intensively discuss the political-economic conditions found for their businesses in the Asia Pacific region (APEC CEO Summit 2000a, 2000b). Here, APEC basically constitutes a dialogue on deregulation and competition among the states in the region.

Conclusion

The chapter opened a perspective to relate research on new regionalism to the broader discussion on global governance. The concept of global governance has been presented as basically being about order – facing the problem of the absence of 'government'. It is basically a question of how the (global) economy is organized politically; that is, how the economy is being embedded in broader politically constituted, social and legal institutional frameworks within which political and economic activities take place. A critical IPE under-standing of order as being related to the specific (and changing) balances between political authority and the market in political economic governance at the national, regional, and global level has been provided. It has been argued that devoting greater attention to the role of non-state actors is of particular importance to increase our understanding of governance in a globalizing political economy. The expansion of markets is one of the central features of globalization, enhancing the power of market actors relative to state actors. A significant degree of global order is shaped by market actors in their attempts to establish (or change) the political frameworks deemed appropriate for the conduct of their global economic transactions. This has been shown with regard to the transition of old to new regionalism found at the regional level. More generally, this transition is linked to the broader structural change in the global political economy at the level of production and the integration of financial markets. More specifically, it is linked to the rise of globally oriented economic actors and the search of those actors for new political frameworks appropriate to their globalizing market activities.

It has been argued that with new regionalism, the predominant politics of the old regionalism found in the international order of 'embedded liberal-ism' of the postwar world is in the process of undergoing a fundamental change which could be grasped as a 'marketization' or opening of the former protectionist regions: opening up towards trade and capital from the rest of the world, with the most competitive region being the one that is most suc-cessful in attracting 'footloose businesses'.[29] The process is bound to the activities of global market actors as globalizing forces organized at the regional level (such as the ERT or ABAC) who have the strength to shape the politics of regionalism.

The perspective of the chapter is taken against the background that there is a general reluctance to place the analysis of regionalism within a wider political economic framework of capitalist development. It draws a link between market actors and deeper historical trends associated with devel-opments in the structure of global capitalism. Hence the attempt of a dynamic perspective focusing on the issues of transformation and change of global order and avoiding static institutionalist analysis based on state-as-actor assumptions. At the same time, the chapter is intended to be a plea not to leave out the regional level when debating issues of global gover-nance. New regionalism is an integral part of the evolving structures of the global political economy. A proper understanding of its nature can be an important building block in conceptualizing global order and assessing the prospects of global governance.

Notes

1 There is an increasing number of studies on 'new regionalism' in fields as diverse as economics, geography, International Relations and International Political Economy as well as studies of identity and culture.

2 For the 'stumbling block' view, see *inter alia* Hart (1992), Lloyd (1992) and Hirst and Thompson (1999). For the 'stepping stone' or 'building block' view, see *inter alia* Anderson and Blackhurst (1993), Dicken (1998), Gamble and Payne (1991), Hanson (1998) and Mittelman (1999).

3 Adoption of the title of Korten's book *When Corporations Rule the World* (Korten 1997).

4 In his earlier work (Rosenau 1987) this is called 'governance II', later only 'governance' while 'governance I' is called 'order' (Rosenau 1992: 3ff.).

5 Kohler-Koch distinguishes between politics of order and politics of process (Kohler-Koch 1993: 117). For the purpose of the chapter, the former is of particular interest.

6 For an overview, see the collection of essays in Baldwin 1993.

7 However, as Cerny (2000: 120) notes, it is not the state as an institutional structure per se that is withering away. It is the logic inherent in the state as a form of political authority that is changing.

8 The term 'global market actor' here is applied to private sector corporate actors that control operations or income-generating assets in more than one country (Jones 1996: 4).

9 Since the early 1990s, there is a vast amount of literature on the phenomenon of the multinational corporate form (mainly in the field of industrial organization as a sub-field of economics focusing on market structures, factors that drive investment decisions, competition, business organization such as intra-firm restructuring, building of strategic alliances and so on). There are only a few studies that integrate political aspects (Dunning 1993; Eden and Potter 1993; Stopford and Strange 1991; Strange 1997). This is against the background that, since the 1970s, interdependence analysis and Marxist studies, there was rather 'silence' with regard to analyzing the role of MNCs.

10 See the collection of essays in Cutler *et al.* 1999b, especially the contributions of Sinclair on bond-rating agencies that have an unprecedented influence over fiscal policy and are increasingly relied upon in international bank regulation; Sell on multinationals and the globalization of intellectual property rights in the Uruguay Round; Spar on private rules of online commerce that govern the activities of internet participants; and Salter on the regime for communication and information technologies.

11 Cutler *et al.* define private authority as the 'establishment of norms, rules, and institutions that guide the behavior of the participants and affect the opportunities available to others' (Cutler *et al.* 1999a: 4).

12 For example, the International Chamber of Commerce, the American Business Council, or UNICE.

13 See also the discussion on multinational companies and the establishment of international rules and on international restructuring of production in Higgott *et al.* (2000a), Part II and III.

14 The same for corporatist literature on private interest government which is focusing at the domestic level (see, for example, Streeck and Schmitter 1985).

15 As representations of the same logic, these 'pairs' are used interchangeably throughout the chapter. However, it should be noted that 'economics' and

'politics' are abstractions in that the distinction between them rests on the theorist's idealization of distinct logical relations whose bare logical forms have no necessary actual counterparts in practical distinctions between economic and political action. They are theoretical abstractions which provide alternative frameworks by which theorists orient and bound their questioning and interpretations of overlapping aspects of the social world.

16 This section entitled 'The postwar order and old regionalism' and the empirical sections on new regionalism in this chapter draw on an earlier version. See Spindler (2003).

17 As Haas already observed for integration projects in 1970: '[P]olitical or social forces...may arise after initiation and deflect (or strengthen) the initial forces *without having been included in the explanation of the origin*' (Haas 1970: 639, emphasis added).

18 Most rationalist approaches still treat them as domestic actors. However, as transnational actors they differ from export-oriented companies with production facilities that are still located at the national level. Their role cannot be captured by domestic level explanations of regionalism. For domestic approaches on new regionalism with a focus on market actors, see Milner (1995), Schirm (2002).

19 At the global level and with regard to the multilateral trading system, globally oriented private sector actors played a key role in promoting policies that stood for an increasingly liberalizing trading order with new political-legal arrangements put in place, the process being underpinned by strategic decisions of firms that led to patterns of increasing economic interdependence (regional and global). For example, see Sell (1999) on the role of the Intellectual Property Committee (twelve business representatives of the most globally competitive industries such as General Electric, Pfizer, and IBM) in bringing about the TRIPs agreement and private sector actors' role with regard to the GATS.

20 Examples where such discussions take place are the Mont Pèlerin Society, the Trilateral Commission, the Bilderberg Meetings, or the Evian Group. However, membership is not always exclusively on business level. See van der Pijl (1995) and Gill (1991) for the Mont Pèlerin Society, the Trilateral Commission and the Bilderberg Meetings. The aim of the Evian Group (established 1995 as basically a 'club of free traders') is to 'provide intellectual ammunition for the strengthening of the open international economic order and the enhancement of the liberal international economy' (Evian Group Webpage).

21 The ERT was founded in 1983 under the chairmanship of Gyllenhammar, CEO of Volvo. ERT members are Chairmen and CEOs of large multinational companies with significant manufacturing and technological presence world-wide. For the members, see *http://www.ert.be*. How the Single Market programme came about and what role should be attributed to the ERT has been a matter of academic controversy. For a neofunctionalist view, see Sandholtz and Zysman 1989. For a liberal intergovernmentalist view, see Moravcsik 1991, 1993.

22 See the ERT vision of an European internal market in their report 'Changing Scales' (ERT, 1985).

23 Since the mid-1980s, more and more of the former 'European' multinationals 'go global', adopting globalizing firm strategies. In contrast to US firms, the majority of European firms only started large scale multinational production through the 1970s (Ruigrok/van Tulder 1995: 128–30). Now, the majority of ERT members' companies are among the Global 500 firms (*Financial Times*, 11 May, 2001: suppl. 4–8).

24 Such a body, called European Competitiveness Council, has been recommended to European governments in ERT's 1993 report (ERT 1993). Among the original

thirteen members were four ERT members, three in the second CAG. See Balanyá *et al.* (2000: 33–5).

25 Created in 1989, the most distinguished achievement that has been reached by APEC was the agreement to the long-term goal of free and open trade and investment in the Asia Pacific by the year 2020. See APEC Economic Leaders (1994).
26 The combination of the four key policies is seen as providing an operational definition of the concept of open regionalism. See APEC (1994: 30); further, Maull *et al.* (1998: ch. 3) and Drysdale *et al.* (1998).
27 PBEC consists of a network comprising senior corporate executives who meet regularly to exchange views on economic conditions within the Asia Pacific region. Its reports provide policy advice and recommendations to APEC Leaders (Woods 1995). PECC brings academic and business sectors into contact with government officials in an unofficial setting (Harris 1994; Higgott 1995).
28 Similar to ERT reports, ABAC Reports are presented to all APEC Leaders in advance of their annual APEC summit and are discussed when APEC leaders meet with ABAC members during the Business Dialogue.
29 Elsewhere (Spindler 2002) and drawing on Cerny's notion of the 'competition state' I have called the new region 'competition region'. Relating the discussion on new regionalism to the convergence/divergence debate in IPE, this type of region has been suggested to be the model on which regionalism worldwide might converge (Spindler 2003).

References

ABAC (2000) Press Release by Office of the ABAC Chair at APEC CEO Summit 2000 taken on 9 June, 2001 from *www.apecceo2001.org/release06.phtml*

Adlan, D. (1998) 'APEC and Asia's Crisis', Speech of Ambassador Dato'Noor Adlan, Executive Director of the APEC Secretariat taken on 1 September 1999 from *www.apecsec.org.sg/whatsnew/announce/feer3.html*

Anderson, K. and Blackhurst, R. (eds) (1993) *Regional Integration and the Global Trading System*, London: Harvester Wheatsheaf.

APEC (1994) 'Achieving the APEC vision: Free and open trade in the Asia Pacific', Second Report of the Eminent Persons Group, Singapore: APEC Secretariat.

APEC Economic Leaders (1994) 'APEC economic leaders' Declaration of Common Resolve', in *Indonesian Quarterly*, 22(4), 378–80.

APEC CEO Summit (2000a) Participants Profile, taken on 9 June 2001 from *www.apecceo2000.com/participants.htm*

APEC CEO Summit (2000b) 'ABAC recommends firm APEC commitment to WTO and new talks round', Press Release 13 November, taken on 9 June 2001 from *www.apecceo2000.com/pr10.htm*

van Apeldoorn, B. (2002) *Transnational Capitalism and the Struggle over European Integration*, London: Routledge.

Ashley, R.K. (1983) 'Three modes of economism', in *International Studies Quarterly*, 27(4), 463–96.

Balanyá, B., Doherty, A., Hoedeman, O., Ma'anit, A. and Wesselius, E. (2000) *Europe Inc. Regional and Global Restructuring and the Rise of Corporate Power*, London: Pluto Press.

Baldwin, D.A. (ed.) (1993) *Neorealism. The Contemporary Debates*, New York: Columbia University Press.

Bieler, A. and Morton, A.D. (eds) (2001) *Social Forces in the Making of the New Europe*, Basingstoke: Palgrave Macmillan.

Boli, J. and Thomas, G.M. (eds) (1999) *Constructing World Culture. International Nongovernmental Organizations since 1875*, Stanford: Stanford University Press.

Cerny, P.G. (2000) 'Restructuring the political arena: Globalization and the paradoxes of the competition state', in Germain, R.D. (ed.), *Globalization and its Critics. Perspectives from Political Economy*, London: Macmillan, 117–38.

Cowles, M.G. (1995) 'Setting the agenda for a new Europe: The ERT and EC 1992', in *Journal of Common Market Studies*, 33(4), 501–26.

Cox, R.W. (1995) 'Critical political economy', in Hettne, B. (ed.), *International Political Economy. Understanding Global Disorder*, London: Zed Books, 31–46.

Cox, R.W. and Sinclair, T. (1996) *Approaches to World Order*, Cambridge: Cambridge University Press.

Cutler, A.C., Haufler, V. and Porter, T. (eds) (1999a) *Private Authority and International Affairs*, New York: State University of New York Press.

Cutler, A.C., Haufler, V. and Porter, T. (1999b) 'Private authority and international affairs', in Cutler A.C., Haufler, V. and Porter, T. (1999), *Private Authority and International Affairs*, New York: State Univeristy of New York Press, 3–28.

Dicken, P. (1998) *Global Shift*, London: Paul Chapman.

Drysdale, P., Elek, A. and Soesastro, H. (1998) 'Open regionalism: The nature of Asia Pacific integration', in Drysdale, P. and Vines, D. (eds), *Europe, East Asia and APEC. A Shared Global Agenda?*, Cambridge: Cambridge University Press, 103–35.

Dunning, J. (1993) *The Globalization of Business*, London: Routledge.

Eden, L. and Potter, E.H. (1993) *Multinationals in the Global Political Economy*, New York: St Martin's Press.

European Round Table of Industrialists (2001) 'Actions for competitiveness through the knowledge economy in Europe, Message from the European Round Table of Industrialists to the Stockholm European Council', March, taken on 15 July 2001 from *www.ert.be/pe/ene02.htm*

European Round Table of Industrialists (2000) 'Proposals for reform of EU competition policy', presented to Commissioner Monti, December, taken on 15 July 2001 from *www.ert.be/pe/ene02.html*

European Round Table of Industrialists (1993) 'Beating the crisis. A charter for Europe's industrial future', Brussels: European Round Table of Industrialists.

European Round Table of Industrialists (1991) 'Reshaping Europe, A Report from the European Round Table of Industrialists', Brussels: European Round Table of Industrialists.

European Round Table of Industrialists (1985) 'Changing scales', Paris: European Round Table of Industrialists.

European Round Table of Industrialists, Webpage, *www.ert.be*

Evian Group (2001) 'Back to the future: Restoring confidence, momentum and vision to the global liberal order', Evian VI Plenary Meeting, Montreux, Switzerland, 20–22 April, taken on 15 July 2001 from *www.eviangroup.org/about.htm*

Evian Group, Webpage, *www.eviangroup.org/about.htm*

Florini, A. (ed.) (2000) *The Third Force. The Rise of Transnational Civic Society*, Tokyo and Washington, DC: Japan Center for International Exchange and Carnegie Endowment for International Peace.

Gamble, A. and Payne, A. (1991) 'Conclusion: The new regionalism', in Gamble, A. and Payne, A. (eds), *Regionalism and World Order*, London: Macmillan.

Gill, S. (1993) *Gramsci, Historical Materialism, and International Relations*, Cambridge: Cambridge University Press.

Gill, S. (1991) *American Hegemony and the Trilateral Commission*, Cambridge: Cambridge University Press.

Gilpin, R. (1987) *The Political Economy of International Relations*, Princeton: Princeton University Press.

Haas, E.B. (1970) 'The study of regional integration: Reflections on the joy and anguish of pretheorizing', in *International Organization*, 24(4), 607–46.

Haas, P.M. (ed.) (1992) 'Knowledge, power and international policy coordination', in *International Organization*, 46(1) (special issue).

Hanson, B.T. (1998) 'What happened to Fortress Europe? External trade policy liberalization in the European Union', in *International Organization*, 52(1), 55–85.

Harris, S. (1994) 'Policy networks and economic cooperation: Policy coordination in the Asia Pacific Region', in *Pacific Review*, 7(4), 381–95.

Hart, J. (1992) *Rival Capitalists: International Competitiveness in USA, Japan and Western Europe*, Princeton: Princeton University Press.

Hettne, B. (1999) 'Globalization and the new regionalism: The second great transformation', in Hettne, B., Inotai, A. and Sunkel, O. (eds), *Globalism and the New Regionalism*, London: Macmillan, 1–24.

Hewson, M. and Sinclair, T. (eds) (1999a) *Global Governance*, New York: State of New York University Press.

Hewson, M. and Sinclair, T. (1999b) 'The emergence of global governance theory', in Hewson, M. and Sinclair, T. (1999), *Global Governance*, New York: State of New York University Press, 3–22.

Higgott, R. (1995) 'Economic cooperation in the Asia Pacific: A theoretical comparison with the European Union', in *Journal of European Public Policy*, 2(3), 361–83.

Higgott, R., Underhill, G.R.D. and Bieler, A. (eds) (2000a) *Non-State Actors and Authority in the Global System*, London: Routledge.

Higgott, R., Underhill, G.R.D. and Bieler, A. (2000b) 'Introduction: Globalisation and non-state actors', in Higgott, R., Underhill, G.R.D. and Bieler, A. (eds) (2000), *Non-state Actors and Authority in the Global System*, London: Routledge, 1–12.

Hirst, P. and Thompson, G. (1999) *Globalization in Question*, 2nd edn, Cambridge: Polity Press.

Holman, O. (1992) 'Transnational class strategy and the new Europe', in *International Journal of Political Economy*, 22(1), 3–22.

Hooghe, L. and Marks, G. (1999) 'The making of a polity: The struggle over European integration', in Kitschelt, H., Lange, P., Marks, G. and Stephens, J.D. (eds), *Continuity and Change in Contemporary Capitalism*, Cambridge: Cambridge University Press, 70–97.

Hveem, H. (2000) 'Explaining the regional phenomenon in an era of globalization', in Stubbs, R. and Underhill, G.R.D. (eds), *Political Economy and the Changing Global Order*, Oxford: Oxford University Press, 70–81.

Ikenberry, G.J. (1992) 'A world economy restored: Expert consensus and the Anglo-American postwar settlement', in *International Organization*, 46(1), 289–321.

Jones, G. (1996) *The Evolution of International Business: An Introduction*, London: Routledge.

Keck, M. and Sikkink, K. (1998) *Activists Beyond Borders: Transnational Advocacy Networks in International Politics*, Ithaca: Cornell University Press.

Keohane, R.O. and Milner, H. (eds) (1996) *Internationalization and Domestic Politics*, Cambridge: Cambridge University Press.

Kohler-Koch, B. (1993) 'Die Welt regieren ohne Weltregierung', in Böhret, Carl and Wewer, Göttrik (eds), *Regieren im 21. Jahrhundert. Zwischen Globalisierung und Regionalisierung*, Opladen: Leske & Budrich, 109–41.

Korten, D.C. (1997) *When Corporations Rule the World*, London: Earthscan.

Lacher, H. (1999) 'Embedded liberalism, disembedded markets: Reconceptualising the Pax Americana', in *New Political Economy*, 4(3), 343–60.

Lloyd, P.J. (1992) 'Regionalization and world trade', OECD Economic Studies 18 (Spring).

Maull, H., Segal, G. and Wanandi, J. (eds) (1998) *Europe and the Asia Pacific*, London: Routledge.

Milner, H.V. (1995) 'Regional economic cooperation, global markets and domestic politics: A comparision of NAFTA and the Maastricht Treaty', in *Journal of European Public Policy*, 2(3), 337–60.

Milner, H.V. (1988) *Resisting Protectionism: Global Industries and the Politics of International Trade*, Princeton: Princeton University Press.

Mittelman, J.H. (1999) 'Rethinking the "new regionalism" in the context of global-ization', in Hettne, B. Inotai, A. and Sunkel, O. (eds) (1999), *Globalism and the New Regionalism*, London: Macmillan, 25–53.

Moravcsik, A. (1993) 'Preferences and power in the European Community: A liberal intergovernmentalist approach', in *Journal of Common Market Studies*, 31(4), 473–524.

Moravcsik, A. (1991) 'Negotiating the Single European Act: National interests and conventional statecraft in the European Community', in *International Organization*, 45(1), 651–88.

O'Brien, R., Goetz, A.M., Scholte, J.A. and Williams, M. (2000) *Contesting Global Governance. Multilateral Economic Institutions and Global Social Movements*, Cambridge: Cambridge University Press.

Ohmae, K. (1990) *The Borderless World*, London: Collins.

PBEC (1998) PBEC co-sponsored APEC CEO Summit, in *Pacific Journal* (Spring), taken on 1 September, 1999 from *www.pbec.org/home/htm*

van der Pijl, K. (1995) 'The Second Glorious Revolution: Globalizing élites and his-torical change', in Hettne, B. (ed.), *International Political Economy. Understanding Global Disorder*, London: Zed Books, 100–28.

Polanyi, K. (1944) *The Great Transformation: The Political and Economic Origins of Our Time*, Boston: Beacon.

Princen, T. and Finger, M. (1994) *Environmental NGOs in World Politics: Linking the Local to the Global*, London: Routledge.

Richards, G.A. and Kirkpatrick, C. (1999) 'Reorienting interregional co-operation in the global political economy: Europe's East Asia policy', in *Journal of Common Market Studies*, 37(4), 683–710.

Risse, T. (2002) 'Transnational actors and world politics', in Carlsnaes, W., Risse, T. and Simmons, B. (eds), *Handbook of International Relations*, London: Sage, 255–74.

Risse-Kappen, T. (1995) *Bringing Transnational Relations Back In: Non-State Actors, Domestic Structures and International Institutions*, Cambridge: Cambridge University Press.

Rosenau, J.N. (1992) 'Governance, order, and change in world politics', in Rosenau, J.N. and Czempiel, E.-O. (eds), *Governance without Government: Order and Change in World Politics*, Cambridge: Cambridge University Press, 1–29.

Rosenau, J.N. (1987) *Governance without Government: Systems of Rule in World Politics*, Institute for Transnational Studies, University of Southern California, LA.

Ruggie, J.G. (1998) *Constructing the World Polity: Essays on International Institutionalization*, London: Routledge.

Manuela Spindler 253

Ruggie, J.G. (1982) 'International regimes, transactions and change: Embedded liberalism in the postwar economic order', in *International Organization*, 36(2), 379–416.
Ruigrok, W. (2000) 'International corporate strategies and restructuring', in Stubbs, R. and Underhill, G.R.D. (eds), *Political Economy and the Changing Global Order*, Oxford: Oxford University Press, 320–31.
Ruigrok, W. and van Tulder, R. (1995) *The Logic of International Restructuring*, London: Routledge.
Sandholtz, W. and Zysman, J. (1989) (1992) 'Recasting the European bargain', in *World Politics*, 42(1), 95–128.
Schirm, S. (2002) *Globalization and the New Regionalism: Global Markets, Domestic Politics and Regional Cooperation*, Cambridge: Polity Press.
Sell, S.K. (1999) 'Multinational corporations as agents of change: The globalization of intellectual property rights', in Cutler, A.C., Haufler, V. and Porter, T. (1999), *Private Authority and Public Affairs*, New York: State University of New York Press, 169–97.
Sinclair, T.J. (1999) 'Bond-rating agencies and coordination in the global political economy', in Cutler, A.C., Haufler, V. and Porter, T. (1999), *Private Authority and Public Affairs*, New York: State University of New York Press, 153–67.
Spar, D.L. (1999) 'Lost in (cyber)space: The private rules of online commerce', in Cutler, A.C., Haufler, V. and Porter, T. (1999), *Private Authority and Public Affairs*, New York: State University of New York Press, 31–52.
Spindler, M. (2003) 'Toward the competition region. Global business actors and the future of new regionalism', in Hülsemeyer, A. (ed.), *Globalization in the Twentieth-First Century. Convergence or Divergence*, New York: Palgrave Macmillan, 119–33.
Spindler, M. (2002) 'New Regionalism and the construction of Global Order', CSGR Working Paper no. 93(02) March, Warwick University: Centre for the Study of Globalization and Regionalization.
Stopford, J. and Strange, S. (1991) *Rival States, Rival Forms. Competition for World Market Shares*, Cambridge: Cambridge University Press.
Strange, S. (1997) *Casino Capitalism*, Manchester and New York: Manchester University Press.
Strange, S. (1996) *The Retreat of the State. The Diffusion of Power in the World Economy*, Cambridge: Cambridge University Press.
Streeck, W. and Schmitter, P.C. (eds) (1985) *Private Interest Government: Beyond Market and State*, London: Sage.
Tabaksblat, M. (2001) 'Liberalizing trade and investment. Business perspective on the need to move ahead', Paper given at the Evian VI Plenary Meeting, Montreux, Switzerland, 20–22 April, taken on 15 July 2001 from *www.eviangroup.org/about.htm*
Underhill, G.R.D. (2000) 'Introduction: Conceptualizing the changing global order', in Stubbs, R. and Underhill, G.R.D. (eds), *Political Economy and the Changing Global Order*, Oxford: Oxford University Press, 3–24.
Wallace, H. (1997) 'Introduction', in Wallace, H. and Young, A.R. (eds), *Participation and Policy-Making in the European Union*, Oxford: Clarendon Press, 1–16.
Weiss, T.G. and Gordenker, L. (eds) (1996) *NGOs, the UN, and Global Governance*, Boulder: Lynne Rienner.
Woods, L. (1995) 'Learning from NGO proponents of Asia Pacific regionalism', in *Asian Survey*, 35(9), 812–27.
World Trade Organization (1995) *Regionalism and the World Trading System*, Geneva: WTO.

Index